Praise for *A Good Day's Work*

"Finally, a business book on ethics that doesn't just talk theory but provides a platform for action. Anyone who considers him- or herself a 'change agent' should read this book, because it illustrates *why* ethics are critically important in today's business environment and gives very practical ideas on *how* to lead organizational transformation to demonstrate individual behavioral integrity. The decision tools provide a framework for analyzing the most difficult ethical dilemmas. This allows us to hold our personal biases at bay while we make the right decisions for the right reasons. This book will be a welcome addition to our company's recommended reading list for our leadership development program."

KEVIN MUNSON
North America Director, Learning & Development
Pfizer Global Manufacturing

"*A Good Day's Work* is a very timely book and meets a critical need in corporate America. Not only does this book do an excellent job of stimulating thought around the topic of ethics, it prompts careful consideration of one's own personal behavior and offers practical guidelines for ensuring ethical motives and actions. As a senior executive, I can assure you that those who desire to take ethics seriously will find that this book hits the mark! Lattal and Clark have done a wonderful job of examining this controversial topic and its relevance today."

LAREE DANIEL
Senior Vice President and Chief Administrative Officer
Operations, Assurant Health

"*A Good Day's Work* provides a comprehensive review of the essence, importance, and value of ethics in the workplace, while pointing out vividly that there is no such thing as 'business' ethics—only life ethics. The authors take on a host of issues relevant to ethics at work, not shying away from controversial or difficult subjects. Many practical and concrete suggestions are made for going from the *knowledge* of the book to *application* of this knowledge on our jobs. I highly recommend *A Good Day's Work*."

RUSSELL JUSTICE
Co-Founder, Transformation Network
Lead Consultant, The Business Excellence Institute
(Consulting arm for the Malcolm Baldrige National Quality Award)

"It is not just doing the right thing in a pluralistic society; the challenge we face today is how to think about doing the right thing in a fast-paced, pluralistic changing world. We need practical models for thinking right about all the stakeholders in the workplace to capture their hearts and minds and engage their desire to belong, do well, and have fun doing it. If you want to be challenged to come up a level or two in your thinking, this book will give you the 'how to' for making these decisions to do the right thing and make a profit. I highly recommend *A Good Day's Work*."

NEIL BITELER
Retired Performance Manager, GTE
Past Chairman, Chicago Chapter of QPMA

"Ethics usually looms small in the business and organizational literature and, sadly, in practice as well. Recent business scandals make the point eloquently. In *A Good Day's Work*, Lattal and Clark set a new tone: ethics is an indispensable dimension of decision making and performance management. The ethical dimension should be considered in every business decision, not only because, with each choice, you are betting your reputation capital, but also because ethical shortcuts usually entail inadvertent costs whether or not one gets caught. Note that this book is not a sermon or a speculative theory, but a 'how-to' manual. Ethics is multidimensional, and Lattal and Clark offer a variety of ethical frameworks that can be incorporated into one's decision making to match the challenge at hand. They also offer behavioral strategies that change agents can use to improve the ethical culture of whole organizations. This is the only ethics book, and one of a relatively small number of business books, that I can fully recommend based on projected ROI."

SHERMAN ROBERTS
Director of Executive Seminars, Harvard University

"Lattal and Clark transform the challenge of workplace ethics from words, words, words to choices, decisions, and actions. Through principles and examples, they guide managers in assessing and changing their own ethical behavior, as well as the ethical behavior of people who report to them. This is a long-overdue book, one that brings ethics to life and teaches us real-world applications. Leaders at all levels, formal and informal, should read it and put it into practice."

DWIGHT HARSHBARGER, PH.D.
Executive Director, Cambridge Center for Behavioral Studies

"*A Good Day's Work* not only offers a framework for understanding and developing an ethical basis for workplace decisions, but also gives clear advice about how these principles can and should become part of any organization's business strategies. In addition, Lattal and Clark offer concrete advice on how ethical behavior can be encouraged and sustained among all employees. In short, this book makes a *very valuable* and practical contribution to the increasingly critical field of ethics in business."

MATHEW B. SMITH, JR.
Retired Manager of Operations and Training
Chevron Year 2000 Project, Chevron Corporation

A GOOD DAY'S WORK

A GOOD DAY'S WORK

Sustaining Ethical Behavior *and* Business Success

Alice Darnell Lattal, Ph.D.

Ralph W. Clark, Ph.D.

With a foreword by Aubrey C. Daniels, Ph.D.

McGraw-Hill

New York Chicago San Francisco
Lisbon London Madrid Mexico City
Milan New Delhi San Juan Seoul
Singapore Sydney Toronto

The McGraw-Hill Companies

1 2 3 4 5 6 7 8 9 0 DOC/DOC 0 9 8 7 6

ISBN-13: 978-0-07-148265-3
ISBN-10: 0-07-148265-2

McGraw-Hill books are available at special quantity discounts to use as premiums and sales promotions, or for use in corporate training programs. For more information, please write to the Director of Special Sales, McGraw-Hill Professional, Two Penn Plaza, New York, NY 10121-2298. Or contact your local bookstore.

Copy Editor: Gail Snyder
Administrative Coordinator: Brenda Jernigan
Production Coordinator: Laura-Lee Glass
Cover Design: Lisa Smith
Graphic Design: Tim Williams
This book is printed on acid free paper.

CONTENTS

This book is dedicated to our children
and our grandchildren,
including those yet to be,
and the workplaces of their future.

ALICE DARNELL LATTAL, PH.D.
RALPH W. CLARK, PH.D.
MAY, 2006

ACKNOWLEDGEMENTS

The cover image, showing chairs pulled up to an elongated conference table, and positioned against a darkened but clearing sky, struck a chord with us as a metaphor for ethical decision making in business. Special thanks to Lisa Smith, who after working with the ideas in the book created a cover that symbolizes the concept of a good day's work.

Thanks to Anne Palmer, excellent agent and wise guide, and to Mary Glenn, our editor at McGraw-Hill, for seeing the potential in publishing this book on ethics at work. Gail Snyder's hand is everywhere in this project, and for preparing the manuscript to deliver to the publisher, we are indeed grateful. Cindy Ashworth and LauraLee Glass read copies of the work as it evolved and offered good advice about how to make it better. Their support is deeply appreciated. Brenda Jernigan's exceptional copy editing made *A Good Day's Work* read much more smoothly. Special thanks as well to Aubrey C. Daniels and to Tom Spencer, each of whom serves as a role model for ethical decision making, always striving to do the right thing in the right way for the right reasons—even when the immediate impact on them is costly. They both have mastered the wisdom of assessing first the greater good. Special thanks for their constant friendship and guidance.

Andy Lattal, special friend and behavior analyst, provided us with a thoughtful critique of what it means to live an ethical life from the perspective of our histories of learning and the conditions in which we find ourselves.

Finally, and of ultimate importance in the writing of this book, we thank the waitresses, receptionists, salespeople, senior executives, carwash attendants, oil rig operators, bank tellers, lawyers, flight attendants, fast food operators, and others in business who, by their everyday acts of integrity, demonstrate the visible impact of ethics at work.

Alice D. Lattal, Ph.D.
Ralph W. Clark, Ph.D.
December 1, 2006

Introduction What This Book Can Do for You

The cosmos is neither moral nor immoral; only people are. He who would move the world must first move himself.

– Edward Ericson, *Wisdom Quotations*

A COMPREHENSIVE GUIDE

Many ethics books discuss what it means to be ethical, but not how to become more ethical. This book is dedicated to the view that ethical change is both realistic and highly worthwhile. Our goal is not just to talk about ethics but to help bring about ethical change. One of us (Clark) has a Ph.D. in philosophy and is a university professor of ethics, while the other of us (Lattal) has a Ph.D. in clinical psychology and is president of a management consulting company. We have combined our areas of expertise to produce a book that is both philosophical and practical. Ethical behavior requires effective ethical thinking, but equally important, it results from practical strategies for saying and doing the right things in offices, factories, salesrooms, and everywhere business is conducted.

Many ethics books discuss high-level questions pertaining to the overall direction of business and society: Should international corporations allow their representatives to bribe government officials in foreign countries where bribery is commonplace? Should the US government strengthen or weaken affirmative action laws at home? In what ways should Congress improve insider trading legislation? Which environmental policies are best? Discussing such questions is certainly worthwhile. However, major policy questions are not the ones faced on a day-to-day basis by most corporate managers, engineers, salespeople, secretaries, shop workers, advertisers, accountants, and so on. For most people in the workplace, less momentous issues, such as how to treat customers, fellow workers, bosses, employees, and suppliers, are the most important. These small matters often underlie the larger ones.

In this book, we discuss ethical questions of all types—not just those faced by the highest levels of management. The advice we offer applies as much to entry-level positions in business as to high-level managerial positions.

Many academically oriented ethics books focus on discussions of ethical theory, but have little or nothing to say about ethical practice. Other books do focus on ethical practice, but do not provide the theoretical underpinning needed if moral advice is to consist of more than mere exhortations. In this book, you will find both. You will find a lot of practical moral advice, and you will also find explanations of the underlying model and decision-making approach we take to solve ethical dilemmas. As everyone knows, when it comes to ethical questions, much is controversial. We do our best, within a relatively short space, to present our view, and we also acknowledge that reasonable and morally sensitive individuals can disagree.

The primary goal for the great number of books in the field of business management is business success, often defined in terms of financial success. While many of these success-oriented books provide valuable advice on how to get ahead in business, ethical issues are rarely given their due. By contrast, the primary goal for books in the field of business ethics is how to resolve ethical disputes; most of these books pay insufficient attention to issues concerned with business success. Our goal is to make substantial contributions in both of these areas—to produce a book that is both ethics-oriented and success-oriented (financial and otherwise). The integrative approach that we take reflects the fact that in this book we combine our three areas of expertise alluded to above, namely, moral philosophy, business management, and behavioral psychology.

Not only do we discuss both ethics-oriented and success-oriented topics, but we provide tools to create the right sorts of workplace strategies designed to make a company both more ethical and more profitable.

THE CONNECTION BETWEEN ETHICAL BEHAVIOR AND PROFIT

Unquestionably, there exists a close connection between ethical behavior and profit. Ethical companies avoid the negative consequences of unethical behavior, such as bad publicity, fines, sometimes even jail sentences, and the legal expenses of defending themselves in court. Ethical companies also acquire all the benefits of a good reputation: loyal employees and business associates, easier recruitment of the most talented people, a stronger spirit of teamwork across all employee levels, higher morale, both new and old customers who are attracted to what the company stands for, suppliers who are more accommodating and reliable, and goodwill from communities in which the companies operate. Ethical companies also benefit in less visible ways, such as through a more open exchange of ideas in the workplace, from an atmosphere that fosters individual initiative and quick responses to problems, and from the ripple effect of having in place many different kinds of positive goodwill within the organization.

At the same time, someone who decides to behave more ethically simply in order to increase profits has failed to grasp what morality is all about. Ethical values are the highest of all values, which means that being moral *for the sake of* profit undermines the very idea of morality. Moral values exist on their own merits, independent of what else is achieved. Ethical actions have "payoffs" that in some ways transcend business, while providing a cornerstone upon which to build and run a business. As far as the profit motive is concerned, the most that can be said is that being moral may be the most profitable course of action. There is no guarantee that it will be. However, being moral is a greater value than being profitable and should never be compromised.

WHAT PRICE SUCCESS?

Let us say first that we want your business and your career to be highly successful. But we do not want you to pay too high a price for success. If success can be attained only by means of unethical actions, then that is too high a price.

Above all, we want you to be inspired by the ideal of personal integrity. Most readers of this book desire to be people of high integrity, striving to do the right thing for its own sake, regardless of monetary gain. Most people want their companies and careers to be successful as well, without cutting corners that have to do with integrity. This book is written to demonstrate in both theoretical and practical ways how we can make a commitment to ethics at work count the most in achieving personal and business success.

If you're an executive, we want your company to flourish. If you're a branch manager, we want your branch to flourish (along with your company itself). If you're a department head, we want your department to flourish; if you're a salesperson, we want your career to flourish; if you're an accountant or engineer or shop worker, we want your job to be financially successful and personally rewarding—and we want all of these outcomes to take place under the umbrella of a thoroughly ethical perspective on life. Most emphatically, we want you to put ethics to work in your pursuit of success, and we devote several chapters to how best to accomplish this goal. But we do not want you to ever sell ethics short—and we devote a lot of space to this goal as well.

OUR APPROACH TO ETHICAL ADVICE

Throughout this book, we make every effort to avoid a one-sided presentation of ideas and advice. For example, we acknowledge the role that religious beliefs can play in a person's moral outlook, but we do not rest our case on the viewpoint of any particular religion. Psychology can instruct us about how ethical behavior is learned, and we incorporate insights from the behavioral sciences. Important developments in the field of business management have clear implications for ethics; an example is the "quality movement," which we discuss for both its positive contributions and its shortcomings. Excellent contributions to understanding ethical thinking and ethical behavior come from various philosophical approaches, such as those found in utilitarian, Kantian, Aristotelian, and other viewpoints. This book incorporates insights from all of them.

Some academically oriented ethics texts say that ethical questions can be answered only when the single best fundamental moral principle has been discovered and applied. A frequently discussed example of such a principle comes from utilitarianism: everyone should strive to bring about the greatest good for the greatest number of people. Another example is Immanuel Kant's "Categorical Imperative": every genuinely moral action will generate its own universal moral law applicable to everyone. We have serious reservations about such single moral principle approaches to answering ethical questions in business, or anywhere else, for that matter. Especially in difficult cases, no single basic moral principle is likely to prove adequate. Instead, several different basic principles usually apply, and sometimes in ways that conflict with one another.

Ethical decision making involves evaluating the potential effects of decisions against the entire set of fundamental values. As we see it, the real world is much more complex and messy than the single moral principle approach allows; we are, therefore, committed to a philosophy of moral pluralism. While the focus of this book is practical, a discussion of practical matters cannot exist in a vacuum. For every discussion of ethical practices, there will be philosophical principles in the background, whether these principles are acknowledged or not. Because we want readers to know what our principles are, we discuss them briefly. Our intention is to say just enough about principles to show that the ethical-decision tools we recommend are, at the very least, good places to start in bridging the gap between theory and practice.

THE CENTRAL PURPOSE OF THIS BOOK

The central purpose of this book is to describe sound ways to make ethical decisions at work through deliberate strategies of self- and corporate management. The advice and examples that we provide are designed to help each of us aim our moral compass in the right direction. We describe how one's moral compass gets set in the first place and what to do if recalibration is needed. One of our goals is to provide a better understanding of how a loss of ethical direction can happen for individuals and for corporations. There are those who do not have a moral compass—and this book will do little if anything to help them. Evaluating your personal moral code in relation to what we suggest makes sense if you already care about how others feel or about how others are affected by your actions. The suggestions offered here will have meaning if you already believe that you have a responsibility for doing the right thing in the right way.

Improvement in ethical actions will not happen easily unless new learning occurs in a number of different areas. In the authors' teaching and consulting, we have come to think of attaining ethical advances in the workplace as being much like jumping over hurdles on an obstacle course. Some of these hurdles have to do with concepts and arguments in moral philosophy. Some have to do with disparities between the values that American culture is said to support and the values that American culture actually does support. Other hurdles exist because of a lack of understanding of the psychology of learning as it relates to people's ethical conduct. Still other hurdles can be overcome by the examination and design of social and tangible incentives within the workplace to promote the integration of ethics-oriented and success-oriented business practices. Hopefully, you already understand some of the varied ways that a deeper understanding of ethics can be valuable to you and your company. To get to the end of the obstacle course successfully, people in the workplace must know what to say and what to do when they encounter inconvenient and sometimes unexpected hurdles along the way.

This book provides a framework for identifying and implementing strategies to improve the ethical climate in the workplace. In addition, it provides the tools of applied behavior analysis to help each of us make changes in our own actions (where needed), to behave in a more ethical and effective manner. This book also serves as a concise, practical text for students of business and ethics.

THE CONTENT

The first section of this book, "Defining Ethics," encompasses Chapters 1–6. Chapter 1, entitled "Demonstrating Commitment to an Ethical Workplace," begins our exploration of what it means for a person to be committed to ethical behavior, both in the workplace and in one's life apart from work. American businesses need to make a great many small changes every day, changes that will add up to an Integrity Revolution. Chapter 2, entitled "Building Moral Integrity," continues our exploration. We discuss answers to a question that is both timeless and extraordinarily timely: why be moral?

A widespread perception is that business ought to play by its own rules. This issue is introduced in Chapter 3, entitled "Is

Business Amoral?" The position we take is that the same moral values that apply in other areas of life are applicable in the world of business. We illustrate our position through discussion of detailed, real-world examples.

Chapter 4, "Respect for Individuality," focuses on the concept of being one's own person while respecting the autonomy of others. An ethical person respects the right of others to make independent choices. Examples of workplace conduct that undermine respect for individual autonomy, and techniques for eliminating such conduct, are described.

In an important sense, all business consists of sales. We sell a product, a service, our talents, our ideas, and so on. In Chapter 5, "Achieving Ethical Sales," we discuss the all-important balancing act that ethical sales require. Many of America's most recent corporate scandals focus on the misleading products and services sold to unsuspecting individuals. This chapter defends the one message that above all others is important for readers of this book. Many of you doubtlessly believe the message already and follow it, but it is worth repeating: financial success in business is a wonderful thing, but it can be achieved at too high a price. Accordingly, a major hurdle that everyone faces in the workplace is learning how to achieve an appropriate balance of values in our business lives. Achieving this balance is especially important in regard to sales. The points made in this chapter are sufficiently general that they apply to other aspects of business as well.

Chapter 6, "Making Ethical Decisions," has more to say about achieving an appropriate balance among conflicting values. Within the context of a philosophy of moral pluralism, basic ethical values are described: respecting individual rights, helping those in need, promoting the common good, and looking out for one's own self-interest. While all of these fundamental values are important, none can stand by itself; each must be balanced against the others. This chapter provides a conceptual framework for making ethical decisions, including a set of tools to help you weigh the choices you make and the potential consequences to you and to others, as well as to the organization where you work.

The next section, Chapters 7–11, is entitled "Ethical Conditions at Work." We discuss a variety of circumstances and factors that have an impact on both how ethical a company is and how efficiently and profitably it is run. In Chapter 7, "Setting the Stage for Ethical Behavior (Part One)," we discuss a number of different ways to make the office setting more conducive to ethical behavior and more conducive to business success. We also discuss desirable physical and psychological environments. In Chapter 8, "Setting the Stage for Ethical Behavior (Part Two)," we discuss strategies for banishing fear from the workplace, for using goals wisely, and for improving the conditions of the workplace in a number of other ways. Chapter 9, "The Constancy of Change," builds bridges between contemporary management practices in addressing change in the workplace while maintaining a commitment to ethics. Chapter 10, "Speaking Up: Defining Loyalty Anew," addresses such topics as company loyalty and whistle-blowing. We discuss how a policy of openness benefits companies in numerous ways. Chapter 11, "Workplace Ethics in a World Setting," explores some of the ethical demands on companies that do business in foreign countries.

The final section is entitled "Increasing Ethical Behavior." The advice offered in the final six chapters reflects current thinking about effective strategies for changing behavior. The chapters in this section offer ideas on how to sustain personal change, and how to institutionalize such change in the organizations in which you work. We suggest that replacing negative motivational strategies with positive strategies encourages initiative, cooperation, and innovation. We describe ways that positive motivational strategies can encourage both more candid talk about ethical actions and more ethically accountable workplaces—in words and also in deeds. With positive strategies, managers are challenged to view themselves as being in a reciprocal relationship with employees, influencing and being influenced by the changes each makes.

Throughout this section, we discuss the necessary steps for creating workplaces that are both more ethical and more conducive to business success. Chapter 12, "The Possibility of Ethical Change," addresses resistance to the idea that such change is possible. Chapter 13, "Behaving Ethically," provides tips on how to manage personal and other types of change effectively. Chapter 14, "Making Ethics a Habit," discusses some of what is known about the development of moral character and how to create effective habits in personal behavior, including ethical behavior. Chapter 15, "Harnessing the Power of Positive Reinforcement," describes the fundamental principles of learning: how the settings we find ourselves in, our histories of learning, current antecedents, and consequences act upon the future probability of our own behavior. Chapter 16, "Accountability and Responsibility for Ensuring Individual Success," looks at the roles managers and individual performers have in sustaining ethical acts at work. Chapter 17, "Implications for Action," supplies the reader with a concise list of steps to consider as you develop your own code of conduct that will enable you to put ethics to work in your company or in your job without ever selling ethics short.

Foreword

For over 30 years at Aubrey Daniels International, we have been very busy trying to ensure that the workplaces of the world demonstrate every day that they value the worth and dignity of all employees. We have demonstrated literally thousands of times that by creating a positive reinforcement culture, organizations can quickly achieve performance levels thought to be unattainable. Because of this success, I had thought that such a work setting would naturally lead to ethical behavior as well. In fact, just by itself, ensuring a positive workplace is not enough to ensure ethical decision-making. The best people and the best intentions are not enough to ensure that we won't do the wrong thing in the name of helping our colleagues, protecting the company we love, or protecting our personal reputations. There is no workplace, no matter how great it appears to be, where the pressures of quality, financial gain, reputation, or relationships do not lead to the potential for unethical acts.

There are many books about ethics and moral character, each extolling us to acts of virtue and assuming that virtue is its own reward—hardly the case. After reading many of these books that focus on homilies and on designing exceptional codes of conduct, it was refreshing to read *A Good Day's Work*. The main difference between *A Good Day's Work* and other books on workplace ethics is that Lattal and Clark not only show you how actions come to be called ethical, but provide you with sophisticated methods for increasing ethical behavior while at the same time achieving business success.

They write about how to shape and sustain ethical behavior at all levels of your company. At no time do they take a simplistic approach to such a complex subject. You will not find platitudes in this book. Rather, they take the teachings of philosophy, the American cultural context, models of business excellence, and—what I believe is most important—the findings of psychological research that demonstrate how to teach and sustain ethical behavior. Lattal and Clark write about the difference between intentions and actions in evaluating whether actions are judged to be ethical or not, and how we, if we are to mature in our ethical thinking and acting, must be alert to the ethical dimensions of business decisions and human relations.

A Good Day's Work provides a decision-making tool that clarifies how, in our pluralistic society, competing values need to be considered and deliberate choices made that balance those competing values. They challenge the notion that we alone are the best judges of what is and is not ethical. No one at Enron wanted to end up doing the terrible deeds that were done, and, in their own defense, those on trial each said they were people of integrity, with high moral standards, intending always to do the right thing.

Lattal and Clark understand the power and the value of profit in American society and how the desire for profit can distort many of the things we do—and yet there are ways to keep ourselves alert to those distortions. They force us to look to standards of self-critique that have stood the test of time.

The authors emphasize that maintaining ethical behavior is a continuous process. It takes practice, positive consequences, an environment that promotes and values debate and evaluation, and the assumption that people can make refinements in their ethical thinking, improving on what is said and done. While some acts require immediate dismissal on ethical grounds, many decisions about business just need to be shaped and refined through wise guidance. Following rules is not enough. We need an opportunity to learn from our experience.

Too few books assume that there is a learning curve to exemplary ethical judgment. *A Good Day's Work* does just that. Obtaining ethical behavior at work requires a belief in the possibility of improvement at all levels, from the chief executive to the front line. It requires a culture where individual and group ethical lessons are celebrated and shared in the same way that financial successes are shared—as critical to the business mission. Being ethical in such a setting is fun—nothing is better to end a good day's work than knowing that we are capturing the best of what we each can be in sustaining those larger cultural ideals in achieving business success. At this time in our society, there is no more important workplace mission for us and for future generations.

Aubrey C. Daniels, Ph.D.
Aubrey Daniels International
July 14, 2006

1

PART

DEFINING ETHICS

1

CHAPTER

DEMONSTRATING COMMITMENT TO AN ETHICAL WORKPLACE

On a personal level, everyone must answer the following question: What is my highest aspiration? The answer might be wealth, fame, knowledge, popularity, or integrity. But if integrity is secondary to any of the alternatives, it will be sacrificed in situations in which a choice must be made. Such situations will inevitably occur in every person's life.

– Murphy Smith, *Business and Accounting Ethics*

OUR COMMON BONDS

As human beings, we are many different people—women or men, executives or shop workers, lawyers or laborers, engineers or clerks, athletes or artists, musicians or mathematicians. We are humorous or talkative or self-assured. Yet, these dimensions of self are not the most important dimensions of human life. Imagine that two people are introduced at a party. Perhaps one is a salesperson while the other is a professional singer; or one is a certified public accountant while the other is a high school English teacher; or one might be an actress while the other is an industrial chemist.

Perhaps one person is extremely outgoing, telling one joke after another, but the other person is quiet. People such as these, momentarily paired off in the midst of life's commotion, might feel they have little in common. However, in reality, they could be more alike than any other two people at the party if they share the same values and similar histories of behaving with moral integrity.

People do not usually talk much about the things that really matter to them, particularly when they have first been introduced. Consequently, it is easy for two people at a party to exchange pleasantries and then move on, never discovering that each shares the same moral values. They never discover, for example, that each believes as much as the other in respecting people's rights, keeping one's word, and honoring contracts. They both subordinate their own interests to other values when appropriate; they act on principle when appropriate, and generally do not take the easy way out. They do what is right for right's own sake. They have a rich history of positive reinforcement for doing the right things.

In the deepest and most important sense, who we are as human beings is a reflection of how we go about making ethical choices in our own lives—what we stand for. Do we have moral integrity? Can people count on us to do what is right? Do we always put our own interests first or do we also look out for the interests of other people? Are we committed to moral principles of rights, helping those in need and looking out for the good of society? Have we thought about these principles and our reasons for following them? Have we thought about what to do when basic moral principles seem to conflict?

The people admired most are those who exhibit the highest degree of integrity in their own lives—those who are committed to values that extend beyond themselves. We admire such people even when we disagree with them. We admire them because of the difference they make in the world. We suspect that their lives are more significant than the lives of people who have not reached out to others to the same degree. In writing this book, we have assumed that anyone who picks it up will have an interest in how personal actions and beliefs can make the workplace more ethical. Without each of us acting as contributing elements to the ethical equation, slim hope exists for creating a better tomorrow at work or anywhere else.

THE WORK SETTING

Events at work affect us in countless ways. The products and services upon which we depend, the communities in which we live, the well-being of our families, our economic security—all are affected by what happens in the workplace. The kinds of people we are (our commitments to one another, how we view competition and cooperation, our sense of personal and social responsibility) are reflected by what we do at work. We also spend a large part of our day at work, so the setting offers an excellent opportunity for practicing ethical conduct.

Yet, few companies require that their leaders analyze the ethical cost/benefit of a particular action in planning a marketing strategy or setting up annual budgets. Candidates for employment seldom describe how they have actually handled ethical dilemmas, providing detailed description of the process of decision making and follow-up action. There is rarely a review of the moral markers for what constitutes a good ethical choice. When managers must make tough decisions about people or resources, rarely do plans for action include the company's ethical obligations. All too often, companies fail to visibly and formally recognize those persons who place integrity above making commissions, or those who refuse to engage in other conduct that they judge to be wrong.

Have you ever heard of senior leadership praising, in meaningful and visible ways, an account executive for losing a sale because of doing the morally right thing? In reality, sales personnel are often punished for losing sales, regardless of the reason. It must be difficult for an ethical salesperson to watch as others receive recognition or a bonus when the very sale that the ethical seller refused would have been sufficient to earn that bonus.

The downfall of Enron, WorldCom, and Arthur Andersen, to name a few, demonstrates that ethics needs to be an on-the-table topic, with the goal of including ethical processes as part of the usual and customary way that business is done.

ACHIEVING ETHICAL COMMITMENTS

Corporate support for ethical behavior in today's companies is mixed or sometimes missing altogether; yet pressure to act in unethical ways is ubiquitous in the world of business. A common method for addressing the subject of ethical behavior at work is to present a vision-and-values statement that incorporates rules of conduct and a plan for disseminating the rules. Often, even if designed to be developmental in focus, performance review processes are used primarily for addressing failures to comply with the rules, such as by written warnings or occasionally by firing on the spot if gross violations occur. If ethical behavior were simply about following rules, then this approach to ensuring ethical conduct might be adequate. Clarity about what is expected and consistent consequences for those who fail to measure up are of course important. However, ethics in business usually goes beyond specific rules and requires careful judgment by individuals in regard to multiple dimensions of a given situation. Rules alone are neither specific enough nor comprehensive enough to cover all aspects of a difficult ethical decision.

Many business leaders believe that ethical commitments are personal and beyond the resources of the workplace to develop; a company's only option is to hire ethical people from the get-go. According to this view, someone either has an ethical commitment or does not. Thus, a company is as ethical as the people it hires. But please note: The executives at Enron and other companies who were in the news for violating the ethical standards of our society—and indeed their own published standards—in all likelihood appeared at the point of hire to be as ethical as anyone else. In fact, it is highly likely that they passed muster in regard to what they said and did across multiple settings up to the point of hire. They may even have presented themselves as exemplars in terms of ethical sensitivity, if the right sorts of questions were asked during hiring interviews. They most certainly were judged for most of their careers to be among the best and brightest in the arena of executive leadership.

Some armchair psychologist might say, "It should have been clear that these individuals were weak, bad, greedy, self-centered, myopic, et cetera. If only I had interviewed them early on, I would have caught their central ethical void." But it is not as easy as that. Judging who will and who will not be ethical is a very difficult task, as later chapters of this book will show. Leaders of businesses everywhere must understand that the real work in creating and maintaining an ethical workplace begins *after* the point of hiring. Hire well, but then continue the hard work of maintaining and improving the ethical direction of your organization and its employees. With the right leader-led structural commitments and consequences in place, companies can guard against unethical behavior while substantially increasing ethical workplace behavior.

SLIPPERY SLOPES

Throughout our careers, even those people whom we view as exemplary ethical leaders may on occasion shock us (or shock themselves) by the actions they take. These may be people whose histories and knowledge are informed overall by moral direction, a strong compass that guides their lives. The tragedy usually begins when these individuals take a small misstep, and end up lost and in disrepute. Such small actions can destroy great companies and harm innocent employees along with the general public. The reinforcing properties of each step along the way can blind an individual to the fact that each step reinforces taking the next step and so on until one is hanging on the edge, with the real possibility of falling off. In many cases of corporate infamy, only a few employees are guilty of deliberate wrongdoing, or a conscious choice to act in a manner that favors personal gain at the expense of others. Most readers of this book probably understand how easy it can be to take that first small unethical step.

Many reasons can be provided to justify one small wrong act, and then another and another. Taking supplies from the office, lying about the completion of a quality-process check in order to finish work on time, or protecting a friend by fudging a timecard—all are progressive and precarious steps down a slippery slope. Just as slippery and perhaps more covertly supported are actions that some might describe as intended for the greater good of the company—for example, ever so slightly inflating year-end sales by showing earned revenues in the present fiscal year when the work will not technically be done for another three months.

Several employees taking a one-time shortcut, or a few employees deliberately and often taking advantage of situations for personal advantage, can harm the company at the same level of impact in a cumulative sense, regardless of the frequency or intention of such acts. Unfortunately, the larger employee base seldom knows that one or two or ten have done the wrong thing until they experience the rapid and terrible cumulative impact on the business as they watch it crumble around them—all of their hard work for naught.

For example, when the giant energy trader Enron collapsed and its accounting firm, Arthur Andersen, came under scrutiny for its complicity in hiding Enron's dubious procedures, the domino effect brought down a few of the guilty but more of the innocent. Enron falsified accounting statements to investors regarding hundreds of millions of dollars. In addition, a Securities and Exchange Commission (SEC) investigation showed that Enron fraudulently avoided income taxes for four of its last five years of operations. Enron's ensuing bankruptcy, the largest Chapter 11 corporate filing in American history, wiped out the retirement funds of thousands of Enron employees, rendering them broke and jobless.

The Enron bankruptcy also dealt the deathblow to Arthur Andersen, one of the Big Five accounting firms. As a result of the SEC investigations, the court found the firm guilty of shredding incriminating documents and failing to report Enron's misleading financial practices. Arthur Andersen, the company, received the maximum sentence allowed by law—five years of probation and a fine of $500,000—a pittance for such an industry giant in terms of money, but not in terms of ultimate repercussions. Arthur Andersen, after eighty-nine years, forfeited its top-notch reputation, and no longer audits public companies. Even worse, the real losers were the thousands of employees who had nothing to do with the Enron dealings. Andersen quickly shrank to a firm of less than 1,000 people, after putting 27,000 employees on the streets.

Unfortunately, recent examples of corporate leadership falling off the slippery slope abound. Arianna Huffington, (2003) in her book, *Pigs at the Trough: How Corporate Greed and Political Corruption Are Undermining America,* provides example after example of business leaders engaging in greedy practices and unethical deeds to line the pockets of senior executives while employees' hard-earned financial security vanishes.

A GROWING INTEREST IN ETHICS

Because of these late twentieth and early twenty-first century events, ethical actions, more than ever before, play an essential role in creating and maintaining company stability and strength. The field of business ethics—as both an academic discipline and a social movement—has expanded significantly in recent years. American businesses are busily restructuring some of their fundamental practices in response to the intense scrutiny and formal investigations of wrongdoing over the last few years. In addition, American businesses are transforming themselves in response to growing competitive pressures from foreign countries. As the world acquires a global economy, profound changes are taking place in the field of business management. These changes have important implications for workplace ethics in the United States and around the world. The global marketplace is becoming more hospitable to common ethical ground rules and, in some cases, more vulnerable to the temptations of power, greed, and regulatory shortcuts pertaining to trade that offer the potential for great wealth.

At the same time, the get-rich-quick excesses of recent decades have encouraged many individuals, both those just entering the business arena and those entrenched in corporate America, to believe that taking care of Number One is good personal morality. Therefore, taking a shortcut, doing minor harm to others, engaging in creative financing, justifying dubious actions to get to the end-goal are, well, just part of the game. Unfortunately, all too many of America's most visible corporate leaders have modeled very poor ethical behavior. As a result, when businesses try to talk about ethics, employees may react with cynicism. There are now, and doubtless will continue to be, vestiges of the greed-is-good mentality of the late twentieth century. Tempting Sirens still seek to lure those who might navigate American business into the treacherous waters of murky ethics. Unhappily, too many of today's business leaders are not lashed tightly enough to the mast to avoid yielding to those devastating songs of seduction.

ETHICAL ACTIONS AND PROFIT

As we have noted, there exists no tight relationship between ethical behavior and profit, except in a principled sense. If only the connection were stronger! While many people, including leaders of business, report that striving to be ethical leads to a peaceful conscience, and is, regardless of financial gain, the right thing to do, the fact is that many profitable companies give only lip service to ethics. Companies that are run according to high standards of ethical conduct are not necessarily companies that succeed. It is also true that companies that practice the highest standards of business ethics may succeed admirably and perhaps beyond even the wildest imaginations of their managers and stockholders.

Some people believe that the business world operates with a separate set of rules, and that success in business is measured by a different standard than in other important domains of life—a less naïve standard that may involve stooping to the same unethical practices as the competition, for example. According to this point of view, business exists within a dog-eat-dog world, and the real successes are those individuals who have the guts to do *whatever* is needed. Such is the true nature of business morality, some people say, and the harsh reality of the marketplace. Indeed, in numerous businesses, people who act unethically are rewarded quickly for such activities, cementing their belief that, in business, ethics is a completely relative term.

Still, as a result of violations they committed for personal gain, some executives now face jail sentences, disrepute, and animosity from their former employees and the general public, certainly another reason that the atmosphere is ripe for improvement. The exposure of unethical activity in our country emphasizes how easy it is to apply a Band-Aid solution to deep ethical wounds that infect many in business. Individuals, not nameless corporations, commit unethical acts. The culture as a whole must take such conduct seriously or the wounds will fester and grow.

American business leaders and employees are beginning to see a rather ugly reflection in the workplace mirror and are realizing that change may not be optional. As a result of recent scandals, the Big Brother of "more business regulation" looms larger. Businesses must step to the front themselves or, very likely, be policed to a greater extent. Open examination and visible changes are necessary for restoring trust in America's business practices.

Even while some unethical organizations are profitable, ethical companies always avoid the negative consequences of unethical behavior, such as bad publicity, fines, and legal expenses. In addition, they acquire all the benefits of a good reputation that we mentioned earlier: loyal employees, higher morale, easier recruitment of good people, a stronger spirit of teamwork across all employee levels, more reliable and accommodating suppliers, customers who come back again and again because they are attracted to what the company stands for, and goodwill from the communities (and even the countries) in which the companies operate. In addition, and for a number of important reasons that we discuss in later chapters, ethical companies also benefit internally in the sense that their workplaces operate more efficiently and effectively. These companies do not necessarily make a profit, however.

As we have stated, being ethical may well be the best path to profit. At the same time, while making an ethical choice will not necessarily pay off in fame and fortune, it will always pay off in a more critically important way—the maintenance of integrity, the most valuable component of character. This is true whether we are talking about ethical choices at the level of personal conduct or ethical choices at the level of management where the intention is to make a workplace more ethical. Because ethical values are the highest of all values, being moral purely for the sake of profit is a debasement of the very idea of morality. However, this does not mean that we cannot put ethics to work in the hope that by running an ethical business, or by conducting ourselves in an ethical manner, we will be rewarded financially. In order to do this without selling ethics short, we must be willing to forego financial rewards if the time should ever arrive when we must choose between doing what is right and doing what is profitable.

Some people believe that the American business system itself must be radically overhauled before significant moral improvement can occur in the workplace. We disagree. We believe that radical change is not needed in the structure of society or in the ways we conduct business, because much of what we do is right. Rather, American businesses need to make a great many small changes every day, changes that can add up to an Integrity Revolution in the workplace. For such a revolution to take place, we must bring ethics into the mainstream of debate and action in corporate boardrooms, managers' forums, and the daily practices of employees.

The commitment to ethics must be visible both inside and outside the corporation. For this to happen in the most effective way, managers of businesses must possess the right set of skills—skills that can be taught, as we demonstrate in later chapters. At the heart of all of these skills is the practice of positive reinforcement, which not only gets the job done but makes life more enjoyable for employees and managers alike. Positive reinforcement is valuable both for itself and for the results that it achieves if used to promote the right behavior; the results themselves can include both higher levels of ethical conduct and a greater likelihood that a company will be more profitable. Surprisingly, the practice of positive reinforcement in the workplace is not at all well understood in corporate America. From the perspective of profitability, positive reinforcement could be used much more effectively in today's workplaces, rather than, as it is sometimes used, to drive undesirable behavior as well as desirable behavior. The use of positive reinforcement sends a strong signal as to what is valued, and what is ethical, at your workplace. It should be a deliberate tool for increasing ethical behavior, used much more often and more wisely than it is by most managers today.

TEACHING ETHICS

A critic might say that you cannot teach ethics, that whether a person is ethical or unethical is a function of character, and character cannot be changed in any substantial way. Our message is that the ability to sort through the issues and make decisions that most people would see as ethical is a skill that emphatically can and should be taught.

When we say that ethics can be taught, we are talking about acquiring new skills just as much as we are talking about acquiring new knowledge. By itself, ethical knowledge is not enough; many people can describe clearly what is and what is not ethical, but still cannot be counted on to do the right thing consistently. This book is concerned with how people actually behave in regard to ethics, not just with what they say, or even what they may believe. To be ethical in the truest sense, a person must say the right things, believe the right things, and also be disposed to behave in the right ways. But behavior in the workplace (and pretty much everywhere else for that matter) is closely tied to incentives or consequences for such behavior. Such consequences include the motivation that maintains ethical actions long after the immediate gain has passed, the motivation that makes a person choose to take a more difficult path in the near-term because of a history that teaches that such actions pay off in the longer term. The payoff may be in personal satisfaction, in being true to oneself. An ethical decision is most challenging when it requires that one make the right choice in the face of covert or overt demands to do otherwise.

The kind of reasoning that lies behind ethical choices may not be apparent even to those who consistently choose to behave ethically, for the simple reason that people do what they have learned and have been reinforced for doing, consciously or not. The workplace must be an environment where ethical acts are clearly valued, and are recognized and rewarded in both subtle and obvious ways.

Clear expectations and consequences imbedded in the workplace can make a profound difference in people's behavior, including their ethical behavior and their effectiveness in translating ethical decisions into actions on the job. This is a point that we cannot stress too strongly: positive consequences for desired behavior in the workplace are extremely important!

Moral leadership, discussion of ethical dilemmas arising from the day-in-day-out pressures and influences of the work environment, examples set by managers and co-workers, training sessions, statements of corporate values, the overall corporate culture, and consequences applied to actions—all can make a most significant difference if they are structured in the right way.

Later on, we discuss in detail how to structure these factors in the right way. We believe that it is completely realistic to expect that the workplaces of the future will embody widespread personal commitments to ethical behavior if the right structures and management strategies are in place.

Apart from the effects of workplace expectations and consequences, individuals strengthen their ethical commitments by means of personal experiences, education, reading, thinking, religious inspiration, and the influence of friends. All of these avenues have value. For corporate America, however, the most important avenue in the world of business is severely underutilized—namely, applying in the workplace practical lessons of performance management and using the science of learning to align our own and others' behavior with a strong moral compass.

INTENTIONS VERSUS EFFECTS

Ethical inclinations and actions can change, increasing in sensitivity and sophistication. Many faulty choices regarding ethical actions occur through a lack of knowledge and skill, not through a deliberate intention to do wrong. However, it is also true that what people say they will do, given certain choices, and what they actually do, are not always the same, as the developmental and social psychology research in Chapters 12 and 13 will demonstrate. In making a choice to do one thing rather than another, some people will do what they think will cause the least harm, but in the end, their actions may still be judged as unethical. They may not harm the majority of their peers, but they may harm the one person who was left out of their equation. The intention may well have been to help everyone, but in fact, the one person who needed help the most was overlooked.

Nevertheless, as far as ethics in the workplace is concerned, it does little good to make post-hoc judgments about other people's intentions. Rather, we need to have in place routine procedures that demonstrate that the company means it when it says it wants to increase ethical sensitivity. This is not to say that actions that are off the mark should be excused. However, staying away from an interpretation of what was intended, good or bad, and focusing instead on the effects of actions, provides an objective means to specifically describe in observable and measurable terms effective or less effective ethical decision-making strategies.

Understanding that people may be more or less skilled in the choices they make does not mean that unethical acts can be ignored. It does mean, however, that companies should work to increase skills in applying ethical tools to 1) reduce unethical acts, and 2) help everyone gain skill in ethical decision making. Both skills provide gain to the company. We hope that by the time you finish this book, you will have already begun to apply the techniques suggested. We also hope that the information within will help you fine-tune your own moral compass, more closely matching your intentions with your actions, helping you to know what to suggest at work to ensure that you and the people with whom you work are not diverted from the course.

2

CHAPTER

Building Moral Integrity

The life of every man is a diary in which he means to write one story, and writes another; and his humblest hour is when he compares the volume as it is with what he vowed to make it.

– James Matthew Barrie, *The Little Minister*

MEASURING SUCCESS

Typically, profits are the measure of business success. Yet, there are other important measures of business success such as how profits are achieved and what employees say about working for their companies. Businesses that are known as companies of high integrity depend on the behavior of their employees to achieve and sustain that reputation. Reputations with customers and stakeholders result from the actions of people who represent those companies. The more stable and broad those reputations, the more companies rely upon employees who are selected because of and then reinforced for making ethical decisions in their daily practices at work and in work-related behaviors that reflect integrity. In short, business is no more and no less than the words and activities of employees at all levels.

It is not that difficult to find American businesses that can be described as exemplars of moral integrity; these businesses focus on doing what is right regardless of expected financial gain or loss. In today's world, however, publicity about companies and their executives more often focuses on the wrong things they do—treating people badly, producing products that cause harm, or acting in other ways that steal from, diminish, or call into question the integrity of the corporate entity.

For example, the print media publish limitless cartoons that poke fun at the scandalous nature and results of unethical business practices. Cartoonist Larry Wright, of the *Detroit News*, depicts a couple emptying a pile of shredded paper from an envelope with the caption, "Enron's accountant . . . just sent us the final audit of our retirement plan." Wayne Stayskal's cartoon in *The Tampa Tribune* shows a cat burglar scaling a corporate building as a security guard assures a befuddled passerby, "It's ok, sir. That's the CEO." *The Philadelphia Daily News* published Signe Wilkinson's cartoon of a luxurious tennis court with the caption "Where our lying, cheating, stealing executives will most likely end up serving." Jeff Stahler of *The Cincinnati Post* pokes fun at the new trend of executive misdeeds with his drawing of a department store greeting card rack with a special section called "Corporate Fraud." A cartoon by Mike Lane of the *Baltimore Sun* sums up this whole media mindset toward corporate America with his drawing of a man in a prison uniform accompanied by the caption "Stripes are IN!! It's the US Executive Look!"

It's difficult to find copy or cartoons about companies that do the right thing compared to those that deliberately take unethical shortcuts for gain, or those that abuse or destroy the corporate trust. Yet, positive events are causes for celebration and there are many such examples. Despite media emphasis on the negative, much of the business landscape is composed of good people doing the right things, and most Americans live a work life of integrity. For many of us, recent events and the standout stories of corruption in business may make it difficult to believe that this is so, in spite of solid financial reports and excellent products and services produced in the workplace. In general, the regular ebb and flow of work life indicates that not every day is a day of moral dilemmas, and not every leader has become a leader by cheating, lying, or stealing.

It is possible and realistic to run a company well from an ethical perspective. Each of us who work in settings where we see the efforts of leaders to do the right thing, where we are asked to work smarter but always with the customer's best interest at heart, and where the consequences for doing so are positive, can attest that many companies do the right thing. Despite the jokes, cartoons, and editorials about business ethics that get their laughs from describing less than stellar acts in the workplace, the phrase *business ethics* does not have to be an oxymoron! The growing cynical bias to see failure in everything that companies do to support moral integrity in the workplace is no more credible than a statement that all businesses are driven by moral integrity.

Fortune magazine's annual list of "Best Places to Work in America" is filled with companies striving to be ethical. This list honors companies based on a thorough evaluation of services, benefits, and salaries, but the real determinant is the result of employee questionnaires that evaluate employees' trust in management, the pride that employees take in their work, and how they feel about their companies.

Organizations such as the International Data Group (IDG), Computerworld's parent company, for example, have made *Fortune's* list. IDG's top executives began an employee stock ownership plan thirty-six years ago that still thrives today with 12,000 employees, and IDG has earned a solid place as the world's top global provider of IT media. Encouraging employee input, sharing in company gains, and regularly recognizing individuals for their contributions are part of the ethical commitment IDG has made. Kelly Conline, IDG's president and CEO, emphasized the foundation of the company's success when he stated that employee satisfaction was considered to be IDG's most consistent measure of a successful company.

The Silicon Valley network publishing company, Adobe Systems, also made *Fortune's* list, ranking in the "Top Ten" of desirable American employers. Adobe's president and CEO attributed the organization's twenty years of success to core values of integrity demonstrated through valuing and recognizing its employees and paying attention not just to what the company does, but how the company does it.

Unfortunately, we do not always know what the underbelly looks like in the good examples. We cannot predict, necessarily, that doing many things right will mean that there are no corrupt leaders or that certain people will not at some point in time decide to do whatever it takes to stay ahead of the competition or to take care of themselves above all else. However, positive examples demonstrate an active awareness by these corporations of their people and acknowledgment of the need for a values-driven performance management system.

PERCEPTIONS OF BUSINESS

A recent corporate social responsibility poll conducted by Environics International indicates that though scandals have produced the negative effect of cynicism and distrust, they have also heightened America's awareness of the importance of integrity and have opened a dialogue regarding accountability. Though those polled expressed a low level of trust in American companies, they also expressed a belief in the abilities of corporations to better not only the business climate but also conditions of the world in general. In fact, two-thirds of those surveyed viewed corporate leaders as capable of bettering social concerns such as poverty and education in other countries as well as our own. The overall findings of the poll reveal that ethical conduct and social philanthropy have a real impact on share value and corporate reputation.

Leaders such as Ford Chairman Bill Ford Jr. and Sir John Browne, BP Amoco chief, take notice of such findings. Both have committed publicly to more environmentally safe ways of doing business even if those commitments take an initial bite out of productivity. The simple fact that publications such as

Fortune each year create the sort of list referred to above, and that Americans are keeping an eye on ethical corporate behavior are very positive signs.

Is it a mere coincidence or are consumers actually paying attention to corporate ethics? The Environics survey reports that 60 percent of Americans own shares in American companies, either directly or through stock mutual funds. Of that 60 percent, 28 percent report that they have purchased or sold shares based on a company's employment practices, community involvement, or business ethics; another 10 percent state that they would consider purchasing or selling stock for these same reasons. Such information indicates that a leader who does the right thing regardless of expected profit is just the person who may make the most money in the long run. Others will judge this person as one who can be counted on, and such trust is fundamental to business success. A business, if composed of many such people, may continue to operate year after year while less scrupulous companies fail. Acting in accord with the interests of others as well as oneself, for the good of the whole and the respect of the individual, and providing safe products and services—these are all key elements to adding value to business success. However, to win, one must be willing to lose. Winning goes beyond what happens with one's business. Winning is also about demonstrating moral integrity in every aspect of one's life.

The loss that each of us must be willing to risk is defined often in financial terms but may also be defined in terms of loss of power or position or even in the retention of our jobs. The statements that leaders make in moments of stress about taking shortcuts, attaining the goal or else, or what the work team itself might say or do, even to achieve the best of outcomes, affect what individuals do. For example, a small unit within accounting may decide, for the long-term viability of that specific unit, to manipulate how numbers on spreadsheets are recorded. This may include doing such things as temporarily re-categorizing or hiding debt, establishing a private, unrecorded payout system, or misrepresenting the true nature of the business. The individuals who do this may view their behavior as consisting of small acts done with good intent. However, such small actions, perhaps described by those who do them as "temporary" and thus not harmful or dishonest, can lead to actions that most of us would never try to justify, and certainly could not justify even if we attempted to do so.

WINNING IN BUSINESS

What is there to win in the business world? This question has a number of different answers. Those who commit themselves to actions based on moral integrity measure winning by more than strictly financial terms. A person who has moral integrity welcomes any profits that result from upholding his or her integrity, but has no serious regrets if profits do not result. The primary motivation for the ethical businessperson all along has been to do the right thing for its own sake. In such a person's experience, many different kinds of positive outcomes have been paired with doing right for its own sake. Such actions become the guiding principle or code of conduct that helps a person weigh the value of the fun to be had right now against the more distant satisfaction of doing right over the course of one's lifetime.

Why should a person do the right thing simply for its own sake? Why should we place a high value or any value at all on moral integrity?

THE ETHICAL PERSPECTIVE

A person with moral integrity wants to do what is right. To carry out this intention, a person needs to have a moral or ethical perspective on life. In the most general terms, this means 1) concern for others and respect for oneself, and 2) an effort to achieve an appropriate balance between the two. Ethical behavior requires that in one way or another, the interests of all affected humans be taken into consideration, including one's own interests. The actions of people who violate fundamental rights of others to promote only their own interests clearly fall outside the sphere of ethical behavior. We may not know what such people believe their own motivations to be, but we can evaluate the effects of their actions. Those who kill others with minimal or no regret, sell drugs to children, or commit violent crimes for pleasure are unquestionably acting outside the sphere of ethical behavior. Fortunately, such extreme behavior patterns are not encountered frequently in the workplace.

We are more likely to encounter individuals who appear to be concerned for other people when in fact their actions indicate that they care only for themselves. On occasion, their actions may benefit both themselves and others. However, when they perceive the goals of other people as jeopardizing a personal objective, such individuals do whatever is in their own interest, regardless of who else they may harm. When such manipulative but successful individuals are encountered in the workplace, they may be lauded for knowing what they want and going after it, for making the tough sales, or getting the difficult contract. When they violate the individual rights of their fellow employees, they may be hailed as gutsy and determined. Aggressive actions are sometimes difficult to address, but when leadership fails to identify and correct inappropriate behavior, others in the organization perceive that such self-serving actions are endorsed, particularly if the person in question brings in profits. Conversely, if someone always treats others thoughtfully, but is less successful in closing sales, that person may be labeled as weak, naïve, unsophisticated, and unable to measure up against those aggressive sons of guns.

At the other end of the spectrum are people who rarely or never speak up for their own interests, as well as refuse to confront issues that, if resolved, might benefit themselves and others. Passive people appear to leave the risks of speaking up to fellow employees. Regardless of the good intentions of these people, their actions are interpreted negatively by other individuals, who may describe such people as unreliable and/or unwilling to provide candid and genuine comments to leadership about needed changes in the workplace. Such people are sometimes viewed as selfish, because they appear to ignore the needs or wants of other employees, but reap the benefits of changes that may come about when someone else speaks out. At the same time, such people seem to be avoiding possible negative repercussions. In truth, such people may simply lack speaking skills and may never have learned to behave in ways others would describe as "assertive" and "confident." They may misread how their passive behavior affects others, and they may harm others unintentionally. Nevertheless, fairly or not, they may still be held accountable for the effects of their actions (or, in this case, inaction) on others.

Concern for others and respect for oneself are requirements for the ethical perspective. As we see it, the most basic moral value is what philosophers call the intrinsic worth of every human life: all human lives have value in and of themselves. Disregarding the interests of others is wrong. It means that we do not recognize that other people's lives are valuable. At the same time, respecting one's own life helps to support the belief that all human life has value. We recognize who we are and how our interests must be balanced against the interests of others. Ethical behavior demands this balance.

WHY BE MORAL?

What if doubts exist, not just about the application of moral principles to business, but also about the foundations of morality itself? In spite of good intentions, we may acquiesce in the face of unethical behavior and end up doing more harm than good. A weak response to even minor unethical behavior will reinforce the idea that morality is on questionable footing in one's company.

Regrettably, moral beliefs can easily appear tenuous. People with the best intentions can fall prey to doubts and uncertainties. For such individuals, the moral perspective may appear to conflict with pragmatic goals. Weak responses by such people undermine moral integrity and make it impossible for these people to be moral guides for others. By contrast, it is easy to have the strong convictions of a moral skeptic. The skeptic is someone who uses the following logic:

> "Why should I look out for the interests of customers, except when doing so is profitable? Why should I pay attention to my co-workers, when it won't pay me to do so? Why should I care about my employer, my employees, or people in my community and future generations? People have talked about morality for centuries, but no one has figured it out—no one has provided definitive answers. However, there is nothing mysterious about my own wants and desires. I know that I need food, clothes, a house, and money for my children's education. I would surely like to have an expensive car, luxurious vacations, and a summer home on the lake. Why should I sacrifice unambiguous values (my needs and wants) for ambiguous ones?"

The advocate of morality in the workplace must go one-on-one against the forcefulness of the skeptic's point of view, as expressed in the previous paragraph. The challenge is a formidable one that can be summarized with this question: why be moral?

This is the deepest and most difficult question in moral philosophy, but it is more than an academic question. At some point in life every reflective person is troubled by it. The person who finds no satisfactory answer to it may have no reason to apply moral standards in any area of life, not just the workplace. Such a person may act morally most of the time but without deep conviction, and thus may more easily try to justify and engage in unethical behavior when under pressure to cut corners. Such a person may lack an interest in making efforts to influence others in the workplace to take morality more seriously.

Moral integrity requires that we strengthen our moral convictions so that we can better challenge ourselves when we are tempted to go astray, as well as stand up to moral skeptics. Clearly, then, it is important to have the strongest possible answer to the question, why be moral? As a matter of fact, several different possible answers are available that are worth considering. Let's start with an "easy" answer.

The Divine Command Argument

This argument says that we should be moral because God wants us to be moral. God wills it, and that is why we should accept moral values as the highest of all values. God wants us to care about all of our fellow human beings—to love others and recognize that everyone is precious in God's eyes.

While this may well be the best answer to the question, why be moral? its practical use is somewhat limited. Not everyone believes in God, and proof of God's existence has been notoriously difficult to achieve for those who do not believe. Moreover, religious doctrines can exist in the name of God (as understood by certain groups of people) where limits are placed on who is to count as precious in God's eyes, restricting the chosen circle to those who profess certain beliefs or share in a particular faith, while opening the door to the persecution of others. In such scenarios, all who fall outside of a special, exclusive circle are branded as unfit to enter God's kingdom. Thus, there is no way to avoid concluding that appeals to religious belief can be highly problematic if we wish to be inclusive, as we do, in our recognition that a diversity of religious beliefs makes important contributions to ethics.

Prominent philosophers and theologians going back at least to the time of Thomas Aquinas in the thirteenth century have said that the ideal basis for morality is a combination of religious belief and rational argument. Let us then turn to answers that do not depend solely on appeals to religious belief.

The Personal Satisfactions Argument

Apart from the religious explanation, one of the best reasons for being moral is the Personal Satisfactions Argument. In essence, it argues that people who choose to live moral lives will find their lives more satisfying than they otherwise would have been. People who are moral in all spheres of their lives, both in their business activities and elsewhere, will be glad that they made this choice, and glad that they were taught how to make such good choices.

There is a catch, though: the satisfaction will likely be felt only some time after the choice to live a moral life has been made. People who already have a deep concern for their fellow human beings will be the ones who understand that virtue is its own reward, but they are not the ones who need convincing. Are there methods to convince people NOW that they ought to be moral or more moral than they presently are? Some philosophers claim that it is simply impossible to appeal to values that a person does not yet have.

> Asked the skeptical question, "But why shouldn't I do actions that will harm others?" we may not know what to say; but this is because the questioner has included in his question the very answer we would like to give: "Why shouldn't you do actions that will harm others? Because, doing those actions will harm others." The skeptic, no doubt, will not be happy with this. He will protest that we may accept this as a reason, but he does not. And here the argument stops
>
> (Rachels, 1985, p. 108).

James Rachels, the author of this passage and a prominent American moral philosopher, appears to be saying that people are locked inside themselves with no way to break out of the set of values to which they are already committed. There is no point in telling someone who puts self-interest first or exclusively that his or her actions harm others. According to Rachels' view, if we attempt to persuade the egoist, as he defines such people, that he or she ought to be concerned for others, we will fail, because the egoist simply cannot conceive that the lives of others have intrinsic value. If Rachels is correct, then the Personal Satisfactions Argument will fail where it is most needed.

Is it true that we are locked inside the circle of values that we presently have? What if we suggested that a person reflect upon his or her own past behavior and then take steps to change for the better? Our argument to the person would be that she would come to understand that the change was for the better at some time in the future after the change had occurred. Why isn't this "try it; you'll like it" approach acceptable? Rachels' argument appears to assume that people's most basic values are unchangeable. We contend that significant changes can be made in how individuals behave and in their interpretations of what they have done; subsequently, these individuals will report a newfound value for ethical actions. After all, it worked for Ebenezer Scrooge!

People develop values through their distinct experiences. Values are taught both directly and indirectly through the actions people take and through the actions that others take toward them. Combined, these patterns of interaction both create and reinforce beliefs regarding values. It is often the case that a person initially does not know exactly what his or her own values are. A child may not know that to wait patiently while other children get their food first can be a very generous and honorable act, especially if the child is hungry herself. Often the child can associate such actions with doing the right thing if we, the adults, help her—through the words we use or the actions we take—to build or reinforce such actions. All too often, adults fail to use the appropriate moment when it occurs to teach a moral perspective by putting into words what we see the child doing—not the simple act, but the values reflected in the act. With adult behavior, also, we often fail to identify and praise, in our own words, those very patterns of behavior that reflect ethical actions and honorable choices.

Knowledge about our ethical perspective can come from studied examination of what is and is not important, and it can come also from examining the choices we make in given situations. If we wish to gain greater knowledge of ourselves in this most fundamental way, we will likely have to enlist the aid of others. They can observe us and describe what values they believe are demonstrated by the choices we make.

It is true that experience teaches us how to get the things we want. At the same time, it also teaches us what we want and do not want. The Personal Satisfactions Argument says that living a life in which we reach out to others will teach us an important lesson about what we will want from our lives henceforth.

Many of us make the assumption that we simply value what we value—change is both too costly and ineffective when it comes to those basic components of our personality that we call *values.* This notion, that values cannot be changed, too often allows us to excuse the unethical behavior of others, not to mention equivocating on ethical issues in our own real-life situations. Changing core values established by long histories of reinforcement is very difficult. However, values follow behavior and, in turn, the values we talk about shape our future actions. (In Chapter 14, this topic and the research on moral development are explored in greater detail.)

Is it true that a more moral life, one that is less self-centered and more other-directed, will eventually turn out to be a more satisfactory life?

Well, if we can believe what the "wisdom of the ages" teaches us, the answer to this question is a most emphatic yes! A singular piece of wisdom from the world's poets and storytellers on the one hand, and from prominent philosophers and scientists on the other, is that the most meaningful and satisfying life is achieved by reaching out beyond the self. People who think primarily about themselves, their own aches and pains, their own accomplishments, their wants and needs and how they will fulfill them, live spiritually impoverished lives. Those who think primarily about business concerns that will benefit them in a narrow sense are the poorer for it, and those around them in the workplace are also less well off. The more someone pursues his or her own satisfaction in a dogged and single-minded fashion, the less satisfaction the person is likely to feel. The self that is tended so carefully will seem to slip away, because paradoxically, self-discovery often requires actions that take one beyond the self.

For those readers who know how difficult it is to change your own or someone else's behavior, a number of strategies for personal change are included in Part Three of this book. These guidelines are based in part on psychological research that tells us that if someone's behavior is changed for a period of time and the person is recognized, in meaningful and positive ways (which, for example, will exist in a well-structured workplace), for making the change, then the person's beliefs will also change to support the new ways of acting. Such behavior patterns, consistently experienced over time, can become who we eventually say we are.

Because our sense of self is shaped by what we do and say, going along with the crowd (groupthink) is more harmful than we sometimes realize. It increases the likelihood that behavior we do not endorse will occur more frequently than if we had not complied with the wishes of others. In addition, much harm can result to oneself and others when individuals fail to speak up for fear of offending someone.

When people compromise valued principles, then their conscience, or learned patterns of what they would call *ethics,* may intercede at first, causing a feeling of guilt. Unfortunately, with practice, such guilt lessens considerably. Scientific research shows this to be so. Any lessening of overt concern for ethical actions by a single word or a single step along the wrong path can be extremely detrimental.

Compromising ethics leads to a compromised sense of ethics. Practicing moral actions leads to consistency of such action. Placing ourselves in situations where moral integrity is expected and reinforced increases the likelihood that we will behave ethically. Companies that do not consistently reinforce ethical behavior reduce the likelihood that employees will act ethically. As a matter of fact, most of us within the workplace have more powerful effects on one another than we may acknowledge or even know. Thus, it is incumbent upon all of us to support and protect the best aspirations of others and ourselves as individuals—as members of a unit, a department, an office, a company, or as part of society at large.

The Pragmatic Argument

At the present time in history, human beings are threatened by weapons of mass destruction and a wide range of new and dangerous uses for technology, such as the possible distribution of poison in our water supply systems, the misuse of electric power signals across the country, destruction of energy networks, and

Internet viruses designed to eliminate our knowledge capital. At the heart of many serious problems facing contemporary civilization is the apocalyptic force of technology itself. Technological forces now exist that could be unleashed in an instant during war or unleashed more slowly in times of peace, polluting the environment and upsetting natural balances that have existed for thousands and even millions of years.

Nevertheless, technology, as much as it has progressed in the last two centuries, is still in its infancy in demonstrating incalculable benefits to humankind—in raised standards of living, improvements in the fields of medicine and nutrition, expanded communications, and global understanding.These benefits are too precious to lose through the consequences of myopic perspectives that lead to destruction. The terrorist attack on the World Trade Center in New York City made the reality of all our fears a part of everyday life. No matter where we live in the world, we are reminded of that threat when we board airplanes, enter high-rise buildings, or hear news about the War on Terror. Over time, the new vigilance may produce insidious destructive elements, including a loss of personal liberties, and daily fears that restrict our actions or limit our sense of freedom or cause our children to grow up with more anxiety and questions about the fundamental goodness of mankind. We have yet to discover the full fallout of recent events, or the extent to which the benefits of technological advancement may be compromised.

Our collective new reality is caused by *behavior*—that simple word describes the acts of immoral human beings who behave without the constraint of respect for the most fundamental of all value-oriented beliefs: regard for the preciousness and sanctity of the individual. Instead, for the furthering of their religious or political perceptions (their interpretations of religious or political beliefs), to gain honor in a subculture that supports their actions, or from their own highly individualistic histories of reinforcement, these people have, in some instances, convinced themselves that their actions are both moral and ethical. In other instances, these people apparently do not care whether their actions are moral or ethical. Individuals who espouse a variety of different views may say that their own worldview represents the only genuinely moral perspective, and that their actions are justified in defense against those who would destroy their way of life. Such conflicts and justifications are at the heart of much of the angst of the twenty-first century.

The human race has much to gain in promoting moral integrity that includes the concept of the intrinsic worth of all individuals in the workplace and everywhere else. It is indeed pragmatic to do so. To have moral integrity, and to promote it, may increase the likelihood that we will take care of one another. In turn, we may refuse to consider other people's worth because of a sense of moral superiority (a most dangerous and difficult justification used quite often throughout history to do great harm), or from greed, selfishness, or on the basis of such criteria as race, religion, or gender.

Contemporary civilization will require great wisdom to overcome the dangers that it currently faces. A most important aspect of wisdom is the idea that all human beings have intrinsic worth, and therefore each of us deserve concern and consideration. Fundamentally, all of us should act with integrity, placing the needs of others alongside other key values and striving to do the right thing even when faced with people whose cultures or concerns are different.

There are many ways each of us can demonstrate real respect for differences while still acting with integrity, without selling short that which we value. The cumulative result of such action is a future society founded on and guided by principles that seek to preserve humanity, including our own.

3

CHAPTER

IS BUSINESS AMORAL?

And he that stands upon a slippery place makes nice of no vile hold to stay him up.

– Shakespeare, *King John*

TODAY, A LARGE NUMBER of publications address ethical issues in the business world. Not only has the number of books devoted to business ethics increased dramatically during the last fifteen to twenty years, so also has the number of journals and newsletters. Many more business schools now require ethics courses; numerous seminars and conferences concerned with moral questions in business are held around the country; and, increasing numbers of corporations write their own codes of conduct and strengthen efforts to enforce compliance with these codes. As a significant component of our lives, the workplace frequently mirrors changes that are currently occurring in society. Perhaps now more than any time in history, people are actively seeking ways to improve the quality of their lives. This effort includes finding personal meaning in the workplace.

Even now, however, large numbers of people remain virtually untouched by, and uninterested in, the business ethics revolution that is underway. They may believe that integrity is something for which one should strive in one's personal life, but that business decisions lie outside an ethical framework. Such people believe that business is not exactly immoral or unethical, but instead that the business of business is business. We encounter these individuals in the workplace all too frequently—their attitudes strongly affect how they treat subordinates, fellow workers, supervisors, customers, and the general public.

PLAYING THE GAME OF BUSINESS

The games of business and of poker have been compared, as have the larger concepts of gaming and business. These comparisons continue to generate much debate. Albert Carr (1968) published the article "Is Business Bluffing Ethical?" in the *Harvard Business Review.* Fritz Allhoff's (2003) subsequent article "Business Bluffing Reconsidered" provides an excellent summary of the debate that was ignited by Carr's article. Allhoff's article includes a discussion of the concept of business gaming and its effect on the subtle differences between lying and bluffing in business.

> Debate has centered on comparing achieving business ends to playing poker—to bluffing . . . commonly understood within a poker game. Such bluffing is friendly and does not distort the relationships among players since bluffing is something we all understand when we play such a game. . . . In business, most of us expect to bargain, to not be told the full truth regarding what the market will bear on the price of a house or a car or any of a number of goods and services. Holding the final price close to the chest is simply being a good player, and such action does not necessarily make the seller unethical—although many people resent the process and, in turn, view business more cynically because of the process of bluffing. This issue does help us gain a better understanding of the conditions for carrying out business negotiations (p. 284).

Let us say first that any attempt to justify lying as a harmless act of bluffing is not a part of good business. Bluffing—or rather, negotiating when all the rules are clear and the conditions of entry to the table are equal (the chances of winning or losing are the same for both parties)—may make the negotiation one of principle and a good game. However, when business bluffing is done to overcome the other party at an unequal playing table, it is equivalent to lying. Then what we have is a game of deceit. It's as though the deck is stacked, or a player pulls the hidden ace out of his sleeve during a game of poker. This kind of game is something that businesspeople cannot afford to play, and should not play. It is clear, however, that many people in business believe that their job is to play this game, whether fairly or unfairly. Let the buyer beware! Such individuals do not think about the conditions of the game, or the rules of conduct that tell us when a win can be declared a fair win.

THE AMORAL PERSPECTIVE

Some would say that businesspeople cannot afford to evaluate business decisions according to ethical criteria. They must play the game of eat or be eaten; get the job done or face bankruptcy. Talk about integrity, acting on principle, moral sensitivity, conscience, and the like, is just so much window dressing. Such talk covers up the reality that the business world follows its own rules, and these practices mean just one thing—SURVIVAL!

The idea expressed above is that business is not so much immoral as amoral. It is exempt from some or all of the rules of morality, in contrast to other areas of conduct. People who express this point of view range from the blatantly dishonest to those who exhibit scrupulous honesty in all areas apart from business. All such individuals have in common the belief that making a profit is either the sole purpose of business or is by far the most important purpose.

Consider the following case, which is admittedly a stereotypical example of ethics in the practices of a used car dealer:

Frank owns a small auto repair shop. On the side, he sells cars that he has repaired. Frequently he buys these cars from customers whom he has persuaded to sell before repairs really get expensive. He might say, even though he knows better, "The engines in that model usually don't go much beyond 80,000 miles; you've been lucky."

Some of the used cars that Frank sells need only cosmetic changes. Other times, they need more work. He tells customers that transmissions are in excellent shape even when they are faulty. He tells fictitious stories about each car's pristine past.

Frank talks about his business practices with like-minded friends, who see nothing wrong with his tactics. "After all, before buying a car, anyone can take it to an independent mechanic to be checked out, but most people are too cheap or lazy to do so," Frank explains. "They want me to fix the cars before I sell them and keep them on my lot where they can get damaged, dirty, and older by the minute. That costs me money. If my customers want cars that don't need many repairs, then they're better off buying new ones. People who buy used cars shouldn't complain if the transmission goes bad right away. What did they expect when buying a used car? If I told them everything that was wrong, I would never sell anything because all the other dealers are telling the same stories I tell."

Would Frank do anything to make a profit? No, of course he would not. He would never embezzle money or rob a bank. He wouldn't dream of committing murder for profit. Moreover, although Frank plays fast and loose with the truth when it comes to his auto business, he would not be any more inclined to lie to his friends or associates than the average person would be. He believes business to be a special exception, to have its own rules, and complete honesty is not one of them. He convinces himself that people have unreasonable expectations and that his customers are not really bad off in the end. He convinces himself that other dealers follow these same practices, while not admitting that his own business practices fall at the low end of the honesty/dishonesty continuum.

Here is another case:

> Mike is a wholesale distributor of produce. At harvest times when fruit and vegetables are plentiful, Mike's business requires a large crew. However, during winter, or when the harvest is bad, or consumer demand slumps for one reason or another, Mike must reduce the workforce. He gives minimal warning before laying people off for weeks or months at a time, sometimes permanently. Occasionally employees show up for work in the morning and he tells them they have been laid off beginning that day—he never informs them for how long nor does he promise them that if the work returns, he will rehire first from his pool of former employees. He simply fills jobs with those who show up on the days when he needs the labor. Most of his employees are people with few skills who cannot find more secure jobs elsewhere.
>
> "I promise them nothing beyond a day's fair wages for a day's work because the market for produce is volatile," Mike comments. "My job, as I see it, is to deliver the best food for the lowest price—period! I'm proud of the fact that I have been doing that for twenty years. I'm still in business, unlike some of my competitors, and believe me, it's been up and down for them, but I've had customers for life. The grocery chains that sell produce most economically can depend on me to have the best produce at the best prices, and because of their loyalty to me, I can offer work, if I have it, to these seasonal workers. That wouldn't be the case if I went out of business. Sure, sometimes people beg for work during a layoff because someone in their family is sick or the mortgage is due or whatever, but that is not my responsibility. It's not that I'm hardhearted, but I want to be around for another day. Look at it this way: if I'm not in business, they'll never get the work again.

> "They complain because I give no warnings before layoffs, but if I told them beforehand, they might look for work elsewhere, before I'm ready to let them go. Anyway, I usually don't know myself how many people I'll lay off until the day arrives, because market conditions constantly change. If I promise someone work for a certain period of time—which I do for the more skilled people I can't afford to lose—then I keep my promise. Likewise, if I say that a shipment of lettuce is fresh, then it is fresh. I tell an absolutely straight story to everyone."

Both Frank and Mike put the profitability of their businesses first, but Frank is largely unconcerned about the well-being of customers and is dishonest while Mike appears uncaring but honest in terms of being truthful to the people he employs and those with whom he has business dealings. He does express concern for the hardships faced by his employees when he lays them off, but he believes that, as a businessman, he should not involve himself in such matters. He believes that he is doing a lot of good for society just because he puts making a profit ahead of everything else by delivering a reliable and valued product and because he is essentially honest, as he sees it.

Mike might justify his actions using concepts similar to those Adam Smith (1776) employed in *The Wealth of Nations.* As Smith saw it, under the conditions of economic freedom, the private pursuit of self-interest through profit making in business benefits the country as a whole. An "invisible hand," said Smith, will direct, unknowingly, the individual toward such activity that will add to the prosperity of society, not simply personal advancement. Mike himself might go so far as to say that individuals like himself are the world's most moral people because they are the ones who get the job done. They are the ones who deliver the food, complete construction jobs on time, keep the country's lights burning, and its wheels turning. In making money for themselves, they benefit the entire country. If morality means actually doing good works, then they are moral because their businesses do a lot of good. Therefore, Mike might ask, "What could possibly be wrong with the way that I operate? Call it amoral if you will, but it's the best way to run a business."

MORAL PURPOSES

We disagree with Mike's point of view. From our perspective, the best way to run a business is to run it as ethically as possible, and that means considering matters other than the pursuit of honest profit as exemplified by Mike's attitude toward business. As we see it, being ethical means having a moral purpose in life—a purpose broader than making profits in an honest business.

Critics might ask, "Does this mean that one ought to sacrifice profits for the sake of morality? If so, then aren't we forgetting about competition?" They may point out that in a competitive economy, every business must do whatever it can to make a profit or it will fall behind other businesses. Only the winners or near-winners stay in the race. This has always been true, but in the global economy of today it is truer than ever before because foreign competition has intensified pressure on everyone. In a highly competitive economy, Mike's point of view may appear to be the only realistic one.

Critics could also contend that every dollar spent on workers who are less productive is charity; every dollar spent on the environment (unless government requires competing businesses to spend as much) is charity; every dollar not extracted from potential customers is charity; every dollar spent on the community that does not result in additional profits is charity. Beyond efforts to increase profits or meet legal requirements, every effort to consider the handicapped, minorities, women, or the elderly is essentially charity.

According to this viewpoint, a company that chooses to engage in charity will soon be out of business; every worker who does not do all he or she can to keep a job or prepare to find another will be at a competitive disadvantage. Businesses and everyone in them must do everything they can to survive. Even then, many will not survive. Companies will go bankrupt. Individuals will lose their jobs and not find replacements. If they do find other jobs, they may take a cut in salary or benefits. The margin for error in this dog-eat-dog world is practically zero.

So the story goes. The world of business is truly amoral. For proponents of this point of view, we too have a number of questions, beginning with one addressed to Mike, the produce wholesaler. We want to know the following: Mike, if making money is your single aim in business, why do you bother telling the straight story to everyone?

He might say that doing so is the secret of his success. People trust him; and in the food business, trust is especially important.

Unquestionably, trust is important in business. People frequently underestimate the extent to which scrupulous honesty enhances profit, especially over the long run. Mike has been in business for twenty years and anticipates being in business for at least another two decades. His reputation is his most valuable asset.

We have a second question for Mike: would you continue to be scrupulously honest if your business was failing and your efforts of two decades were going down the drain? Food wholesaling is a fiercely competitive segment of the business world; hard work and a good reputation do not guarantee continued success. Suppose Mike answers no. In a crunch, he says that he might be willing to abandon his policy of strict honesty. If this is his answer, then being honest may be the secret of his success in the good times, but it has a caveat attached to it. A person who is honest only as long as honesty is profitable may find that the need for immediate gain overrides honesty, especially in situations where competition is fierce. Therefore it is unlikely that honesty actually is the secret of Mike's success. More likely, his secret is opportunism and the effectiveness of using honesty as long as things are going well.

Let us suppose instead that Mike truly is scrupulously honest and that his answer to our second question is yes. He would be honest at all times, even if he found himself in bankruptcy court. If competitors hit his business hard by using innovative methods that he was not able to adopt in time, he still would remain diligently honest rather than cut corners in quality and service.

Our third question, then, is this: Mike, why would you remain honest if you could salvage your business by fudging on the truth? Ideally, Mike will say that he tells the truth because it is simply the right thing to do. That is the kind of honesty that can be most counted on—the individual who is honest has learned that such integrity offers the greatest benefit. It is the right thing to do whether or not it can be measured in precise business-oriented terms. Bona fide honesty, like other aspects of morality, exists for its own sake.

Therefore, if Mike really means it when he says that he is an honest man, he can answer our third question by saying that his life stands for something other than merely making money or pursuing his own interests. He stands for honesty first and making money second. He will not sacrifice the first goal for the second.

This leads to our fourth and last question for Mike: if you place honesty above profit making in your scheme of values, why aren't you willing to place other values above profit making as well? We are referring to values such as kindness toward employees and regard for the well-being of people in the community. Perhaps because of competitive pressures, Mike cannot do much more than he is now doing along these lines. However, at the very least, the well-being of his employees should count along with his concern for honesty. Furthermore, understanding as he does the cyclic nature of the food business, he could reconstruct his rules about his employees and what they are allowed to know, particularly if he thought differently about them as an experienced labor pool—a pool that he can promise to contact first should work return. The small extra effort to consider first the good skills of those he knows before hiring again, rather than simply hiring whoever comes to the door, might provide to the worker in his industry some sense that the worker's efforts are valued. Mike may well understand that many of the workers in his industry are migratory and the likelihood may be slim that they would still be available. Nevertheless, the promise to consider them first if they are available is a valuable commitment to the workers. He even has the option to earmark a small part of his annual profits as a fund for his employees based on need when he lays them off. Doing this is not necessarily either good or bad business practice since he loses some money that could be his, and he may only have gained a small amount of loyalty from those who move frequently and whom he may never see again, or from someone he helped out at the time of a layoff. Indeed, he may reap little or no tangible reward, but he may enjoy the intangible reward of feeling better about himself. What he has done in this scenario is to reach out to those who helped make his business profitable in the first place. These suggested acts are about doing the right things for the longer term. They may make a difference only in how his employees believe he feels about them as valued human beings. Yet, any realistic actions (directed toward employees) that acknowledge their contributions to the success of the business are actions that increase moral awareness and ethical behavior.

Presumably, those who defend the claim that business is amoral and who admire the way Mike does business would have us believe that honesty is somehow in a class by itself: honesty is merely a ploy to consider in playing the game of business, not a higher value. When viewed from this standpoint, the decision to be honest is just one more factor in the pursuit of profit. For Mike, understanding that employees are subject to the volatility of the marketplace and thus at his mercy, and then acting benevolently toward them is part of acting morally. The actions that one might choose in such circumstances are varied and do not necessarily require cash outlay, or even much effort beyond acknowledging the impact of hard times. But, it is never enough to say "Let the employee or the customer beware!" as justification for less than moral actions.

THE DILEMMA OF BUSINESS ETHICS

Defenders of the amoral view of business tend to paint a black-and-white picture: either a company does all it can to make profits or it totally abandons the pursuit of profit in order to engage in something other than business. For purposes of the examples we have been discussing, charity is that other something. The choice is not this stark, however. In other areas of life no one lives by a single value. Why, then, should business be an exception?

Devoted parents put a lot of effort into raising their children, but usually find time for other pursuits as well. If they do not, they may seriously jeopardize the environment they provide for their children. Dedicated physicians, scientists, musicians, actors, and athletes put a lot of effort into their careers, as people must in any competitive field. But the person who subordinates everything to his or her career appears, at best, single-minded and, at worst, a fanatic. If the person goes so far as to totally neglect duties to dependents, then clearly the reach for success has gone too far. It is no longer simply an autonomous search for high achievement but is, in fact, an abusive disregard for others. Success can be achieved at too high a price—almost everyone knows that, and the business world must not be excluded. However, the dilemma of business ethics is often put this way: if a business is moral it will lose out to competitors; if it fights for survival, it will be driven to sacrifice morality.

Perhaps the key to resolving this dilemma lies in the value of products and services that a company produces and the commitment of the company to its employees, investors, the general public, and its other stakeholders. After all, business and ethics are intertwined. From the first moment a company decides to sell a product or provide a service, its approach to these activities begins to establish an ethical framework, or lack thereof.

Factory Closings

Consider the situation of a corporation that must close a plant for sound economic reasons.

> Sharon manages a factory located in a small community. Closing the factory will affect not only the employees of the plant and their families, but also people who run support businesses such as stores and gas stations, employees of local schools and government, and those who depend on revenue to the local economy and tax base provided by the company. The harm caused to the lives of all these

> people, if the factory closes, will be direct, immediate, and in many cases, severe. Moreover, if the plant is closed, the company at large will be harmed. For example, anger expressed by displaced employees may jeopardize the company's public image as well as lower the morale of its remaining employees. But foreign competition and a downturn in the economy have made the plant unprofitable. What should be done?

First, before the company takes any official action, Sharon should carefully assess the ethical problems she faces as the plant manager, the one who will implement company decisions. She needs to evaluate the issues of power and how decisions about such massive events as plant closings will affect others. Regardless of what the company may do, Sharon has her own responsibilities. These responsibilities are all the more significant because she, in acting for the company, is expected to achieve the closing as smoothly as possible. She would do well to consider her own personal ethical obligations as a first step in addressing the question of what should be done.

Leaders of companies sometimes appear to be insensitive to the consequences that their exercise of power has on others. Such insensitivity is not unique to people in business. Business managers may abuse their positions of authority, but so can people in government, the military, medicine, law enforcement, or education. In implementing change, those with power have a special responsibility to handle themselves carefully and to approach important decisions with as much visible respect for the well-being of others as is possible. This is essential in situations such as the closing of a factory, or actions that in other ways risk the livelihood of many individuals.

Perhaps the most important word is *visible.* It does matter what and how things are said. It does matter that leaders speak forthrightly to their employees. It does matter whether or not they have a plan that evaluates the "people costs" and that they do what they can to address those costs. Even when the closing of the plant must occur regardless of the harm to individuals, it is important that a review be conducted, and its conclusions seriously considered when anticipating the change. While others may misunderstand the motives and concerns of the company, it is essential that those who have fiduciary responsibility do what they can to minimize damage. It is wrong for them simply to make a decision and walk away.

Defenders of the amoral view of business say that in the tough competitive markets of today, businesses cannot afford to engage in charity that may lead them into bankruptcy. It does not matter whether the beneficiaries are select individuals or groups, employees, local communities, the environment, or future generations.

Our position in this book is that most businesses can afford to be moral and that such acts will not put them in jeopardy of bankruptcy. We advocate that companies combine the pursuit of profit with moral values in every situation where such values are relevant. This engagement in moral actions that give back to others shows concern for the employees, but moral actions geared to support the long-term health of the company should also be evaluated against pragmatic concerns.

Admittedly, a company will not be around long enough to act morally if it gives back so much of its margin to employees that it has little capital left to upgrade equipment, invest in new facilities, or take innovative risks. A company that does good works through what it produces has a moral obligation to manage itself wisely. It looks out for the long-term well-being of its stakeholders (as well as its stockholders), the community, consumers, employees and their families, and its investors.

What about companies that sell questionable products, use misleading advertisements, or engage in other objectionable business practices? There is no good reason why such businesses ought to survive in a tough competitive battle with other companies whose products and practices are superior. As an example, the world would unquestionably be better off without Frank's used car business.

What about companies that produce a combination of worthless and valuable products or services? If they cannot make a profit without selling products or services that are worthless (or even harmful), then, from an ethical perspective, they cannot justify their existence.

A Helping Hand

How much help should a corporation give to those who are harmed by the shutdown of a factory or other crisis? No precise answer to this question is possible, just as no precise answer is possible to the similar question of how much each of us as individuals ought to give to charitable causes. Many factors are relevant in making such decisions. A necessary question to ask ourselves when deciding how much we as individuals should give to charity is simple enough: how much money do we have available for this purpose?

In turn, an executive who faces a plant closing must ask, "What cash reserves does the corporation have? What are its credit lines at the present time?"

As individuals we should ask, "What personal obligations do we have to families and friends and others that may conflict with giving a significant part of our income to charity? What have we given already to other charities? What have we done to help others?"

An executive might ask, "How much good has the corporation already done to help its employees and others?"

A corporation that has a good track record of doing the right thing for its employees and customers must still evaluate its situation in light of new needs or hardships created by such events as that of the factory-closing example that we have been discussing. It should at least have in place procedures and programs that benefit employees who face termination, and take special care to protect those programs. Good companies try to provide a strong retirement system, a training and development program that keeps employee skills up to date, contingency funds to see people through periods of transition, and effective coordination with union officials to ensure that trust and communication are built into the fabric of the operation. Furthermore, unfavorable developments should be managed before the major crisis of a closing. This would greatly facilitate damage control. Companies that have never faced up to such obligations will have a more difficult challenge in managing the closing of a factory or enterprise in an ethical manner.

It's Lonely (And Powerful) at the Top

Corporate executives need to constantly remind themselves that they can abuse their power, even if, as is usually the case, they acquired it legitimately. Indeed, power acquired legitimately is likely to produce complacency both in those who wield it and in those whom it affects. Most executives have risen to positions of authority as the result of talent and hard work, and it is appropriate for them to feel a sense of accomplishment. However, this feeling may lead to false assumptions about their unique contributions to the organization. The danger of a personal belief in entitlement because of company success (or even by some in the face of company failure!) has occurred all too often at the top in many corporations, leading to outrageous excesses in executive compensation, benefits, and other dispensations from the corporation.

In addition, executives are often cut off from a full evaluation of their effectiveness. Quarterly profits and losses provide them with significant feedback, and such information is an admittedly appropriate and often tough measure of accountability. However, many executives can go through their entire careers being measured only by this yardstick, no matter what else they may or may not do. Other yardsticks of success exist. If executives evaluate and act on factors such as how well they have treated employees or the ways they support doing the right thing in spite of temporary loss of business, they may actually increase profit. An executive may further find that measures of what he or she deems worthy behavior across the spectrum of activities provides personal, as well as professional, benefit.

Executives often do not receive the kind of candor they need from those closest to them. Those who tell executives only what they appear to want to hear do not serve them well. Executives absolutely must arrange their workplace environments to ensure that they will hear from those who speak candidly. They need challenges to the daily judgments that come with being an executive, such as informing people of company activity and enlisting the support of others. Executives need to deliberate with those with whom they disagree, being open to new ways of looking at traditional activities, and always examine their actions in terms of ethical implications. Unfortunately in today's world, some of these activities are typically viewed as outside the usual lines of accountability. Executives must seek out ways to hear from everyone about their actions and give audience to exceptions and critical comments. Those statements that describe concerns, even if raised by a few, should be considered as instances where some truth may reside, instead of being dismissed as concerns coming from a disgruntled few.

Seeking moments of reflection should not be optional, but should be a part of the fabric of a chief executive's life on the job. This is especially true during very difficult times of transition such as factory closings, mergers and acquisitions, or reductions of the workforce. Without deliberately putting reflection ahead of other activities, most people, including executives, get caught up in the tumult of rapidly approaching events. The best time to consider actions that have ethical implications is before the storm; then again during the storm to assess how well one is managing the situation, and finally, after the storm has passed. Post-hoc reviews are excellent vehicles for discovering improvement opportunities. If senior executives accept this in-depth accountability, employees will likely have a clearer understanding of the leader's interest in workplace issues of common good, fairness, and integrity.

The Interests of Stockholders

Sometimes people say that corporate executives have an obligation to their stockholders to make as much money as possible. If stockholders want to give to charity, they could do so directly, rather than invest in the company. However, consideration of the role that stockholders play in business does not change any of what we have been saying. We need only ask ourselves this question: would the stockholders, in their own lives, choose to put all their efforts toward single-minded endeavors regardless of the costs to others? Most would not. Then why would they want their financial investments to be any different?

We allow a depersonalized sense of ownership to work its way into stockholders' perceptions when we do not inform them of all the costs and benefits of business decisions. As described earlier, some evidence exists that individuals are willing to invest in companies that combine the pursuit of profit with a firm commitment to moral values. In any case, it is the right thing to do.

Speaking Out Loud

Most corporations have published statements about their values and commitment to ethics—considered to be not only good but necessary policy. In most large corporations you will find a solid set of policies, statements of commitment, codes of conduct, clear sanctions against violating ethical principles, and other written documentation indicating that ethics is a seriously regarded topic. These statements of intent are highly desirable and good—but they are not sufficient. Effective ethics is a personal event as well as a structural one. For example, in setting up conditions for ethical actions, too few business leaders make important statements about monitoring their own behavior openly in terms of very real ethical sensitivities that come with positions of power. One worthy exception was reported in the Minneapolis/St. Paul business community, as described by Dave Beal (2003) in the *Pioneer Press:*

> Thirty-eight local business leaders here have signed on to an evolving set of principles designed to help restore the public's confidence in the practices of American corporations. The principles deal with four topics: executive compensation, balancing short-term gain with long-term value, corporate responsibility and corporate governance (p. 2).

The statement grew out of concerns voiced by David Koch, retired chief executive officer of Golden Valley-based Graco Inc., and others about the need for corporate leaders to speak out on such issues (Beal, 2003).

It is time for business leaders to start talking out loud about the ethical nature of how and why their companies do business and their personal willingness to engage in self-monitoring as well as corporate monitoring—to indicate that they, above all others, understand the dangers of the slippery slope to which we referred earlier. It is important for businesspeople at all levels of authority to vigorously challenge the amoral view of business.

To ensure that business operates from a less impersonal viewpoint, the fundamental principles of the worth and autonomy of each person, including ourselves, must be established. Unfortunately, many times the Golden Rule is ignored, except when it comes to a consideration of our own worth and autonomy. Treating others as we would be treated is such a nice thing to say, but it is rarely among the first things evaluated in how we do our work. Stockholders, employees, and consumers must recognize that they have a stake in maintaining such a vision.

4

CHAPTER

Respect for Individuality

The plague of mankind is the fear and rejection of diversity: monotheism, monarchy, monogamy and, in our age, monomedicine. The belief that there is only one right way to live, only one right way to regulate religious, political, sexual, medical affairs is the root cause of the greatest threat to man: members of his own species, bent on ensuring his salvation, security, and sanity.

—Thomas Szasz, M.D.

We as a nation speak often and fondly of the rights and dignity of the individual. We speak of our right to privacy and our need for trust and caring for one another as individuals. We say that we value the creativity of the individual and the unique styles of our colleagues, and we speak of the value of diversity. Yet, as much as we talk about recognizing individuality, what we say and what we do often conflict. This chapter explores interpersonal dilemmas against the backdrop of what we need to know in order to recognize individuality.

Following are some examples of what might get in the way of our doing the right thing in regard to recognizing individuality. Many of our actions in the business world impede the rights or dignity of someone, and we often act without thinking about the impact of our actions. It is difficult at times to separate our own wants from the wants of people around us. For example, we typically find ourselves doing more for our friends than for the stranger who works down the hall. Is this a violation of fundamental ethics? In all probability it is not, but the question is worthy of consideration in our efforts to protect and respect individuals.

FOLLOWING THE RULES

Let's look at the behavior of several employees, all of whom are considered good people, and all of whom believe that they are doing their jobs effectively. They would all say that they respect and protect the rights of others.

Joe, who is an office manager, assigns an easier work schedule to his friend Henry than he does to Stan, someone he has no ill feeling toward but does not know very well. Both employees share the same job description. Stan has asked questions about the various assignments, but appears to accept Joe's answer that he depends on Stan to put in extra effort since Stan is so good at what he does.

Jennifer, a typist, continually finds excuses to leave her desk to check her makeup, get a drink, stretch her legs, and so on. It seems to her office mates that she is often unavailable when needed.

Jack, an accounts manager, takes printer ribbons, mailing envelopes, rolls of tape, and other supplies home for his personal use. He takes so many supplies from the office that he has enough to give to his children and friends. He considers the "free" supplies as job perks.

Lucy, who handles purchasing, often misses work for the slightest of reasons and frequently on days when she knows the workload will be the heaviest.

Trisha, the business development and marketing specialist, is often late for work, for meetings, and even for luncheon engagements with clients and colleagues. She waits for long periods of time before calling people back and then pouts when confronted and complains about how busy she is. She wastes a considerable amount of other people's time.

When you read about or encounter examples of workplace conduct such as these, what is your response? More than likely, you will ask yourself questions and have thoughts such as the following:

1. Why is Joe unable to see that he is abusing his position of authority? He is increasing the friction between himself and Stan and contributing to resentment between Stan and Henry. This interferes with effective office operations, thus short-changing the company he works for. He is not playing the game according to long-established rules of fairness that are essential in a civilized society.
2. Why can't Jennifer see that she is violating her employment contract and therefore is not playing by the rules? It makes no difference ethically whether the contract is written or oral, implicit, or explicit. A person who takes a job agrees to work with a certain level of diligence, a level that Jennifer has fallen below.
3. Why can't Jack see that he is violating one of society's most basic rules, the prohibition against stealing?

We can submit similar questions about Lucy and Trisha.

All of these responses refer to the idea of moral rules. These moral rules have much to say about how we are supposed to treat one another and what we owe to others through our own conduct. Such rules can generate red-hot reactions in many of us when we merely think about how people sometimes treat one another. In earlier chapters, we said relatively little about moral rules. While they are extremely important for living in a civilized way they are not enough to maintain moral actions. In addition, they do not guarantee that if we only follow the rule, the outcome will be an ethical one. These points are frequently misunderstood.

People sometimes make the mistake of supposing either that moral rules alone constitute morality (morality means following rules and nothing else) or that the essence of morality is "following your feelings" and rules do not count. Even beyond that, many people believe that once we are provided the rules we follow them because we should. However, people learn the rules by doing things that are reinforced by others or by the events that occur in the environment as a result of behaving according to the rules. The reinforcement from others often includes a verbal explanation about how good it is to follow the rule—respecting others, putting someone else ahead of oneself, and being honest.

Sometimes, until we hear or see the effects of our actions, we may not think in terms of following a moral imperative or taking an ethical stance. These understandings come most fully after the actions have taken place. Over time, we do come to do certain things consistently, finding reinforcement for being on time, returning phone calls in a timely fashion, talking straight to a friend about why favoritism at work is not possible, even for the friend himself, and so on. Rules are statements we make about a whole set of behaviors that we have been taught and reinforced for doing. We discover through our own interactions that a rule is a handy way of summing up a great many different behaviors that belong to a particular class of behaviors, such as those that fall under the heading of *respecting others.*

Achieving ethical improvement in the workplace requires, among other needed changes, increasing respect for moral rules. They regulate our interactions with others, providing protection for the autonomy and dignity of each of us. One method for increasing respect for moral rules is to bring such rules to the attention of people in the workplace. For example, publish and conspicuously post a company "code of conduct" that defines rules regarding company and individual property rights, the honoring of business and personal contracts, the protection of personal, and in some cases, corporate privacy, or other aspects of the workplace. Keep in mind, though, that it is not the rule that is controlling behavior over time. Codes of conduct are good initiators of what is desired, but behavior is changed and maintained by the consequences that follow actions. Most people do what they are reinforced for doing on a daily basis, rather than doing what they see posted as written codes of conduct.

From a philosophical perspective, rules belong to the "surface" of morality; the essence of morality consists of deeper values, such as the belief in the intrinsic worth and dignity of all human beings (discussed below) and rights and justice (discussed in Chapter 6). It is not enough to focus attention on rules, because as just stated, morality consists of much more than rules. In addition, it would be difficult in a manageably brief code of conduct to list all the rules that should be taken into account. If a rule is not explicitly listed, does that mean it is unimportant? After all, most of us understand that the commandment "Thou shalt not kill" doesn't imply by the absence of comment that mutilation and physical abuse are acceptable. Perhaps the most important first step that anyone can take to encourage ethical improvement in the workplace or anywhere else is to talk ethics—to explore options, debate choices, defend ethical conduct, praise what is right, and condemn what is wrong.

Effective ethical talk must be broadly focused, pushing people beyond the surface phenomena of moral rules. Rules help define and summarize appropriate actions, but they are not sufficient to produce ethical behavior. In judging others, many people all too often may apply a rule before they ensure that the performer knows what the rule is or even how to follow the rule. It is wrong to then accuse that person of violating the rule. Nevertheless, this is something that parents do all too often with their children. For example, as children, we were given many rules: Wash your hands before meals. Never run into the street. Finish your homework before you go out to play. Come home before dark. Do not step in puddles. Make your bed before breakfast. Turn off the lights. Be quiet when others are sleeping.

The rules of childhood seemed endless, and people forever carry their childhood rules with them in one form or another, along with for some, an inclination to rebel. It is helpful, therefore, when explaining rules to children or to any of us, to understand that as a rule giver, you can increase effective ethical talk by focusing on the reasons behind rules as much as on the rules themselves. Ethical talk defines umbrella values that are broader than a specific rule, such as consideration for others and personal responsibility. Such explanations help to put the rule in a larger context.

In each instance of ethical choice there exists a hierarchy of values, some more important than others. Children, as well as the rest of us, learn shorthand descriptions for what is important, not from being told to follow a rule, but by having what we do positively reinforced or punished as well as talking about why a rule is important. It is amazing how quickly little children grasp the meanings behind rules if parents and teachers discuss the larger meanings of the rules with them.

Of course, all the talk in the world will not help a child learn a rule and its value-based meaning, if what is said is very different from what is done. If we were told to wash our hands, but our parents ignored our dirty hands at the dinner table, even if they helped us understand the need for the rule, we learned sooner or later that hand-washing was a stated rule but not a valued rule. The word *rule* became something else—an annoyance or a small inconvenience—not meant to be taken too seriously. Thus, rules that are stated, such as in a code of conduct, but are then not attended to through consequence management, undermine all other rules, ultimately undermining the clarity of what is said to be important.

People do not always realize that if rules are not reinforced positively when children first begin to learn them, or are treated as irrelevant one day but taken seriously the next, then children learn that many of the directions given to them can be ignored. Very often, entrenched rule-violating behavior patterns start with the initial ambivalence that parents show regarding the importance of rules with their young children. These patterns often are accompanied by an equally damaging failure to recognize the children's efforts to follow the rules. When they attempt to wash their hands in a sink they can't reach, or wait quietly to be called on even when bursting with excitement to speak, adults should acknowledge their efforts. Finally, all too often, parents do not, or cannot, identify the fundamental moral code behind following the rule in the first place. Their overt actions in regard to the underlying principles tell the child as much or more than the occasional word of praise for doing the right thing. While parents may fail to comment positively to their own children who are working to do the right thing, managers are even less likely to see or say anything to their employees who model outstanding personal performance according to a published code of conduct.

These very small actions of neglect by parents or managers undermine the two fundamental values of intrinsic worth and individual autonomy that must be upheld in all efforts to act ethically. These values must always be considered and reinforced as part of what is valued. Moreover, these two values, when ignored, can erode the ethics of society.

INTRINSIC WORTH AND INDIVIDUAL AUTONOMY

The most basic of all moral values is the centrality of the intrinsic worth and the autonomy of all human beings. In the history of civilization, the highest kind of moral advancement has been the increasing recognition that in the most profound moral sense, all human lives count equally. Josiah Royce (1885), an American philosopher of the late nineteenth and early twentieth centuries, said that other people are "selves like us." They are valuable to and for themselves just as we are valuable to and for ourselves.

Most systems of morality in earlier times were tribal in recognizing the intrinsic worth of at least some of the members of one's own society (women and children did not always count) but not the intrinsic worth of people outside one's own society. Past and current human rights movements highlight our country's ongoing struggle to shape a moral world. As a society, Americans are concerned now more than ever before about civil rights, women's rights, the rights of children, of the elderly, of homosexuals, and the handicapped. We are concerned about the rights of individuals and we are concerned about individual expression.

Understanding the full implications of the inherent equality and worth of all human beings is in its infancy. Yet, in the opening years of the twenty-first century, almost all national and global organizations at least acknowledge the inherent equality and worth of all human beings; of course, there are exceptions. Some people believe that individuals must earn and retain equality through their actions and that they can lose their equal-worth status. For example, angry debate continues on what fate should be imposed on those who commit murder or do other terrible acts of harm against their fellow human beings and especially against the more helpless, such as children. The underlying issues are difficult ones to reach a consensus on, and involve a host of values that individuals in this country hold dear. As a society we seem to be moving away from the death penalty but there does not yet seem to be a "moral consensus" that we can all agree with, other than the news that innocent people have indeed been put to death. We have not yet come out and said that as a society the taking of life is never justified, even if that life took another. It may well be a long time, if ever, before we do reach anything like consensus on this subject, because both sides see righteousness on their side.

The recognition that people have intrinsic worth as individuals means several different things; the most fundamental is respect for autonomy. A rough definition of *autonomy* in this context is "being one's own person." An autonomous individual has opportunities to make his or her own choices, even wrong ones, within a broad range of actions. Yet, we must have rules regarding property rights, privacy, honoring contracts, truthfulness, and so on, if autonomy is to be respected and protected.

As individuals we have different interests, wants, and needs that can and do conflict. Life is full of hardships, deprivations, and imperfections. From various religious perspectives (Judeo-Christian, Muslim, Hindu, and many others), life is a testing ground for everyone, a harsher testing ground for some than for others.

In a world like ours, individual autonomy requires the existence of an impersonal structure to life that only rules can provide. The rules must not depend upon the whim, or even the considered judgment, of others. For each of us to be our own person day in and day out, we must be in a position to expect that most people will follow rules regarding autonomy generally.

Rules give us space to be ourselves: if it is my property, then (within established limits) I can do what I want with it. Because one's sexuality belongs within one's own private sphere of life, a person can make of it what he or she wants. Invasion of another's privacy is intolerable. Unless we keep promises and honor contracts, we will be unable to carry out plans that involve interactions with others. If we do keep our promises and honor agreements, then cooperation is possible even with people who do not share our specific goals.

Because human beings too often fail to follow moral rules, a legal system is required to apply constraining influence when and where appropriate. The laws of the land, provided they are good laws, are often an extension of moral rules and are equally essential for the protection of individual autonomy. Thus, belief in the intrinsic worth of one's fellow human beings goes hand in hand with respect for rules and laws. The fundamental message is that we will treat others as we would have them treat us, as independent beings. Each possesses his or her own talents, achievements, hopes and aspirations, fears and uncertainties, and all of the burdens that humans endure, both self-imposed and those resulting from each person's unique station in life.

WHEN GOOD PEOPLE BEHAVE UNETHICALLY

Most people have a pretty good idea about what goes wrong when a bad person behaves unethically. The person lies, steals, reneges on contracts, takes advantage of others' weaknesses, and so on. This is blatant disregard for ethical norms. Good people also behave unethically, less blatantly but nevertheless in ways that can cause a lot of harm to other human beings as well as to themselves.

One of the most frequently occurring ways that good people behave unethically involves violations of individual autonomy. Examples include well-meaning parents who choose hobbies, colleges, careers, or life styles that they attempt to force upon their offspring; spouses who do not give each other enough room to develop as individuals; conscientious people who attempt to push their political or religious beliefs on friends or fellow workers; and employers who perceive female workers stereotypically as not being able to handle tough decisions. It is all too easy for one person to fail to perceive the uniqueness of someone else. Even people who strive to be ethical can fail, as seen in the following examples.

A boss might have a rigid moral guidepost that requires him to treat everyone equally. He imposes an inflexible vacation schedule on his employees. One of his employees wins a free, one-week trip to Paris. Even though she is not crucial to company activities for that week, the boss will not let her go.

A manager sometimes transfers subordinates arbitrarily in order to keep things running without any kind of disruption to production. This may require that employees move from the downtown location to one of the branch operations. The manager doesn't consider how the transfers may impact the personal lives of employees and makes no attempt to work out problems. In some cases the transfer will mean increased costs for transportation and an extra hour of travel to and from work, extra childcare expenses, and more time away from home.

A company climate that grows out of positive team spirit may compel employees to work longer than the normal workweek. The implied, but not necessarily proclaimed, rule is that if you are really part of the team, you will put in a lot of time after regular hours and managers will take notice of those who go home right at five o'clock.

As far as the examples listed above are concerned, it probably does not occur to the decision makers involved that they have unreasonable expectations. Nor are these examples clearly of a life and death ethical nature. "I do it this way to achieve a greater good as I see it" is the prevailing attitude. It is important to bring to the attention of such people how an impersonal process such as unconditionally following rules can affect the autonomy of others. The individual who refuses to help a colleague facing a deadline by doing a simple task such as filling the copying machine with paper, for the sole reason that "it is not right to do people's work for them" may be responding to rules learned early in life that at a rather simple level are correct. But when put in the context of cooperation, empathy, and respect, such absolutes lose their moral strength.

Ethical behavior in the workplace is more than just being true to one's own values. Just as much, it is a matter of having the right values in the first place. The highest level of ethical behavior requires an awareness of moral rules and the values they represent. We must weigh the relevant principles, gather all necessary information, and ask ourselves whether or not we are being morally sensitive to all the people we affect. We must decide when to follow rules strictly and when to make exceptions.

CONSCIENCE

Many people believe that morality means following one's conscience. Philosophers sometimes refer to the conscience as the moral sense. They have debated at length about the role that it plays in ethical decision making. Conscience, from the perspective of behavioral psychology, refers in shorthand to our personal histories of reinforcement for conforming to certain societal standards of right and wrong.

Following one's conscience is a skill that can be strengthened and put to good use, but a person's moral feelings can and sometimes should be changed—at least nudged in a more favorable direction. A person's conscience is not an absolutely reliable guide for making ethical decisions. Consider the well-known anthem "My Way" the English version written by Paul Anka and popularized by Frank Sinatra (1969). The following stanza sums up the individualistic view that many Americans hold regarding decision making:

For what is a man? What has he got?
If not himself—then he has naught.
To say the things he truly feels
And not the words of one who kneels.
Let the record show I took the blows,
And did it my way.
Yes, it was my way.

If we are to respect the individuality of our fellow human beings, we must follow our conscience in an enlightened way, not always our own particular way. The adult conscience often must reach beyond rules that do not apply exactly to the situations in which we find ourselves, and we must be willing to consider questions of morality that extend beyond our unique personal experiences.

EVALUATING BEHAVIOR AGAINST AN ETHICAL FRAMEWORK

Too often both employers and employees do not know how to evaluate their actions against the elusive and difficult framework called *ethics,* but it can be done. The ideas we have discussed in this chapter (moral rules, intrinsic worth, individual autonomy, and conscience) provide a beginning point in evaluating the importance of individuality and of being aware of the measurable standards against which to evaluate ethical choices. Using these ideas to assess and validate our actions are the first steps toward being more fully accountable for ethical behavior at work. The chapters that follow will detail additional steps.

Unfortunately, discussing aloud the ethical criteria against which we measure our actions or those of our company is rarely done. In this age of public accountability, it behooves both individuals and corporations to pay close attention to ethical decision making and what it involves. Everyone must go beyond simple mission declarations or guiding statements that proclaim that the company always strives to do the right thing, and look to his or her own behavior as a central part of the ethical landscape.

WHAT WILL A COMPANY DO FOR PROFIT?

The first tangible evidence of how a company operates at an ethical level often comes in its practices in selling its products and services. Without adequate sales, businesses would soon lose out and disappear. If businesses are to survive, they should not go about selling their services and products without a careful analysis of how they are promoting and supporting the right actions. In the next chapter, we discuss the practice of selling—to customers, to our stakeholders, to one another—and its central role in defining the world of business. To know how centrally your leadership places ethics in your company, start with a careful examination of the actual practices of those who engage in selling and how those practices are supported or shaped. This analysis is often as close to a corporate mirror as you can get when first examining ethical practices at work.

5

CHAPTER

ACHIEVING ETHICAL SALES

There were some nice days…when he'd come home from a trip…or on a Sunday, making the stoop… finishing the cellar, when he built the extra bathroom and built the garage…You know, Charlie, I think there was more of him in that front stoop than in all the sales he ever made…He had the wrong dream…all, all wrong.

—Arthur Miller, *Death of a Salesman*

ALTHOUGH NOTHING HAS GREATER importance to any business than selling its products or services, it is difficult to find a more ambiguous area of contemporary life. Without sales, a company loses its reason for existing. Yet many people have mixed feelings about the sales profession. Should they admire it or despise it? Should they view selling as a necessary evil, a marginal good, or a praiseworthy activity requiring a high level of skill?

A century ago, horse traders were distrusted, while employees of Great Britain's East India Company, who engaged in foreign trade on a grand scale, were admired. Willy Loman, the main character in the play *Death of a Salesman,* struggled to make a living in a rough and tumble, no-holds-barred world, caught in his personal definition that equated a meaningful life with achieving success in business, his American Dream. The story of his quietly desperate life evokes empathy, yet the used car salesman, whose plight is similar to Loman's, is distrusted and made the butt of jokes. By contrast, "sales engineers" for large corporations are treated as members of a corporate elite who fuel the American economy. As people try new techniques for avoiding or resisting various sales pitches, books such as *The Art of the Deal,* describing effective sales techniques, become best sellers. Especially within their own companies, successful salespeople may be heroes, but they are just as often mistrusted and maligned. Employees may advise one another not to be taken in by their "sophisticated" sales colleagues whose skills are equated with the manipulative, self-serving strategies of the snake that tempted Eve to eat the apple.

When it comes to sales practices, people are fascinated, envious, repulsed, grateful, embarrassed, and even angry, depending in part on whether they gain or lose from the sales process.

Selling, in a broad sense, permeates and reflects life because life is full of ambiguity, conflict, and controversy. Almost everything that people want in their lives requires convincing someone else to help provide it. It might be money, goods, services, friendship, security, or the wide acceptance of a cherished belief. Usually, when we want something, we must convince others that they ought to give it to us, sell it to us, help us make it, help us obtain it, or help us keep it. This means that we must make a case to attain their assistance or compliance; we must sell our point of view. All sales involve a "sales presentation," even if this amounts to no more than placing ourselves in a position where we may hope that others will notice our needs and wants.

So, although some may argue otherwise, the ethics of sales is not a separate branch of ethics with its own special rules (as when people say, "That's just a sales pitch.") As we said in Chapter 3, the world of business is part and parcel of the world itself, not an amoral entity existing apart from the world. The sales arena does not constitute a separate domain but rather is an important (perhaps more vulnerable) thread in the fabric of work life; the vulnerability exists because of the inherent and unique pressures that come to bear upon a sales career. For this reason, business leaders are especially obligated to design the financial incentives and goals of salespersons in a way that doesn't prompt, condone, or reward inappropriate actions.

WHAT GOES WRONG

Selling is the pulse of the business heart. There is nothing dehumanizing about selling goods, services, one's labor, or anything else—unless it requires the selling of one's integrity. Of course, selling one's integrity involves a different sense of the word *sell.* A career in sales does not make a person materialistic, greedy, grasping, or superficial. It need not teach a person, as Oscar Wilde (1890/1892) said in a somewhat different context, "the price of everything and the value of nothing." A career in sales can be as honorable (or dishonorable) as any other.

Unfortunately, pressures unique to sales can present more temptations to act without honor. Far too often, short-term contingencies, bonuses, commissions, expensive trips, and prizes drive sales activity. Not making the sale, regardless of the reason, is almost never rewarded financially. Has an ethics credit ever been placed in a salesperson's file for placing integrity above commission? (We don't know, but if so, we bet it's not a common practice. In fact, the salesperson who forfeits a sale for reasons of integrity would more likely be punished, not rewarded, for doing so.) Almost everyone realizes that salespersons sometimes reassure customers that a particular sale involves no commission. Even if such a statement is true (which it may not be), the need to make the statement indicates that something clearly is wrong in many sales/customer relationships—something of greater concern regarding the seller, the customer, and self-interest.

An unspoken division frequently exists within a company between salespeople and other employees. The division may occur because other staffers feel that salespeople are treated differently by management regarding status, training, and the degree of risk-taking expected and condoned. Yet, common values shared by salespeople with their fellow employees are the most important in the long run, and in the vast majority of sales those values are critical to everyone's success. Some of those common values include courtesy, sympathy for others (especially for those in need), respect for the individuality of other people, and a desire to make a contribution toward improving the world. In other words, salespeople, like all other employees, are obligated to protect people's rights, alleviate suffering, and make efforts toward improving society overall, even in the tasks of routine business life. Salespeople must be concerned about the well-being of others while also looking out for their own interests in a responsible fashion. The basics of ethical behavior apply to salespeople as well as to everyone else.

Ethical issues arise in everyday practices, and sometimes unfold in unexpected ways. The following is a typical example of sales behavior.

> Jane sells real estate. Not long ago, she sold a small house to a single parent, Sarah, who recently moved into town with her two children. Sarah received no child support from her ex-husband and was struggling to make ends meet. She told Jane that she wanted to buy a house, in part, to build financial security—a correct observation several years earlier when the real estate market was unusually strong, but not as certain now. In Jane's town, real estate prices had been falling, but had not bottomed out. As was her practice with every potential customer, Jane said nothing negative concerning the real estate market to Sarah; as far as Jane was concerned, that was not her responsibility. If she were to tell potential customers that real estate was not a particularly good investment at the time, fewer people might buy property, the market could get worse, and Jane would lose income and possibly her livelihood.
>
> The house that Sarah showed the most interest in was one that had many small problems. Sarah was inexperienced in issues related to building construction, furnaces,

wiring, plumbing, and other areas where deficiencies can occur. Jane said nothing about small problems that Sarah did not notice herself, even though the house was most suitable for owners who could make a lot of minor repairs themselves. The house was a fixer-upper, but Jane did not tell this to Sarah.

In her own mind, Jane justified rushing Sarah into buying that particular house, in part because she was not pushing Sarah into offering the highest possible price for the property. The owner had listed the house for $72,000, but Jane knew he would accept an offer as low as $60,000. To make a quick sale, Jane told Sarah that the owner had turned down an offer of $60,000 but would probably accept $63,000. As Jane saw it, it was better for her to quickly sell two houses at the low end of their price range than to take a long time to sell one house at the high end.

The world is full of individuals like Jane—salespeople in every field who are not totally wrong in their moral thinking, but who fail to achieve a proper balance among values. They believe that customers should look out for themselves, which is largely true, but Jane was aware of Sarah's background, her lack of knowledge regarding home repairs, and her limited income. Jane should have honestly revealed the fixer-upper status of the property to the customer. However, as far as Jane was concerned, she met her own goal, thus helping her real estate agency, her own family, and her career.

FINDING AN APPROPRIATE BALANCE

Consider what Jane told Sarah about the real estate market. A positive pitch about the product on the part of salespeople is not morally wrong. Salespeople are essentially advocates for products or services; their job is to present what they are selling in an appealing light. Yet Jane, in persuading Sarah to buy the house, went beyond that. She took advantage of someone who was struggling financially and who would probably have been better off not buying a house at the time or buying a house that needed fewer repairs.

Sellers need not mention every last defect in a product or service, but should mention more of them than Jane did. From an ethical, as well as legal point of view, they absolutely must mention all major defects. They have an obligation to make a significant effort toward matching up the right product or service with the right customer. For Sarah, who had little money available for repairs and no skills in home repair, all of the small problems with the house taken together amounted to a major problem. Jane ignored this issue in her eagerness to make a quick commission.

Salespeople have a stronger obligation to the people who buy from them than Jane recognized. Jane should have strived for a more appropriate balance among the interests of the customer, the real estate agency, the seller, and herself. If Jane had been more candid with Sarah, she would have produced a more satisfied customer and, in the long run, a more successful agency. She could have even increased her income potentially, stemming from positive references from Sarah and other customers who would talk about how fairly and thoughtfully Jane treated them.

Why are there so many people like Jane? Is it because the United States, and much of the world, is so highly competitive that people are driven into behaving unethically? Is it that we espouse short-term goals and quick fixes? Is it that our society strongly endorses self-interest and individualism, and successful individuals are measured to a great extent by the money they make and the things that money can buy?

Certainly, societal emphasis on competition and winning (two highly acclaimed components of American business) might be interpreted loosely to justify selfish acts, but this emphasis is not the true culprit. On the contrary, there is great value in a free, or relatively free, market system where business is open to competition. Whether or not competitors will in actuality fight one another tooth and nail is another question. Within a market system that allows as much competition as possible, those who compete should deliberately choose to strive for an appropriate balance of interests. A competitive marketplace does not preclude cooperation; it merely shifts a part of the ethical burden to participants within the market. In later chapters we discuss further the role that cooperation can play within a competitive marketplace.

Competition for sales does exert strong pressures on salespeople such as Jane, but there is nothing unique about these pressures. Similar pressures bear heavily upon people in other lines of work. Physicians are pressured to spend less time with each patient; researchers are pressured to cut corners in collecting data; professors are pressured to grade students' papers too hastily; farmers are pressured to use excessive amounts of pesticides; composers are pressured to be continually creative and sometimes to even claim other's work as their own…and the beat goes on.

The pressures that are to be found in each of these situations can lead to shortcuts that contain ethical issues, some small, many large. In every walk of life conflicting values must be balanced, particularly in cases where success requires measuring up to the achievements of other people or to monetary goals. There are temptations to spend too little time at one's job in order to be with one's family. There are also temptations to spend too much time at one's job and too little time with one's family. There are temptations to favor one's employer over one's subordinates, and there are temptations to do exactly the opposite. Everyone in the workplace faces pressures from many different and conflicting directions.

Some say that the pressures in a sales career are unique because they are often one-dimensional; all of the pressures are exerted in the direction of sales volume (measured in dollars or numbers of orders). These individuals may contend that in other areas of life there is recognition that conflicting values do and should exist. For example, we expect people to seek a compromise between time spent with family and time spent on the job. The same applies to time spent on student's work and on one's research in academia, or between loyalty to one's employer and loyalty to one's subordinates, and so on. However, defenders of separate sales ethics assert that salespeople are often expected to focus exclusively on volume sold and money received.

If focusing solely on volume and cash were a correct characterization of all sales practices, such practices would be amoral or flat-out immoral. It would be appropriate to liken the amorality (or immorality) of sales to the amorality of war; both have been described as possessing a single motivation, namely to win at all costs. As the saying goes, "All is fair in love and war." Yet, the mark of a truly civilized world is the attempt to civilize warfare. We produce rules of war, as expressed in the Geneva Convention. These outlaw a considerable number of abhorrent practices, such as shooting prisoners and using chemical and biological weapons. Hence, not even war should be one-dimensional: even when one's life is at stake, not everything is permissible. If war can be civilized somewhat, then certainly sales practices can be.

The point is that sales need not be one-dimensional. Indeed, many salespeople do have a keen sense that they are selling not only the product or service of their company, but also the commitment, promises, and follow-through they exercise as individuals. Salespeople, perhaps more than most other employees, represent themselves when representing the company. This perspective is not lost on the majority of salespeople who sell with honesty and personal integrity. The long-term effects of what is said and done as a salesperson build that person's reputation, along with the protection of one's reputation. This, along with the protection of one's own values, provides a safety valve that makes many salespeople unwilling to mislead customers. This is especially true when sales are based on personal relationships. Salespeople usually understand that the personal codes of conduct they demonstrate elsewhere in their lives contribute integrally to their success in sales.

Consequently, a company that hires and sends out its sales representatives must make clear what it expects from them. The sales plan must be part of a larger, more comprehensive marketing strategy. The company must insist on delivering what is promised and ensuring that the interaction between sales and service is paramount. At no point does ethical decision making become more important than in building moral fiber into the sales operation.

An example of the need for building ethics into sales relates to high-tech companies that, as we know, are pressured by the marketplace to get to market fast, in secret, and with something novel and better than anything competitors are selling or are about to sell. To have the revenues needed to keep the research and development cycle going, the company may covertly or overtly pressure their sales personnel to promise product specifications and unreasonable timeframes for products that have not yet been produced. The engineers then must try to design/produce the specifications under high pressure. Often, the specs and/or timeframe cannot be accomplished, resulting in angry customers, angry staff, and angry management. Yet, we might assume that the sales staff should be generally happy. They pocket the commission from the up-front sale and move on to the next customer. Still, that cash may be a heavier burden than we think.

Most salespersons do not want to sell through deception or fraud, but they are often the people who are put out there to keep companies financially viable, creating unique pressures to ensure company success. From such pressures come statements, or an implicit understanding, along the lines of the following slogan: "Promise them anything but get the contract!"

RECIPROCITY OF EFFECT AND THE LONGER TERM

A reciprocal relationship exists between the individual and the business. Neither one can truly win if the reputation of either is harmed by the assumption that winning outweighs character and ethical action. A company must consciously make ongoing and sincere efforts to strengthen its salespersons' justified concern for the customers, clients, suppliers, the general public, and even future generations. For example, does the product they are selling have any potential to do significant harm? The company must promote and follow codes of conduct regarding how they recognize ethical sales behavior, and provide example-based case studies, awareness training, and role playing sessions for its sales force on this very topic.

Almost all of us can create ways to sell good products and services with honor. Granted, no one is perfect, but the moral requirement is that we should attempt to always move in the right direction. When more and more people move in the direction of "civilizing" sales practices, those practices, over time, will bring about considerable overall improvement in the world of sales. These small improvements will eventually lead to broader progress in the long run, since each new level of improvement will become the standard against which future improvement must be measured.

Yet, without a motivation to adopt this broad, longer-term perspective, and with so many positive consequences in place for doing otherwise, unethical conduct happens, whether in sales or other areas.

Clearly, seeing the big picture from an ethical perspective allows businesses to better assess the meaning of their actions. In scientific research, if numerous practitioners were corrupt but little was done to remove their corruption, this would place pressure on the other researchers to likewise make use of inadequate data, accept support from interested parties, or sensationalize their findings. This sort of thing did happen in the Soviet Union a generation ago, when, for a time, faulty biological research and findings nearly extinguished legitimate biological science in that country. Similarly, in our society, bad sales practices have tended to drive out the good ones, more so for some products than for others. Unquestionably, unethical practices can and frequently do drive out ethical practices.

Why has this phenomenon so often been associated with sales? Part of the answer is that people have not adequately integrated the world of business into their lives as a whole. Centuries-old biases against commerce still hold sway; with the consequence that business is judged to be amoral. As we stated in Chapter 3, a widespread belief persists that business can follow its own rules. It is no wonder that sales practices, residing at the heart of business, should have suffered the most in this regard. All too often, commerce lives up to our cynical expectations, but we all pay a high price when we wink at, and then ignore, unethical and immoral practices.

Further explanation for why there are so many individuals like Jane lies in part with how we identify and teach values to America's youth. Parents are often poor role models, and advertising and media barrage our children with materialistic messages. However, the most important part of the explanation lies in the business systems that improperly reward sales efforts—those that 1) do not reward salespeople for placing integrity over commissions, and 2) fail to integrate ethical business strategy with sales practices.

MEASURING ETHICAL CHOICES

The next chapter defines how a set of core values can be used to assess how well, in given circumstances, you apply a principled perspective to decisions you make. It gives you a tool for measuring impact before the act, and a method for assessing, after the choices are made, how well you did in taking the actions you did. Businesses that adopt such a model have an independent measure, rather than a strictly situational one, to assess actions.

Without an external standard, the temptation to apply situational ethics arises, greatly reducing the probability that actions will be evaluated against a variety of contexts—the good of society, the good of those affected by the practices of the company, and finally, the good of the company. Never make the mistake of evaluating ethics without an external standard. Remember the slippery slope discussed earlier—there is good (for me) and then there is good (for the right reasons). A company that truly desires to be an ethical company must always remember that self-justification for the good of the business is a shaky platform upon which to stand.

6
CHAPTER

Making Ethical Decisions

A people that values its privileges above its principles soon loses both.

—Dwight D. Eisenhower, *Inaugural Address*

There are two possible models for ethical decision making: (1) the single moral value approach, and (2) moral pluralism.

When following the first model, every ethical decision boils down to determining how to apply a single value, such as the one espoused by the moral philosophy of utilitarianism. For utilitarians, every ethical question must be answered by determining which action will bring about the greatest good for the greatest number of people.

Large tariffs, customary gifts to key managers, and special perks can all be thought of as bribes; they are objects of value or privileges that buy special favors pertaining to trading rights for certain interest groups. Should companies doing business in foreign countries offer bribes for the right to do business in those countries? A utilitarian would answer that offering bribes is acceptable if doing so will bring about the greatest good for the greatest number of people. Which sales practices should be followed by real estate agents such as Jane (discussed in the previous chapter)? Here again, the utilitarian would say that Jane should follow sales practices that will bring about the greatest good for the greatest number of people. This kind of single-principle answer resolves many questions, but it also can lead to many additional questions.

Offering bribes may allow a US company to work inside a foreign country that is in other respects removed from any involvement with America. That may be a good thing, but offering the bribe may be the start of greater or different types of bribes involving labor laws or even foreign policy. It may be that by giving monies or other forms of bribery to do business with a particular company, an American company ends up supporting child labor. In spite of the conflicting values of the greatest good versus the harm to children, it still might be true that for the good of the two companies involved, or the countries involved, the decision will be to pay the bribe (most likely described as a tariff or gift). In all likelihood, good is defined in terms of economic gain in this scenario. Often, the greatest good is seen as a very pragmatic, near-term concept tied to benefit or financial gain.

Such a single pragmatic, economic focus can leave many important, even critical values-related questions unresolved. Also, when other values-related questions are not explored, we may find that we have opened a hornet's nest of unexpected ethical questions that can come back to bite us.

When the second model for ethical decision making is followed (moral pluralism), ethical questions are not answered by appealing to a single basic moral value. According to moral pluralism, no such value exists. Instead, in this philosophy, several basic moral values must be balanced against each other for ethical decisions to be made most effectively. How is this done? As you might suppose, the answer to this question is somewhat complicated; moral pluralism is a more complex model for ethical decision making than the single moral value approach. However, we believe that moral pluralism is the better model for ethical decision making. Bear with us while we briefly describe moral pluralism and offer our reasons for preferring it.

Distinguishing right from wrong is sometimes the easiest thing in the world, as, for example, when someone is tempted to pad an expense account. Doing such a thing is wrong, and virtually everyone knows that it is wrong. In other cases, making an ethical decision may be extremely difficult. Consider the case of a manager who must decide what to do with a long-time employee whose performance has become a problem for the company but who has been allowed up to now to perform in the same manner for many years. In especially complex situations, such as corporate mergers or acquisitions where the interests of many individuals are involved, it may seem virtually impossible to do the right thing for everyone.

One of the strengths of moral pluralism is that it helps to explain why making ethical decisions is sometimes extremely difficult. According to moral pluralism, as we said above, there is no single basic moral value or principle that can be appealed to; instead, several different fundamental values exist that may conflict with one another. Making ethical decisions requires that an appropriate balance be found among these conflicting values. Potentially at least, this is a difficult task.

Of course, even in reference to a single basic moral value, ethical decision making can be challenging. Whatever the basic value is taken to be, it must be interpreted and applied in individual cases. Even doing this can be problematic. Many people do believe in a single value. (At least they say that they believe in a single value.) We have mentioned already the basic utilitarian value as bringing about the greatest good for the greatest number. Other examples of the single moral values approach are doing God's will on earth, "looking out for Number One," and, in the limited context of business decisions, maximizing the investments of stockholders. For each of these examples, difficult questions need to be asked: What will bring about the greatest good for the greatest number? What is God's will? How do we maximize stockholders' investments? What should we do to look out for ourselves and do a good job of it?

We would be the first to acknowledge that in committing ourselves to moral pluralism, we have compounded the difficulties to be found in ethical decision making. Why have we done so? The answer to this question, at least, is simple: no single basic moral value or principle by itself is satisfactory as a basis for making all-important ethical decisions, because no single principle works in every case.

UTILITARIANISM

The basic decision-making principle of utilitarianism can be stated as follows: answer every ethical question by determining which course of action will bring about the greatest good for the greatest number of people over the longest period of time. Critics have been quick to point out that a lot can go wrong in following this principle. For example, utilitarianism is open to the charge that, in principle, it neglects the moral rights or special needs of individuals and minorities. If the goal of our actions is always to look out for the greatest number of people, then the interests of individuals and minorities are left essentially unprotected in situations that conflict with the common good.

In a worst-case scenario, utilitarians have no way to show, for example, that slavery is wrong in principle. It is possible to imagine the existence of a hypothetical country where enslaving a few people helps to achieve the greatest good for the society as a whole. Another objectionable scenario might include a policy of "socio-economic triage" where the neediest individuals in a society are killed off because doing so benefits the group as a collective whole.

In defense of their view, utilitarians have attempted to show that policies such as slavery and killing of handicapped and/or indigent people do not contribute to the greatest good. Among other negative effects, these policies would demoralize society as a whole; if some people were made slaves or were sacrificed, then practically everyone in that society might worry about becoming slaves or being sacrificed. These bad effects outweigh whatever good might be accomplished.

Nevertheless, this utilitarian response is not satisfactory because, as we see it, the moral value of individual rights needs to stand alone and not be subordinated to the principle of the greatest good. Slavery is always a violation of individual rights and is always wrong, no matter what the circumstances. In addition, there are other values that should be considered as part of the construction of an ethical perspective. It is necessary to then consider the common good and its impact, independently and also in consideration of the rights of individuals, along with these other values. The moral value of justice, in the sense of helping those who are most in need, must be added into the decision-making design. Furthermore, self-interest, when properly balanced against these other moral values, is a core value to consider.

Thus, we are committed to the view that ethical decision making requires achieving a proper balance among four different fundamental values: individual rights, justice, the common good, and self-interest. We will define these values more precisely and discuss their application later.

First, however, a caveat is in order. Ethical improvement in the workplace can occur at a number of different levels, some of which have little to do with moral theories or the controversies surrounding them. Moral pluralism is a controversial theory, just as is utilitarianism. The same is true for all of the numerous other theories that compete with these two (theories we will not elaborate upon here) that are based more strictly on theology or on the philosophies of Aristotle, Immanuel Kant, John Rawls, and others. Business people who are honest and concerned about the individuals they deal with can do a lot of good, regardless of whether they believe in moral pluralism. They can do that good if they are utilitarians, Kantians, or advocates of a strict rights-based moral philosophy. At the level of basic honesty and decency, the foundations of these and other theories do not conflict with such principles.

The primary purpose of this book is to provide guidelines for ethical change in the workplace, not to win converts to moral pluralism. In the authors' opinion, moral pluralism does provide the best overall guiding moral philosophy for ethical decision making. It certainly is not the only moral philosophy that can benefit the workplace, and the core values we have selected in this book are not the only ones you might consider in constructing a philosophy of moral pluralism. These values do, however, cover a lot of ethical ground.

MORAL PLURALISM

We have referred to moral pluralism as though it were a single theory. That is not actually the case. Different versions of moral pluralism are possible depending upon which basic values are included. The version recommended in this book is based on the following four values:

1. Individual Rights
2. Justice
3. The Common Good
4. Self-interest

In earlier chapters, we discussed autonomy and the intrinsic worth of every human being. The four values listed above are not intended to be independent of these other two values, but instead to provide an analysis of them. As fundamental values, autonomy and the intrinsic worth of everyone need to be interpreted before they can serve as effective guides to human conduct.

In Chapter III, the factory manager in our example was faced with closing a factory in a town where the factory was the mainstay of the local economy. Suppose we were to say to the manager, "Every human being has intrinsic worth; everyone should be treated individually." Saying this would not help much in the manager's search for answers to all of the difficult questions that she faced. She would know little more than that the interests of everyone concerned with the shutdown ought to be considered in some way, which is true and important, but constitutes only the first step in ethical decision making.

A manager who believes that business is amoral or that corporations have obligations only to stockholders has not yet taken even that first step. Once the step is taken, numerous conflicts among people's interests come into play. Regardless of whether the factory closes or stays open, someone's interests are jeopardized, whether it is the interests of displaced employees, members of the community, stockholders, or future employees of the company.

What should the manager do? From the perspective of moral pluralism, the answer lies in finding an appropriate balance among the four basic values listed above. When the right balance is found, then and only then will proper recognition be given to the autonomy and intrinsic worth of all people.

How will the factory manager know when she has achieved the proper balance among the four values? To this question there is no hard-and-fast answer, but there are guidelines that provide direction. She cannot provide incontrovertibly correct ethical answers, nor can anyone else. Moral pluralism gives due recognition to a certain degree of openness, or indeterminacy, that is unavoidably present in ethical decision making. Such openness is one of the strengths of moral pluralism.

This is a subject that will be discussed later in the chapter. We will also return a bit later to the example of the factory manager. Before doing that, a further analysis is needed regarding the balance of the four basic values of moral pluralism and how to know when one or the other might stand alone as the primary value in any given decision.

THE INTRINSIC WORTH AND AUTONOMY OF EVERY HUMAN BEING

The world contains several billion people. Their interests, ambitions, hopes, fears, needs, and aspirations vary greatly. Some people are moral, some immoral. Some are law-abiding; some are criminal. Some are hard working; some are indolent. Some people cooperate with their fellow human beings; others do not. Yet all people have intrinsic worth. From a religious perspective, all people are precious in God's eyes.

How can anyone sort and work through all the actual and potential differences in people, and still view each of them as possessors of intrinsic worth and autonomy? Moral pluralism provides a framework for answering this difficult question, or rather for acknowledging that no single, definitive answer is possible.

Only when taken together do the four values of moral pluralism express what is meant by a commitment to the intrinsic worth of all people as autonomous beings. This is not only a commitment to protect the moral rights of every person, but also an acceptance of the concept of justice and the obligation to give help in response to greatest need. It is an acceptance of the duty to make the world an overall better place; and a recognition of the unique value that each of us has to ourselves.

THE FOUR VALUES

Writers, philosophers, theologians, and thinkers from many fields have for centuries discussed the concepts of rights, justice, the common good, and self-interest. For brevity's sake we must content ourselves with somewhat rough-and-ready descriptions of the four basic values:

1. The concept of *individual rights* is the idea that all people are in a fundamental way equally valuable. We ought to consider everyone on an equal basis, and protect their individuality.
2. The concept of the *common good* means that sometimes the interests of a few will be subordinated to the interests of the human race as a whole (or a subset of the race in a given setting—company overall versus unit—and so on). Sometimes, because we cannot be all things to all people, we should attempt simply to do our overall best.
3. *Justice* means many different things and has unique meanings in philosophy as well as in law. In the present sense, the concept of justice requires that we selectively help those in most need, or in other words, help the most those who most need help.

4. *Self-interest* is the idea that sometimes and in some ways we should put ourselves first, not treat ourselves as one more face in the crowd. Our self-interest does matter; treating ourselves as special does not necessarily make us selfish, although it may sometimes make us appear selfish. We must consider ourselves within the moral equation and make a conscious decision about where our interests do lie. In some situations, the correct moral answer may indeed lie with supporting the common good at the expense of our immediate self-interest. Sometimes, supporting the common good, or justice, in the short term will serve our self-interest in the long term.

Individual Rights: Whose Rights?

At the present time in the United States and in much of the world, the sharpest controversies concerning rights are focused on their political dimension, on whether or not and to what extent the government should guarantee particular rights.

Political dimensions of a country's ethical code are shaped by cultural practices, history and the roots of belief, social and economic pressures, and underlying assumptions about what that country should look like. The rights to life, liberty, and the pursuit of happiness (which in most formulations includes the right of citizens to buy and retain property) are least controversial in this regard; virtually everyone in America believes that it is government's job to protect those rights. Rights to benefits such as medical care and welfare assistance are among the most controversial. The focus of this book is on the ethical, not the political or legal, dimension of rights, insofar as they can be separated. In the workplace, a basic political or legal idea of rights is equal protection, and that works well for the underlying moral value of individual rights.

Justice: Definitions of Need

The moral value of justice, in the sense of helping people in proportion to their needs, enjoins us to give special help to the most needy. In the workplace, if managers were to consider only the concept of rights, they would treat all employees in a wholly impartial fashion regarding such factors as race, gender, age, disability, poverty, or affluence.

However, managers should not be wholly impartial in these matters. Instead, managers should consider what the implications are for their ethical acts of giving or not giving special consideration to individuals or groups who have special needs, such as employees who have suffered from discrimination based on race, gender, physical handicaps, or sexual preference. Similarly, when a factory must be closed, managers ought to give special consideration to those who are hurt the most by the closing; again, complete impartiality is usually not appropriate.

The Common Good

The moral value of the common good enjoins us to examine larger and larger wholes. In the workplace, if managers go too far in their efforts to help victims of discrimination or anyone who has suffered deprivation, then the managers' actions may undermine the common good or threaten the rights of other individuals. But sometimes a manager will find it necessary to forego providing both equal protection to all and special benefits to those in greatest need. The manager must do so to achieve the common good by strengthening the corporation, as when a struggling company closes its weakest factories but does not have the resources to help displaced workers. In such a case, management does what it can to avoid bankruptcy, which would be harmful to the company as a whole and perhaps to the community of which it is a part.

Balanced Self-Interest

In finding an appropriate balance of values, self-interest must be balanced against all three of the other values reflective of concern for others (rights, justice, and the common good). Reciprocally, values of rights, justice, and the common good must be balanced against one another and against self-interest. These balancing acts prescribed by moral pluralism cannot be neatly distinguished nor separated from one another because a person's self-interest cannot be neatly distinguished from the interests of other people. For example, if you act to protect rights in general, you are also helping to protect your own rights; you, as well as others, are benefiting from your actions. The same may be true regarding helping people in need and acting for the sake of the common good. Nevertheless, the overall thrust of actions directed toward rights, justice, and the common good is usually toward helping other people more than oneself. Acting solely for the sake of self-interest typically does not involve concern for basic ethical values as much as it does concern for one's own career, business, hobbies, or personal life.

THE "PRINCIPLE OF PRINCIPLES" IN MORAL PLURALISM

The only "principle of principles" in moral pluralism is the requirement that a reasonable balance be found among the four values. In every ethical decision, each value must at least be considered. Someone who says, "I care nothing for rights" or "I care nothing for helping people in need" or "In certain instances, the good of society does not matter at all" or "You should never think of yourself but only those whom you serve" is wrong.

None of the values should ever be totally disregarded as you pursue the right course of action. Sometimes you will find that one or two dominant values leap out. In those cases you may well find yourself acting on just one or two values. It is in the *consideration* of all the values that the principle holds, not in the necessity of including all elements in the actions you take.

We must point out that what we have just said is oversimplified, a universal danger in discussions of ethics. For example, helping victims of discrimination is a good thing to do, not only because the individuals may be in special need of help, but because helping them will likely contribute in its own way to the common good and may, in addition, help to protect their rights. The points we have made are intended to illustrate just a few of the important ways that values sometimes conflict. We also hope that these points help you to begin using moral pluralism as a decision-making tool.

INCREASING SKILLS IN MAKING ETHICAL DECISIONS

One of the ways to become better at making ethical decisions is to practice making them. Also, it helps to pay close attention to the moral decisions of others. It helps to talk and act in ways that are described by objective observers as more empathetic, more focused in terms of the impact on individual and group needs.

Moral decision making is an art, not a science. Two people can be equally well informed, sensitive, and experienced, but still end up in disagreement. When such disagreements occur, an external third party may be able to guide the individuals who disagree toward finding a better solution. Even when there is no disagreement, ethical decision making in the workplace requires openness to public scrutiny and review. A peer review system is one effective strategy for providing accountability that will help management better assess the ethical components and effects of corporate decisions.

Examples for Discussion

These examples illustrate the need in ethical decision making to find an appropriate balance among conflicting values.

Example #1

In the computer store where you work, you need to make a big sale to meet a monthly quota. Occasionally, uninformed customers want to buy software for their computers. One of your customers is a determined, but naive man who wants to buy a particular brand of desktop publishing software for his office computer. He wants it to work in his laptop as well. He describes a number of programs that are currently loaded on the laptop, all of which he considers essential.

In most such cases you would ask the individual to bring his laptop to your store to make sure that the memory capacity is adequate for the program. You do not offer this option to your present customer but instead yield to his impatient demand that he purchase the best desktop publishing software available for a contract he is completing. He has read about the brand in question and that is what he wants. You are reasonably certain that he does not have the equipment needed to start the program. You mention once that you could sell him a different program that would do the job he needs for less money, but he is not interested. You do not object further but let him buy the product he wants, without making much of the fact that he may have to buy a few more things to make it work.

It is close to the end of the month, and your sale of the software will put you over the top of your sales quota. By the time the man either returns the software or buys more equipment, you will have received temporary credit for the sale. This sale will keep the sales manager off your back while you make new sales. You are not positive the customer can return the program, but he is so certain regarding what he wants and impatient with your advice, that you skip discussing this point. Next month you may have to make up for this sale, if the customer can and does return his purchase, but you will think about that later.

For now, you have met your needs and satisfied your customer's immediate concern. What should you have done differently, if anything? Did you balance self-interest and the interest of your customer sufficiently in arriving at the decision to sell? If you submitted a report of this sale to an outside review, what would others say about your efforts?

Outside ethics reviewers might approve your sales transaction if you had informed the man of all possible repercussions of purchasing the software. You should have told him that you would be more comfortable if you knew the necessary information about his computers, so that you could determine if this was the best product for him. You also should have informed him that using the product might require him to purchase more equipment. Finally, you should have insisted that you be given time to verify the store policy on returns and exchanges before completing the transaction.

Example #2

You have completed interviewing a woman who has applied for a position in your firm as a design engineer, and you have decided not to hire her. For the interview, she brought with her a computer disk containing information on her recent work. She showed it to you briefly on your computer, and you found it to be most interesting and potentially valuable to your firm. You would like to have had time to study the specifics of the information on her disk. As it happens, you now have a chance to do just that because she has forgotten the disk, leaving it behind in your computer. It would be an easy matter for you to copy it before calling the woman to tell her that she should come back to pick it up.

If you were to do this, there is almost no chance that you would ever be caught. Moreover, as far as you know, the woman who owns the disk would not be hurt in any substantial way by your theft of the information, while you have reason to believe that you and your company would benefit significantly. At the same time, you also know that the owner of the disk would not voluntarily give you the information even perhaps if you were to hire her. You do not want to hire her because you have another candidate for the job who will fit much better into your operation. What should you do?

Any civilized society has strong prohibitions against theft. Laws and moral rules against stealing tell us that these acts are wrong regardless of who will benefit and who will be harmed by the theft. Such rules are needed for the protection of individual rights and for the sake of the common good. Therefore, if in the above example you are to act on principle, then you will not steal the information. A person who adheres strictly to professional codes of conduct is acting on principle. Such a person does not lie, cheat, steal, or in any way violate the basic moral rules that are a part of civilized life.

Could you justify copying the disk as supporting your company's increased knowledge, as a higher order of value than the rule against theft? If you were to copy the disk, could you sincerely assert that the principle you were acting on is promoting the greatest good for the greatest number?

Sometimes rules that protect individual rights should be broken for the sake of the common good or to help people in need, but this example is not such a case, partly because the rule against theft plays such an important role in civilized society. An unusually strong reason is needed to justify stealing. For example, most people believe that when other resources fail, it is morally permissible to steal a loaf of bread when doing so is necessary to feed a starving child. The child's need is as great as can be imagined, while the harm done to society by the theft is relatively slight. To allow the death of a child rather than take the loaf of bread because of the possible consequences of stealing to the individual who takes the bread (getting caught and perhaps going to jail) also seems to be morally wrong. Putting self-interest ahead of justice (helping the most helpless) is not justified in this case, from our perspective.

Ethical choices are not always easy choices even when they involve poignant examples. You may remember the dilemma of Sophie in *Sophie's Choice,* the story of a Holocaust survivor. Sophie was forced to choose which of her two children would live, and which would die. One might argue that Sophie had no real choice; but she did choose within a terrible frame of options, and the choice did save one child, at least for a short while. (The saved child later died in a concentration camp.) One might argue that Sophie could have let both children die to avoid the pain of making such a choice visible to the one she sacrificed, protecting the child from having to know such isolated terror. Suffice it to say, decisions that people make are not always easily understandable, but that does not mean that some very hard moral considerations were not involved. All of us must be careful that in evaluating the choices of our fellows, we examine the circumstances and the outcomes reflected in their acts. We often cannot really know intent—only effect. More will be said about this issue later on.

> **Example #3**
> James has recently graduated with a degree in business administration. He is offered two jobs, one with a building supplies firm and one with a tobacco company. Work conditions, benefits, and prospects for advancement are similar for the two jobs, but the tobacco company is offering a significantly higher salary. James has recently married and plans to have a family. Which job should he take?

The primary moral conflict here is between James' self-interest and the common good. The job with the tobacco company will do him more financial good, while the job with the building supplies company will presumably benefit society to a greater extent or, at the very least, contribute less to the proliferation of a product that has been shown to cause harm to health. His moral choice would appear to be relatively straightforward: he should take the job with the building supplies company. However, to make a balanced decision—if ethical concerns are indeed directing him toward the construction company in place of the tobacco company—he should take an additional step. He should also obtain information pertaining to the record of the building supplies company regarding the organization's history of pollution control and other business practices that affect its employees, suppliers, customers, and society.

At the present time, prospective employees may feel reluctant to ask ethical questions in employment interviews; but since a great deal of information about many organizations is available in libraries and on the Internet, such questions may not be absolutely necessary. We hope that in the future people will feel freer to ask ethical questions of potential employers about the organization's product and that product's impact on society.

Since this is a book for the workplace, we must face head-on the fact that many products and services are controversial, and in many different ways. Warheads and weapons are built with the primary purpose of destroying enemies—which may overall be a good thing, but of course could overall be a bad thing instead. Alcoholic beverages may bring pleasure for some but result in abuse and addiction for others. Pharmaceuticals that help cure illness or alleviate pain for many may be produced in a plant that pollutes the atmosphere; and, there may be insufficient information available at a given time as regards harmful side effects of taking certain prescription drugs. In some cases, natural treatments are available that are superior alternatives to prescription medications that are large profit makers for a particular company. Extensive advertising campaigns for prescription medications may influence people to choose treatments that are not the best for them.

Needless to say, deciding to work in industries such as defense, alcoholic beverages, or pharmaceuticals does not mean that the person who does so is unethical or giving in to some flawed choice. A commitment to a particular belief about the necessity of war and being prepared does not mean the person making such a choice is a bad person. Making wine, enjoyed by many, is not a bad thing, even if many abuse it. Prescription medications are absolutely essential in the treatment of numerous illnesses—and so on. This entire area of discussion can open up a lot of debate and the possibility for strong disagreements. In no way does working at a particular plant or job setting—unless its products or services are indeed vile and without social purpose—make the person who works there unethical. It is imperative, however, for the person who is looking for a job to make a balanced and clear-eyed choice. In addition, employers should help prospective employees feel comfortable about asking questions regarding ethical practices at that workplace, and about the ethical implications of the products and services produced there.

Making ethical choices based on the performance of companies that are ready to hire us is difficult. Remember, however, that the way we conduct ourselves, regardless of our intentions, will be judged as to how our conduct affects the common good, the rights of individuals, justice, and self-interest. Remember also that the materials or components produced in a given factory may be used at times for end products that the people on the factory line know little or nothing about. Services may be provided that are later shown to be corrupt or intended as a means to steal from the unwitting customer.

But, what if employees do know about the harm their companies do? Does that change the moral equation? Many people who work on an assembly line producing cigarettes do so with an apparently clear conscience, without concern about the ethical implications of their actions. They may or may not believe that cigarettes cause cancer. They may put the good of family and a steady paycheck above everything else.

Sometimes, even when we feel the most indignant because we see people doing things that we believe are unethical, we are unaware of the issues those people face. We can make a judgment that producing cigarettes is harmful. We cannot make the judgment, if we are to be fair, that all people who work in cigarette factories are unethical. As the authors of this book, we are sure that many readers will disagree with us on this point. It is difficult to compare the harm to the larger society that results from the manufacture of cigarettes against the needs of an individual employee to keep food on the table. However, we all must understand that it is difficult to not judge others for the choices they make, or for failing to refuse to make the choices we believe to be right.

Remember that the choices we make become the acts by which we ourselves are judged, often in spite of our good intentions. Workers in cigarette factories may well be judged harshly as more and more people die from smoking-related cancers even if they choose that work to feed their families. That will not necessarily absolve them of responsibility for the harm their work creates. Some of the executives in the corporate scandals of the early twenty-first century are finding that their seemingly easy-to-make and unintended missteps have redefined everything about their professional histories. Would they not call themselves, fundamentally, good people? Yet, all that they have stood for is now gone—including, for some, their freedom.

Example #4

You have been asked to inflate sales figures "just this once" by the manager of your division, who says that his job is on the line and that he will never ask you to do it again. You would like to help the man out because he is otherwise hard working, fair, and kind to you, and has always acted responsibly as far as you know.

This is another example involving moral rules, where acting on principle requires that you refuse to lie on the man's behalf. Rules against lying play an essential role in the protection of individual rights as well as in promoting the common good. In terms of justice (as we are using the word) you ought to help the most those who most need help. The manager of your division does need help because he is about to lose his job, but that is not a sufficiently strong reason to justify lying and compromising your personal integrity on his behalf.

You will likely feel some remorse about your inability to help the manager, but you can instead offer your support by making positive statements about his leadership to those who manage him. You can take responsibility for whatever part your actions or failure to act may have played in the reduced sales. If you lie, however, you put many people in jeopardy, including yourself. Even if you believe that the man has been given an unfair sales target or that the company employing him and you is impossible to work for, altering the sales figures is wrong. You must define the issues as you see them; consider justice, the marketplace, the skills of yourself and your colleagues, the leadership of the manager, and the requirements of the company. After making those analyses, tackle any and all of these issues in a responsible and sensitive manner.

Example #5

Mary has just returned from a trip to New Zealand and it is early on Friday morning. She has single-handedly set the stage for establishing a new branch office in New Zealand for her New York firm. She has met with the pertinent people and obtained their written agreement as needed on all the essential matters, except (as she discovers once she is back in New York) for one thing. She has forgotten to get an authorized (original) signature to release for shipment the contents of a warehouse that her company is taking over.

Getting this signature seemed the least important matter that she had to attend to while in New Zealand, and in fact is really only a formality. She knows that she can get an original signature sent to her company by Monday or Tuesday of the next week. However, that will be too late to present a complete package of documents for the new branch office at the special board meeting this morning (Friday) in New York. She remembers that the man who needs to sign the document mentioned as she was leaving New Zealand that he was getting ready to take a long-awaited, three-day weekend fishing trip in a remote area where no one would be able to reach him.

Because Mary's boss is a stickler for details, she knows that not having the signature will be an embarrassment to him and to the Senior Vice President of Distribution and Logistical Services who has flown in from Texas. She believes that not having the complete documentation package ready for distribution will hurt her career. Mary, tired from her long trip and wanting the session today to be a strong kick-off, is confident that forging the signature herself will hurt no one's interests, and she is certain she can simply request the signature and get it easily when her customer returns from his trip.

In this example, it is possible that the requirements for acting on principle, for following strictly the rules that society needs to protect rights and advance the common good, are not strong enough to outweigh the benefits that forgery would bring—to Mary especially. Is a consideration of Mary's self-interest strong enough to outweigh other ethical concerns? If she does sign the document, what else need she do, if anything, to improve the ethics of the decision? Are there any other actions she could take that will help her respond to the concerns she believes are there? Does her company have specific guidelines about signing for others? How can she address the matter and still succeed at her meeting that Friday morning? Should she sign and wait until after the meeting to address the additional issues? What else should she consider in making her decision?

The option of forgery is not a good one, because even in seemingly innocent circumstances, it can lead to serious problems, even criminal charges. The first step toward resolving Mary's dilemma is to rule out the *prima facie* unethical and deceptive choice of forgery, which would then allow her to consider other options. The answer to this dilemma may be simple but the issues are real.

Corporate board meetings, especially where senior vice presidents fly in, are not taken lightly. Those who are presenting at such meetings are expected to show well. These are the kinds of moments when *walking the ethical walk* is put to the test. Many people do things under these circumstances that give them temporary relief, but that usually leads to future problems.

It is possible that in the long run, Mary could gain the trust and admiration of her customers and even her boss, for being both honest and thorough by adopting a different strategy. She might go into the meeting and submit the unsigned document, pointing out that the individual whose signature is required is on a fishing trip and will be back Monday morning when she will be able to get his signature both faxed and mailed. This seems the easy, correct and ethical response, even if she does not mention her failure to obtain the signature when there. Others may ask her why she did not get it when there and that requires a simple statement of fact such as "I forgot. I apologize." Negative consequences are still possible, but such a direct approach may lessen the damage, if there is any at all.

Example #6

David, who is in charge of product planning for his firm, meets Cynthia at a convention. (Both are single.) She is his counterpart at a rival company. After chatting with her, he makes two discoveries: first, he is attracted to her, and second, his own company clearly has the inside track on new products for the coming year. He is in a position to do his own firm a lot of harm if he were even to hint at his company's plans to anyone outside of the organization. If he asks her for a date, particularly before the new product line is released, he would be violating his company's code of conduct. At the same time, he trusts himself absolutely not to give away any company secrets. He judges that no harm would result if he violates his company's code of conduct, except possibly by the example he would set. If he were to date Cynthia before the release of his company's new product line, he would be discreet. Probably no one would ever find out.

Should David act on principle or should he put his own interest first? Who might be affected by his actions? How should he weigh opportunity for himself against responsibilities to his company? If he were to date Cynthia, what concrete steps could he take to ensure that his actions would be discreet?

One answer might be that, first of all, David may be assuming a lot! Before he falls into the throes of soul-searching he should first find out if Cynthia reciprocates his interest in a possible relationship. Honesty could easily be the best policy here; it would require that David say something like the following: "I'd really like to ask you out but my company and yours might frown upon that under the circumstances. After the new product lines are released, would you be interested in going out to dinner with me?" With this approach, David has considered all parties involved by giving Cynthia an out if she isn't interested (perhaps because her company wouldn't approve), by remaining loyal to the interests of his organization, and at the same time pursuing his own self-interest in a balanced manner.

As you think about the examples that we have just discussed, bear in mind, as was stated earlier, that ethics is an art, not a science. There is room for disagreement between two individuals who possess the same high degree of moral integrity, are morally sensitive, and possess all relevant information. The examples above may appear to be simple but they open up avenues for going down a slippery slope. It's all too easy to assume an "oh well" attitude, or to say, "It's such a small point. What difference does it make?" While the lack of precision and certainty in ethical decision making may be frustrating, it is also true that one of the things that make ethical decision making interesting and even profound is just this room for equally ethical individuals to see matters differently.

The circumstances that surround an ethical act are important if you are to become more alert to the requirements for being ethical. You need not only the right stuff, but a cool head, and a method for evaluating your acts against a larger standard, not simply the circumstances of the moment. The right choices are not always easy—and the subsequent measure of your acts by others will not always be made with compassion. Unfortunately, many good people in our corporate landscape have gotten caught up in a situational analysis of the moment, and have done things that in retrospect they would never have done. Now, they cannot turn back.

2

PART

ETHICAL CONDITIONS AT WORK

7

CHAPTER

SETTING THE STAGE FOR ETHICAL BEHAVIOR (PART ONE)

To feel complete, we must know that we made a contribution somehow. Something that will remain when we are gone, a mark that we can leave to show we were here.

—Rabbi Harold Kushner, *The Masters Forum*

ADDING THE PHRASE *in bed* to the reading of fortune cookies often gets a good laugh. "You will have good luck—in bed." "You are a most creative person—in bed." It also offers comic relief from the idea that the cookies could contain anything really serious about our futures or fortunes. Nevertheless, there is often a ritual of reading the fortunes aloud, agreeing, disagreeing, or wondering why such inanities as "The tulips come up in spring" have to be the type of fortune you, if you are like the authors, always receive. But what if we play this same game adding a different phrase to our cookie fortune? To a fortune such as "You make life worth living," try adding the phrase at work. Does it provide the same comic relief?

If we are told that someone makes life worth living, we would not normally suppose that the setting for such a noble endeavor is the workplace. Making life worth living is a grand notion, not bound by walls, clocks, computers, cubicles, timetables, and such mundane tasks as reading monthly progress reports or completing margin analyses. A life worth living, many believe, refers to LIFE—that thing that starts for many people when they leave work.

Yet, based on a famous German phrase, two things make life worth living: *lieben und arbiten*—love and work. Some may say that it is incumbent upon those who own businesses and obtain their wealth from other people's efforts (as well as their own efforts) to ensure that they create an environment that makes life at work worth living. And, indeed, there are those who, by virtue of their positions and skills, can make life worth living at work. They are the people at the levels of management who direct and control much about how worthwhile the daily experience of work really is. For at least 220 days a year, large chunks of our lives occur from the time that we take our first sip of workplace coffee until the end of the workday. If we fully understood how strongly these hours at work impact us, not only physically but also emotionally, and realized how so much of our lives pass by at work, we would all want our workplaces to be settings where life really is worth living.

Granted, when basic minimums are met (comfortable temperatures, safety, smooth and well-understood processes for completing work, a regular and as equitable a paycheck as possible) then most people report that the work site, the physical conditions of work, are at least OK and often the owners of such businesses are judged to be OK as well. Many business owners may not supply nice-to-have, but non-obligatory extras for their employees. These extras may not be essential and their absence alone does not differentiate an ethical business owner from a less ethical business owner.

In a book about ethics and the workplace, it would be easy to examine all decisions made by the boss in terms of the ethics of those actions. However, there are more strictly economic concerns as well. A boss may balance financial gain over adding something of value to the work setting, but even if the choice is to delay or not to add a work-site benefit, it does not mean that the boss is behaving unethically. More is required before that judgment can be made. Nevertheless, based on how and what decisions are made about the physical conditions of work, employees may spend hours whispering discontentedly or quietly raging about the boss's ethics when such perks as the midday free sodas are removed or the company changes its free day-care policy. Of course, we know that not all issues in life are ethical issues, even if they affect one's everyday enjoyment of work.

Yet, a smart business owner understands that the benefits of nice-to-have additions to the workplace are more than goodwill, but also play a part in achieving maximum profit by promoting the discretionary efforts of employees. Under the normal conditions for running a business, making the workplace a setting where a life worth living unfolds is a decided advantage in achieving maximum return on the investment owners make in the design and operation of a company.

Discretionary Effort, when used in its specialized meaning (trademark Aubrey Daniels International) refers to the rate at which positive performance accelerates when employees *want to* versus *have to* perform and they are receiving positive recognition for their efforts. When the positive conditions necessary to produce discretionary effort are in place, workers report feeling pride and worth in the work they do. Discretionary effort occurs through the extraordinary power of positive reinforcement used effectively. Positive reinforcement is not just about recognizing the efforts of employees in ways that matter to a particular employee, but encompasses every condition of the workplace that makes it more likely that a person will repeat a behavior again with ease, and rapidly gain the skills needed to continue to do the work at a high-and-steady rate.

SETTING UP POSITIVE WORK SETTINGS

This chapter describes the start-up conditions that employers can put in place to ensure that the work environment is in itself reinforcing and thus invites the best efforts people have to give. It also examines the areas where the strains and pressures of business management can lead to faulty decisions, fatigue, and unethical acts, all in the name of perceived best practices. Because the behaviors of employees are the primary determinants of business success, the settings and conditions of work in which behavior occurs do matter. By providing the best work design for employees, organizations set the stage for the best work behaviors.

It would be ideal if all aspects of the workplace could be physically arranged to improve the quality of worklife; however, this is not absolutely necessary. What is necessary is an awareness of task and teamwork requirements of the workplace and an awareness of what is being asked of an individual to achieve the expected goals. All of us who have tasks to do, deadlines to meet, and goals to achieve, understand the value of the setting in which we work and the management approach that is intended to guide our actions. Most employees are keenly aware of the extent to which the company has attempted to do the right thing for its employees.

You may be fortunate enough to work in a setting that has been designed to ensure that your success can readily be achieved. There are few to no environmental barriers to your success—no loud noises distracting you, no bad lights, and no computer meltdowns. You have a phone that works, and colleagues who know what they must do to help you and themselves succeed. There is great variety in the elements that might be contained in such a design. The context of work, to be maximally effective, must contain at least one thing: a lot of readily available positive reinforcement. Generally speaking, good work environments make the reinforcing properties of the work itself easier for employees to access.

The context of work has at its base the potential to build reinforcement into the very act of entering the office, answering the phone, turning on the computer, making a good cup of coffee, and sitting in a comfortable seat. Those companies that consider employees' work comfort are way ahead of those that let the work setting form like oozing lava—taking on unpredictable shapes as it flows throughout the space provided, then settling and hardening in ways that may not serve the best or most efficient outcomes.

Positive benefits result when certain working conditions are met. These conditions require a commitment to evaluating daily work life. Such an evaluation does not have to do primarily with the beauty of the workplace, although this may be pleasant to have, but rather with how work is managed. Many successful and caring companies are housed in old warehouses or in unattractive buildings, but the people inside, doing their work, find the setting to be just fine. Many businesses start in basements or garages, but if the tools to do the job are present, then work can be very good. Some people work in cubicles that provide minimal privacy but do allow for a sense of individuality in the space provided. In many ways, the workplace affects the ability of people to do their work. It helps them perceive themselves as part of an organization that in its very design encourages a commitment to ethical actions.

A company that works hard to bring out the best in its employees by considering the environment in which work occurs is more likely to be perceived as committed to ethical standards than a company that disregards the needs of its employees. While the ethical commitment of the senior leadership is not necessarily tied up in the physical and psychological settings of the workplace, establishing conditions for ease of work, fair treatment, and special regard for the rights of employees does create the expectancy that such a company's leadership will put a priority on doing the right things in the right way for the right reasons.

The Physical Setting

A fundamental question that an employer must ask is, "Do employees have the resources to do their jobs?" Employees who have at hand all necessary equipment and supplies and are working in a comfortable environment will look forward to work each day. Under these circumstances, most employees find work easier to do. In turn, they talk about their workplace as a good place to be. They often reciprocate by giving extra effort—doing the very best work they can and, if they are also recognized and feel appreciated at a personal level, such employees are very likely, in spite of what we hear about unstable workforces, to remain loyal to the company.

The physical layout of an office or other workplace has a great deal to do with how people behave in that environment. The convenient location of essential equipment and supplies, desks that are matched to the work, the selection of lamps, chairs, tables, even artwork—all must be taken into account and made appropriate to their users. Consider temperature, air quality, and noise levels. The physical arrangement in which people find themselves either encourages them or discourages them from including the little extras that can spell success or failure for a corporation. The physical workplace setting displays in a visible way management's commitment to the well-being of its employees.

Research tells us that employee involvement in the design of the workplace is a key indicator of high job satisfaction. Employees report that jobs that provide opportunity to them, jobs that require them to think about the work and how best to do it, create high job satisfaction. In turn, employees with high job satisfaction

1. believe that the organization will be satisfying in the long run;
2. care about the quality of their work;
3. are more committed to the organization;
4. have higher retention rates;
5. are more productive (Bavendam Research, Inc., 2000).

The Psychological Setting

William Shakespeare wrote, "To business that we love we eagerly arise, and go to with delight." Much has been written about the psychology of the workplace and the manager's unique role in creating a good place to work: reduce threats; drive out fear; involve people in high-performance teams; respect, collect, and use employees' ideas; celebrate and have fun with small tokens of recognition and reward; demonstrate that you value their contributions to business success.

Studies that compare workplace environments in which employees are treated as valued contributors to the organization with those workplaces where employees are simply given a job to do and are never asked to contribute to the larger organization, reveal a profound difference in the employees' psychological outlook toward work. Employees who are treated as valued members of the organization enjoy coming to work, more readily participate in team activities, and offer solutions to problems. They also describe their workplace as being a caring place, a place where people are valued, a good place to work, and so on.

Many books over the past several decades describe a new management philosophy that is actually based on ideas that go back at least to the early 1950s when W. Edwards Deming, widely known as the "quality guru," went to Japan to teach his management philosophy to key Japanese business leaders. Deming advocated then, and continued to promote until his death at the age of ninety-three, a non-authoritarian approach to management. He taught that managers should motivate not through fear but through respect. In place of constantly looking over an employee's shoulder, checking and testing for the correct behavior, managers should give employees broad responsibility for producing high-quality products that meet genuine customer needs. Deming was on the right track.

THE QUALITY MOVEMENT

The quality movement continues to be a very real focus of American management practice. Quality (in the sense understood here) and ethics appear to be logical partners. Some of the major tenets of the quality movement are the following.

1. Poor quality products and services are not usually the fault of individual employees. In most cases, the fault lies with systems of management.
2. *Total Quality Management* (a phrase coined by J. M. Juran) requires systems where every detail is oriented toward satisfying customers. This applies to external customers who buy products and services from the business, and equally to internal customers—those co-workers sitting one desk over or in the office next door.

3. Business success requires high levels of cooperation. Coordination between producers and suppliers, employers and employees, designers and manufacturers, is essential.
4. Understand that superior quality products and services that best serve customers almost always cost less in the long run.
5. Supplement short-term goals (management by objectives) with greater reliance on long-term goals.
6. Push decision making down into the ranks from top levels of management, and eliminate middle-management layers whenever possible.
7. Replace motivation based on fear with motivation based on pride in a job well done.
8. "Empower" people to do their best by encouraging them to take the initiative and by removing barriers to their productivity and problem-solving abilities.
9. Minimize the possibility of human error through the improved design of all workplace procedures and systems; these include manufacturing, delivery within the company and to clients, and informational systems. For example, whenever it is feasible to do so, design parts so that they cannot possibly be assembled incorrectly.
10. Guard against the domino effect in product use and design—a fault in one area should not cause problems elsewhere. For example, choose a non-corrosive material that can withstand possible chemical leaks from adjacent components of a machine.
11. Reduce pollution and improve health and safety for workers and consumers.
12. Improve morale and productivity by making workers' jobs more meaningful.

The overall direction of the quality movement supports an ethical perspective. Making work more meaningful, increasing cooperation in the workplace, enhancing autonomy, improving conditions for health and safety, and making the workplace more participatory, are all goals of the quality movement that are laudable from an ethical perspective. From the perspective of this book, the most important maxim of the quality movement for leaders of corporations is the following:

> Treat everyone well: customers, employees, fellow workers, suppliers, stockholders, and stakeholders—which includes people in the communities where we work, the countries where we trade, and the society we represent.

Deming's powerful ideas are echoed and elaborated upon by an ever-growing number of contemporary management experts. However, Deming failed in one important area relevant to his considerable knowledge and his valuable message: human behavior was not an area that he understood very well. While he was famous for advocating that fear be driven from the workplace, much of his philosophy dealt with the people who got things wrong: management. He clearly saw failure as a problem of management. In Deming's model, trusting employees usually meant giving them a clear set of expectations and then leaving them to achieve these outcomes, an important part of what he believed good managers should do in order to achieve excellence.

The problem was that when this rather passive method of management did not work or people failed to achieve certain outcomes, Deming did not have more details to offer. Fear is all too often the cornerstone of how quality practices are, in fact, managed. It was not until many years after the advent of the quality movement that managers began to examine human behavior with the same rigor as quality processes.

Control of the intricacies involved in reducing the extent of variance in human performance was the one area that eluded Deming in his long and distinguished career. Yet, if more managers understood human behavior (especially how human behavior can be changed in a positive direction) they would also know how to translate a slogan such as *driving fear from the workplace* into active and relevant practices that actually succeed. They would clearly understand how the physical and psychological processes of the workplace can be designed to encourage employees to act with integrity when representing their company.

Murray Sidman (1960), a leader in research into human behavior and author of *Tactics of Scientific Research,* spent years of his life researching the effects of escape from, and avoidance of, threats and fear. In his book *Coercion and Its Fallout,* Sidman (1989) takes a strong philosophical stand in arguing that any use of coercion in managing people is wrong. It is wrong as much for its effects on those who use coercive strategies as for its effects on those who are the recipients of such strategies.

Other psychologists who study learning have said that coercion is an inescapable part of life. Something as simple as the necessity to get out of bed in the morning is coercive: if we do not get out of bed, we will not get to work, and eventually we will lose our job. Every workplace is at least implicitly coercive since it contains an understanding that we must "do this or else"; we must arrive on time or be penalized; we must work on tasks assigned or lose our job; we must exceed our sales quota for the month or not receive a bonus, and so on.

However, in fairness to Sidman, we need to point out that he is not talking about these kinds of circumstances that exhibit a kind of *passive coercion* (our term); after all, even a doorknob is passively coercive because you must turn it or else the door will not open—but, of course, we don't want to do away with doorknobs.

As we understand his argument, Sidman is talking about more of an active process in which the mode of interaction between a supervisor and a subordinate is coercive, such as when the supervisor says to a productive employee, "Get this service contract completed today even if you have to stay all night or you're out of a job." Other threats can include only the perception by the worker that she can lose her job or receive a bad review regardless of her overall work patterns, or receive disfavor if she does not stay late or do things that go beyond the job for the sake of pleasing an irrational boss, or the fear of being ignored during the next round of promotions if she complains that work is being assigned to her that seems irrelevant.

When Sidman says that the use of coercion in managing people is always wrong, he is not talking about mere passive coercion, as in turning doorknobs or in how an individual's history might create a misperception of coercion to a reasonable request. He is talking about something much more direct, even if done without the intention to be coercive—the use of threats and fear to produce actions.

Is Sidman correct? Sometimes threat and fear are necessary—they alert us to danger; they help us redirect our behavior along a more productive path; and they can force us to do things that we don't want to do but that must be done for the good of others as well as ourselves.

What Sidman says is correct for managers who are working to establish positive and sustained behavior patterns and create positive goodwill. Most importantly for this book, Sidman's view is correct for managers who are working to make ethical behavior a habit. In addition, non-coercive strategies exist that not only get positive results but have solid side effects in creating a better place to work. Unquestionably, coercive relationships should not constitute the dominant method for changing behavior. Coercive relationships can be drastically minimized. In taking the stand that managers should *never* use coercive strategies on others because to do so demeans everyone and is unethical, Sidman turns a bright light on how we treat one another and compels us to examine typical management styles and their possible debilitating effects. Managers are often trained in the "do it or else" school or not trained at all in terms of how to apply positive management techniques to human performance.

Another enlightening discussion of the power of non-coercive approaches to management can be found in books by Aubrey C. Daniels. *Performance Management: Changing Behavior That Drives Organizational Effectiveness,* first published in 1982 and now in its fourth edition, (by Aubrey C. Daniels and James E. Daniels) summarizes for managers how to apply the findings of the science of behavior to achieve business success. Daniels' philosophical stand is that, in the main, positive strategies for managing people are best (2004). Daniels backs his beliefs up, as does Sidman, with findings from the scientific literature. These findings are somewhat controversial, however, since some writers argue that it is not possible to define, based on what science tells us, which type of consequence system is most effective for motivating human beings (Perone, 2003).

Like us, both Sidman and Daniels maintain that the question of whether to use coercion is both a scientific and an ethical issue. The strongest case against the use of coercive management strategies is made when both science and ethics are considered together; this is the essence of the integrative approach to creating a values-based business environment that we mentioned in the Introduction.

Managers' choices of strategies to promote performance may appear to be deliberate, but all too frequently, managers do not realize the full implications of what they are doing in managing performance. They do not realize the extent to which they are using strategies of fear and threats, as opposed to strategies that utilize positive reinforcement. All too frequently, managers are taught virtually nothing about the science of learning and the conditions that motivate success.

Only recently have managers had the opportunity to learn about management tools, such as those provided by Daniels, that offer pragmatic help to make Deming's mandate to drive out fear more than a slogan. We are now in a position to compensate for the major shortcoming in the work of Deming and many of his followers—their lack of a clear understanding of human motivational systems and the causal relationships between behavior and its effects.

In the mid-twentieth century, Thomas Gilbert (1978) studied human performance and began to identify the types of variance in human behavior that could keep a company from achieving optimal performance, not only by the top performers but also by others in the organization. He wrote about his findings in *Human Competence: Engineering Worthy Performance,* a gem of a book that has long been ignored by American business.

Not long after the publication of this book, Daniels took conclusions drawn by Deming, Gilbert, B. F. Skinner, and other scientists and researchers regarding human learning and applied them to performance at work. Daniels' application of the science of learning to work settings has made a significant difference in the way business views human capital. Daniels shows how important conclusions about quality, variance in human performance, and the psychology of learning can merge to dramatically shift the way work is structured to achieve the best business results via the best in human performance.

TOTAL COMMITMENT AND AN INHERENT DANGER

The quality imperative states that employees must be integral parts of the companies they work for, both in how they function within the system and in terms of their attitudes and commitments. Employees who more fully understand the company as a whole can help solve its problems and contribute to its long-term success. For its part, the company must tap all of the problem-solving capacities that its employees possess. Quality-driven companies make maximum use of their employees' talents, energy, and dedication. As much as possible, these businesses enhance each employee's sense of belonging to the company.

The danger here is that the corporation may swallow up the individual. As David Kirp and Douglas Rice (1991) are quoted in *Workplace 2000,* "What so-called *work hard, play hard* companies want is nothing less than total responsibility and over-the-edge loyalty" (p. 40). A person's individuality can be lost in an organization that requires an excessive degree of loyalty and commitment. In striving to elicit the absolute best from every employee, managers may demand too much. And it is not just managers who may do this; employees may demand too much of one another and of themselves. From a moral perspective, it is essential that businesses adopting "quality management" remember that employees have their own lives apart from the company.

In an atmosphere designed to elicit new ideas, managers should allow employees to express differences of opinion about office procedures and corporate goals, particularly those opinions that diverge from company perspectives. It is equally essential that managers help individual employees assess the need to take time for themselves. In turn, managers need to be alert to their own needs in this regard. As Deming himself said, "We have to restore the individual" (Aguayo, 1990, p. 122).

Ethical behavior in the workplace requires finding a balance among potentially conflicting values: work versus family, need for leisure time versus the need to complete job assignments promptly, and loyalty to the company versus commitment to social causes that may conflict with corporate goals. Respect for individuality requires not glossing over or ignoring these conflicts.

8

CHAPTER

SETTING THE STAGE FOR ETHICAL BEHAVIOR (PART TWO)

Warren Buffet said . . . that trust is like the air we breathe. When it's present, nobody really notices. But when it's absent, everybody notices. Trust Is a Must: In the eyes of employees, investors, clients and the public at large, honesty is the only policy that will do.

—Chris Sandlund, *Entrepreneur Magazine*

WORKPLACE EXPECTATIONS

What conditions might lead to unreasonable expectations in the workplace? The following are prime examples: time frames that are unrealistic; tasks that are assigned unfairly and inappropriately in relation to skills, knowledge, and the abilities of particular workers; production standards that are arbitrarily shifted. In these situations, a point can be reached beyond which expectations are destructive or at least excessively stressful. From the perspective of profit making, unreasonable expectations are likely to backfire. Unreasonable demands produce a variety of negative reactions, including resentment, anxiety, fatigue, compromise of product quality, and, most damaging, the absence of trust.

Even if setting unreasonably high expectations were the most profitable strategy, following such a course of action establishes, for many, an unethical subtext in the culture because of the behavior required to maintain good standing. We have said it before: success in business can be achieved at too high a price.

Sometimes, enthusiastic managers say, "We set high standards around here. Anything less than 100 percent is not acceptable—100 percent both in terms of your effort and your output." Such hyperbole is in fact quite common, and most employees understand that it is not meant literally, but rather as inspiration. Such talk can reflect endorsement and enthusiasm for the hard work of everyone. But if such talk is meant to be taken literally, then it is out of place except for unusual circumstances. We expect a football team in a national championship to do its absolute best; but under normal conditions of life, even regarding football players, demanding the idealized, unmeasured, absolute best from oneself or one's employees (or one's players) can place an intolerable burden on the individual. Virtually no one can maintain perfection for extended periods of time.

Words create their own reality. When hearing the manager's high expectations, employees may think in terms of perfect performance. They may read even more into their manager's statements and add their own unreasonable requirements for such things as production quotas and number of service calls required. Employees who fail after setting these self-imposed conditions often feel inadequate or guilty. They may begin to slightly inflate figures and receive praise for doing so. Management strategies for the new millennium require the most careful review of expectations and outcomes. Failure to make the best use of stretch goals lies not with employees' misperceptions but with a manager's failure to examine the effect his or her words have on employee actions—particularly those effects that might lead to unethical actions in the name of company productivity goals, such as lying about available service to get a sale before the end of the month in order to meet a quota, and so on.

BANISHING FEAR

The establishment of unreasonably high expectations is a more sophisticated version of the old authoritarian style of managing. In the old style, a boss said, "We tolerate no more than five defective products per one hundred." It didn't matter what the real causes of the defects were or whether they were under the control of the individual employee. He or she was simply told "No more than five defects, period." How was this level to be achieved? Somehow! If it was not achieved, then the threat of recriminations was constantly present. Employees worked in perpetual fear, or if not in fear, then certainly without enthusiasm.

Achieving 95 percent error-free production is not even a consideration for many companies in America today. Many of today's top companies might say that 98.7 percent error-free is tolerable, but only tolerable. The goal is not necessarily wrong. It is the style in which the goal is stated and the negative consequences implied for not meeting it that we believe can impede all kinds of top performance. In some companies managers have found out how to have high standards and high performance without inflicting fear. However, in most cases, the fear of job loss is a familiar companion when it comes to productivity and company expectations.

People know that failure to achieve company objectives threatens their jobs. Elimination of fear requires that employees fully understand the conditions of their employment and that those conditions be predicated upon fair practices. Management must carefully and clearly define corporate and unit goals and help employees understand what they are required to do in order to achieve their particular goals. Changes in strategy or operational focus require explanation as well, if the company's actions are not to appear arbitrary and capricious. For example, downturns in business may lead to job loss. Keeping employees informed of the marketplace or having them labor in a threat-based work culture are two very different ways of managing the same issue.

A good manager expects that each employee wants to do a good job and can improve. The manager is equally committed to the idea that the employee can help the manager improve his/her performance as well. In such a system, managers do not create employee dependency on managerial favoritism, but instead create environments that invite problem-solving efforts.

Robert Eisenberger, professor of social psychology at the University of Delaware, and his colleagues report that employees who perceive organizational support for their contributions demonstrate greater degrees of emotional commitment to the company, and such companies experience less turnover. These employees report that they care about the well-being of their organizations, and they attribute human qualities to their organization as if the company has their concerns at heart. The work of Eisenberger et al is vital to understanding how recognition and reward for effort that conveys social regard for the needs of employees has long-term sustained benefits (Rhoades, Eisenberger, & Armeli, 2001).

PRIVACY AT WORK

Another area where corporations have an opportunity to set up a strong, positive context for work involves removing unnecessary invasions of employees' privacy. Of particular concern is the use of tests such as polygraphs and personality profiles, especially when ill-trained people are allowed to make assumptions about the future potential of individuals. The use of such tests is not always wrong, but the heavy reliance on such tests as primary hiring tools can be counterproductive in the long run. Such tests can generate mistrust and ignore individuality. They often predict general behaviors based on statistical analysis of traits. Furthermore, the results may only confirm preconceived ideas and not reveal the truth about how an individual will respond in a new setting. Does this mean that companies that need to hire large numbers of people will move away from this kind of profiling?—probably not.

If valid and reliable psychological tests are administered by trained individuals who understand the limitations and benefits of each test, the company and the individual will, in most instances, obtain useful information. As a bare minimum for the ethical use of such tests, there must be a clear understanding that the individual will receive his or her test report, fully disclosed, including how the information will be used, who will have access to it, where it will be filed, and how long it will be considered of value. Many tests have short-term validity because people and circumstances change over time. In some cases, test results follow performers around for years, a fact usually unknown to the performer. All too often, fair disclosure policies are not standard practice; in fact, in some companies the data banks of information about employees are treasure troves of potential invasion-of-privacy liability. Old and thus invalid, unreliable results may be used by uninformed individuals who falsely believe that the test results they find in a personnel file represent a greater reality than do a worker's skills and aptitude demonstrated in daily work life since the many years when the test was first administered. In today's workplace, this sort of scenario is highly likely. The kinds of data banks to which we are alluding do exist, and their contents are often viewed and used by untrained (even if well-intentioned) individuals who make decisions about promotions, selection for certain tasks or jobs, and even advancements in compensation based on not what *is* happening but what was reported—sometimes years before.

Do many company HR departments actually throw out a test result after the six or twelve months that indicate the limits of its validity or reliability? Are records purged of old data on a regular basis? You owe it to yourself, if you have ever had a psychological test administered at work, to find out just what has become of this information, who has it now, if it still exists, and how it has been used. You have the right to know whether the people who use the data are trained and careful with the test construction guidelines, or instead, are like many who keep and use pills in their cabinets long after the expiration date.

Often skill and aptitude tests are used as preliminary screening to sort through the hundreds of applications a company may receive when a relatively small number of job openings are advertised. In general, such tests provide good information about core knowledge that a person brings to a demanding job.

When a company has a problem with turnover it should not start by replacing one set of employees with another set of new hires by using a testing procedure in the hiring process, but should first address the workplace reason for the high turnover. Address the reason for a lack of motivation in your current employees before you replace them with another group of motivated employees, then another, and another.

You might say in defense of psychological testing, "Pilfering of supplies has gotten out of hand. We have thousands of employees, so we must have a quick way to screen them for honesty." Again, some pre-screening can help.

However, honesty is a very difficult quality to determine through testing. Again, we should say that, in the right hands, testing can give you some indication of who will be honest and who will be dishonest. It can help you eliminate the very obvious bad choices, but testing alone will not adequately fill every space in your employee pool.

Testing at the executive level—another common practice—can provide a rich source of data about a candidate's interpersonal skills, for example. However, making decisions about the person's future based mainly on a test, in essence, means discarding years of solid observational data; it is one of the sadder uses of such information in making senior-level advancement decisions. Many executives never know exactly what their tests showed, nor do they have any opportunity to deal with the issues that were raised by the test results.

In summary, our advice to managers is to be careful how you collect any kind of personal information about your employees, and make sure you have a process for keeping such data current. Be sure as well that you describe fully how you will share findings with the individual, and fully inform the person of the implications of taking a particular test so that an informed choice can be made. If for some reason data cannot be made available to the individual, be sure that you have a good reason for withholding the information, and that the reason is told to the person before he or she elects to take the test. Although we are focusing here on testing, we should point out that there are other private data sources that companies can access, such as credit histories, family and health information, and other files that can be destructive. In this age of easy access to information that has long been considered private information, we have an even greater responsibility for how we treat private aspects of a person's conduct or beliefs.

SAFETY

Another area that requires a high degree of ethical diligence within organizations is on-the-job safety. Here, full disclosure of all information pertaining to safety is the most important moral requirement. All information about hazards, safety equipment, and possible long-term risks in the workplace must be disclosed when known—and companies must actively seek out such knowledge. While employers cannot of course totally eliminate health risks in the workplace, a policy of full disclosure does allow for informed consent. Someone may object that full disclosure does not go far enough because many employees are forced by economic realities into taking or keeping a job regardless of workplace hazards. There is some truth to this claim.

So, how should a corporation dedicated to ethical behavior respond to workplace safety issues? No one can promise the total elimination of all health risks; all workplaces have hazards of one sort or another. Some dangers are quite minimal but not outside the realm of possibility, such as slipping on damp tiles in the washroom. Others are potentially lethal, such as working with underground mining machinery or in oil fields in a foreign country that harbors hostile individuals or groups. Reduction of health and safety hazards will in the long run result in savings for most companies, but there is no guarantee that this will happen.

A company has the moral responsibility to eliminate as many hazards as possible on an active and ongoing basis. If employees are sent into potentially dangerous settings, the company must provide the protection needed to ensure safety to the degree possible under the circumstances. It is not enough simply to warn the employees.

When the immediate elimination of a particular risk is prohibitively expensive, the morally correct course of action for an individual company is to move as far as possible in the direction of greater safety. A company that does this and also advertises its changes can help to persuade the entire industry to reform or invest in research to reduce the risk. There are many fine examples in today's business world of companies working to make the workplace as safe as possible. Unfortunately, some companies continue to place their workers in harm's way. As regards the latter, external watchdogs are needed to put pressure on company leaders who carelessly expose their workers to danger. State and local inspectors charged with community oversight of plants and other operations must put the good of the worker above the economic gain of allowing such practices to continue. In unsafe work settings, workers are often unable to speak up for fear of losing the work that they may badly need. These are instances where external review is absolutely necessary.

CORPORATE CULTURE AND ETHICAL ACTIONS

A corporation's culture is no more, and no less, than the sum of what employees in the company say and do—what they are reinforced for doing according to stated and unstated rules of conduct and contingencies of the workplace. We cannot stress enough the need for an explicit reference to ethical values in a company's vision statement. Every company stands for something, either by choice or by default. Why not make what the company stands for explicitly ethical? Public statements that define the corporation's ethical standards increase the probability of ethical behavior. In turn, the company is sometimes saved from the expenses of unethical conduct.

At heart, ethical behavior is a kind of mind-set, an attitude that includes respect for all persons and an endeavor to find an appropriate balance among important values. Some or all of these values ought to be an explicit part of a company's vision statement. For all companies, Deming's observation is pertinent: "A company exists to provide goods and services that help improve the standard of living of mankind." At any given time, a company will be following specific procedures for the manufacture of its products and the provision of its services. A company should also have in place specific guidelines for enhancing its ethical conduct toward employees. All of these procedures and guidelines should be open to modification whenever better ways are found to manufacture products or to treat employees well.

In today's global marketplace, corporations more and more recognize the need for specialized services and for listening to and fulfilling customers' specific needs. Success depends upon listening well. Such a focus requires a painstaking assessment of what the company does well and what it does not do well. For example, some companies will master the design, manufacture, and marketing of products with extremely short turnaround times and an even shorter shelf life, such as personal computers. The resultant fast turnover of products becomes part of the corporate culture, or how they do business. Other companies' products have long turnaround times, or they take many risks in marketing new products, or fewer risks, or they endeavor to meet people's existing needs, or they create products first and then persuade people to want them. There is no right or wrong among any of these options.

Similarly, companies can specialize internally in meeting employee needs. Within a wide range of corporate policies and structures, there are many different ways to do this. For example, where one company gains a reputation for providing excellent day care for working parents, another company may offer extensive optical and dental insurance and another may offer greater flexibility in the scheduling of working hours or the assignment of tasks. Not all companies can or should put equal effort into all of these spheres, or into programs for retraining laid-off workers, or into finding special niches for older employees, or into including exercise rooms, health food in cafeterias, preventive medical checkups, and so on. Both practical limits and limits imposed by employee needs help the company's management make the best choices. For example, childcare is not usually an issue for a company of older employees, nor is elder care necessarily an issue for a newly formed youthful enterprise.

Beliefs about what a company should give its employees play a part here, and deciding that services such as those mentioned in the previous paragraph are not part of the company's commitment does not mean, again, that the company leadership is unethical in its choices. It may choose to put its resources primarily into growing the business in order to sustain employment, for example.

As part of doing business, every company should be dedicated to treating everyone well. This dedication should be a part of stated company policy—a prominent part of what the company stands for in the eyes of its employees, customers, suppliers, competitors, and the world at large.

Businesses that spend any amount of money beyond the bare necessities to create a better environment, a better product, or a finer service, can be viewed as demonstrating to some degree an ethical commitment to doing the right thing in the right way. Many companies spend large amounts of money on designing business practices for the common good, and striving to do the right things in the right way. Companies invest in process and product redesign and in finding new and better ways of meeting quality, service, productivity, and health and safety requirements.

These investments do, very often, benefit the bottom line and end up helping to make the workplace a better place to be. They can also, if considered carefully, create a visible sense of management commitment to the individual and to ethical actions across the corporation in achieving profitable business results. Companies must first work to ensure some profitability, of course, before they can go too far down this road, ensuring that there is, indeed, a workplace in which to enjoy these benefits.

MANAGEMENT BY NUMBERS

Managing by numbers (volumes, rates, dollars, frequencies, and percentages of a goal) is clearly understood by workers because those numbers relate to the deliverables for which they are in part responsible, but it is not a completely adequate approach to management. While quotas and other numerical goals are often used as measurement tools and do serve a practical function, when they are treated as the sole criterion for success they are misleading and limit achievement. Suppose, for example, that a company requires each salesperson to close forty new product sales per month but asks nothing about how the sales are made. The company may get the numbers, but this tells us nothing about the quality or impact of the sales on customers. When a company emphasizes closing a very high number of sales or an unreasonable quantity of a certain kind of product sale, then the likelihood of questionable practices to make sales is much greater.

Producing high quality goods and services requires an examination of multiple dimensions of business management. Volume is one of them, preparation and content another, and follow-up or outcome a third. Management must state corporate goals in such a way as to include all of these dimensions. Measurement that focuses on a single dimension will eventually compromise quality and can compromise integrity as well.

FAIRNESS TO WOMEN AND MINORITIES

Another area that requires sensitive management is the area of minority and gender diversity. We all feel demeaned when we receive stereotypical treatment as members of a group rather than being treated as unique individuals with our own special talents and interests. Women often face obstacles in the workplace that are brought upon them not by their performance, but by their gender and others' preconceived views. Minority group members have problems based on the biases and perceptions of others. Once again, performance is not the issue—their minority status is (unfairly) the issue. A sensitive manager must be aware of such problems.

Members of minority or disadvantaged groups may be reluctant to take full advantage of structures that support advancement, particularly in systems dominated by the majority. For example, the personnel department may hire a woman as a technical assistant in an engineering department composed only of male engineers. She then shows an aptitude for her job but waits for someone to point out that she would do well as an engineer. Not only may she be less likely to ask for support to take engineering courses to advance herself, but it may be the case that others rarely think of her in terms of advancement and self-improvement in the same way that they would think of a man in the same job position. A good manager will not ignore this differential, but will provide additional encouragement and actively support the woman's efforts at self-improvement and advancement.

Similarly, a good manager is alert to communication problems, whether written or oral. Such problems may affect minorities whose primary language is not English or who have insufficient training in the proper use of English. A good manager will not ignore such difficulties or allow them to worsen but will offer the necessary help to improve the employee's communication skills. A manager serves the employee poorly when the manager ignores the employee's continual errors of speech or written communication. Not wanting to offend the employee is no excuse for the manager's negligence, which ultimately will mean that both the employee and the company lose out.

Thus, we are not advocating a gender-blind or color-blind management policy. This is one where a manager purposefully ignores problems associated with distinctions between men, women, majorities, and minorities. Such a manager might say, "All people are treated equally here." In reality, equality in the workplace does not exist in this sort of context. The treatment that people receive is almost always dependent at least to some degree upon membership or perceived membership in one or more groups. Sensitive management must strive to understand and respond ethically to both the advantages and the disadvantages of group membership. That membership may not be related to traditional categories like race or gender, but other factors such as differing social or political associations that form inside a workplace.

If the right conditions are set for men and women, regardless of their particular ethnic origin, gender, or age, performance from all groups can excel far beyond what many companies experience, even when companies have in place policies that focus on ending discrimination. The company's focus may be on changing language (not using sexist terms and so on), which is good in and of itself, but the real focus should be on building skills, assuming that an employee is capable of advancement, and designing into the workplace recognition for managers who help employees gain skills as well as recognition for the employees who do so. In short, managers should create more reinforcement for learning and doing, and focus less on the differences that either stand in an employee's way or perhaps unfairly propel the individual forward.

At one level, the approach to workplace diversity takes its cues from focusing on differences inherent in our labels—black, white, Asian, old, female, male, and so on. These differences should be treated with respect in terms of culturally ingrained practices. We must become more neutral, however, about workplace management practices and manage employees from a clear set of expectations by skill level and experience, requirements of the job. The differences of cultural history can enrich the ways we look at what others do and how we view our businesses, but the labels we attach to others can also set up the most biasing of conditions.

Many managers will say that a problem with a particular worker is "not fixable" because it is part of that person's cultural history or ethical value system. Such passive approaches to good people generate great unfairness, and in the end the very individuals we are working to support find themselves in dead-end jobs or losing jobs because management never got "real" with them about unacceptable practices. This is no small problem in American business today.

If our goal is to make the workplace a more level playing field for diverse individuals, then we must look less to the label than to the accomplishments and potential of each person. Whenever we see in a person's workplace patterns an indication that the person's background plays a role in their approach to their job, then we should recognize this fact about the person and be alert to it. But we should always be on guard against allowing our treatment of individuals to reflect any biases or assumptions that we may have as to what is to be expected on the basis of age, race, cultural background, gender, and so on. Look to what you can see and hear people saying and doing and apply reasonable standards of performance to them.

Consider the following example. A national fast-food chain wanted to increase the number of Hispanic females who were promoted to leadership roles (positions above that of franchise owner) in their Southwestern operations. In terms of the culture and, it must be said, biases of the time, women from Hispanic backgrounds did not have sufficient knowledge about how to "get ahead" in the traditional ways that lead to promotions in this company. These women did themselves report that it was contrary to their culture for them to speak up in meetings about the larger corporate structure, for example, or share ideas about how to improve the company's assets. They were excellent as local franchise managers or owners, and pursued opportunities at that level, but they were rarely considered for, and even more rarely applied for, further advancement. Many of the men who oversaw their work assumed that they did not want to advance beyond the local operation, perhaps because of time demands that interfered with home life. However, in interviews with these women, it became clear that they did want to advance.

When these women received training in how to approach opportunities for advancement, and regarding what was expected of individuals seeking advancement (training directed at both the women themselves and also their bosses in how to encourage and develop leadership skills required by the fast-food chain), promotions began to occur and the labels and faulty assumptions about Hispanic women and their leadership abilities lessened.

Cultural diversity is a hallmark of our society. It is one of the best things about American culture. How we approach one another in terms of our common humanity is another valuable part of our culture, and learning to do it well and with respect is essential in the workplaces of our future. We need never discount or abuse the rich backgrounds we bring, but likewise we must never use these backgrounds as a reason for limiting potential or opportunity in an ethical workplace. Our society, our workplaces, our place in the world—all of these are undergoing important changes. Managing people in the midst of our changing perceptions, customs, and demands is another area where ethics and business management come together.

9

CHAPTER

THE CONSTANCY OF CHANGE

Nothing endures but change.

—Heraclitus, *Diogenes Laertius*

And this too shall pass away.

—Abraham Lincoln

MANAGING CHANGE SUCCESSFULLY

Initiatives to implement new strategies and strategies to fix those very initiatives are a constant of the workplace. These endeavors, sometimes sarcastically called the *flavors of the week, the month, or the year* pop up continually in business. Not only is there an ongoing search in the business marketplace for new product ideas and innovations, it is clear that the most frequent motivation for the search is to find ways to inspire people to work more effectively. The search may be driven by financial outcomes, but it can also be about morale, about finding ways to recognize, reward, endorse, and empower workers. Companies are searching for ways to make work easier, and for new ways to delight the customer.

The search may take the form of a program to help retain top people, provide work-friendly methods for lone workers, or promote a commitment to diversity. This search for new ideas and innovations may be viewed as, at its core, strictly financial—the competitive edge. Yet, the search can reasonably be viewed as a noble quest, a thirst for knowledge and continuous learning, and a desire to treat employees well—going beyond the status quo to find new ways for the company and its people to excel. Innovation and highly praiseworthy business often results from these explorations.

Nevertheless, many of today's companies have in place numerous distracting and overlapping theories and initiatives about how to reach business goals. Regrettably, no control center has yet been designed for effectively eliminating bad ideas that most probably should have been recognized as spam on the hard drives of business decision making. For example, a company recently sponsored a three-day retreat for senior executives (guided by an external consultant) to build a behavioral roadmap for successfully implementing business strategy.

Early in the session, the team listed the competing and distracting events that demand employees' attention yet divert them from what they really should do to meet key targets. By the time the list was complete, the leader team had uncovered thirty-seven different initiatives in active stages of implementation at the company—initiatives that demanded time and resources, and, in some cases, contained competing and overlapping objectives. Other companies have come up with even larger numbers of ongoing initiatives.

Several of the initiatives on the list were in fact working well, meeting their objectives and considered to be worth the effort. Many other initiatives on the list caused raised or furrowed eyebrows, as leaders worked to remember a particular consulting team from the past, or a strange acronym that everyone had been so excited about only weeks before. Was it just fourteen months ago that they had started their *Innovation through Inquisition* Program?

The burden of the initiatives looming on flip chart paper, mostly promises all, became the first order of business. The group used process tools from the quality movement (thanks to Deming, Ishikawa, and other quality pioneers) for sorting, prioritizing, and deciding among the initiatives. Soon they had identified the overlaps, the insignificant, and the worthy—reducing the number of large initiatives to three, and the number of smaller initiatives in various areas of the company to fifteen. A new tomorrow!

Sadly, after about ninety tomorrows, the list had once again grown, this time to twenty-six initiatives, with seven of those additions fitting the *large initiatives* category. Ultimately, no initiatives were eliminated or completed during that three-month period following the initial reduction to the critical fifteen at the road-mapping session. Once again, incomplete, unattended to, and distracting initiatives lay strewn around the corporate entity, creating cynicism about the possibility of change, and significantly as well, creating in employees a sense that there is little care put into what is asked of them and little reward or follow-through on what they try hard to complete.

A CRUCIAL COMPONENT OF SUCCESSFUL INITIATIVES

When a company considers investing in a new initiative to promote the most effective change, company leadership does not make the decision to invest unless it believes that recommended processes will bring good things to the company and its employees. Still, in the end, many things that are done in the name of doing the right things in the right way fail or fade. Is this just the way it must be—that we must try and try again, experiment, redesign, implement, evaluate (or not), and then start over? Could there be, underneath the striving and redesign, a fundamental error in the way continuous improvement is approached in the workplaces of America, leaving out a critical component of analysis, a component that is fundamental to determining what should change in the first place?

Many of you work in companies where you can list the types and slogans of multiple initiatives that are all actively moving along. You may say that they provide focus for employees, retain jobs for taskforce members, and that they create genuine excitement about doing things in new ways. After all, continuous evaluation and change are all part of the fundamentals. We must be willing to examine, to change, and to improve.

If you see your company's initiatives as good things, you may well be right. Large companies have areas of business that require great care, and undertaking a well thought-out initiative can be beneficial. Organizations may have large-scale, multiyear projects costing millions of dollars as well as smaller initiatives focused on near-term needs. The number of initiatives is not the critical issue. However, when leaders find that many of these initiatives produce little to no actual return on investment, these shiny new initiatives lose their luster. Why does this happen?

The problem is that the processes that generate new initiatives often ignore the fundamental element for success: changing the predictable patterns of human performance. Human behavior, when not completely ignored, is the most fundamental yet most incorrectly analyzed element of the workplace.

Whether in ancient Rome or in today's America, people behave lawfully and predictably. Unfortunately, and almost always, a systematic examination of patterns of performance is left out of the initiative equation. The analysis focuses on something not directly related, such as "better teamwork to get more productivity" or "process changes" in an already superbly designed process flow analysis; it can't simply be a question of more effective management of performance. In fact, in many so-called new initiative events, it turns out to be that simple—the new process flow works no better than the old one; teams do not necessarily produce better results over time, and so on. Then, the cycle starts again. New initiatives are needed, again leaving people's patterns of behavior out of the equation.

If there was, as a first step, a systematic, measured approach to behavior analysis as to why the current initiative is not working, it would almost certainly demonstrate that changes can be made that will immediately improve performance in the areas that many initiatives are designed to target. Surprisingly, the science of behavior usually plays no defining role in assessing why a performance problem exists even in initiatives with names such as "People Power" or "Putting Our People First" or "The Power of One."

Each time a new initiative is undertaken and then left to fade or drift, a certain kind of cynicism is bred, the kind that says, "You cannot trust this company. They foolishly introduce new ways of doing things. We, the workers, learn these new ways—we have no choice. The leaders then just move on, stop measuring, recognizing, or remembering what we are doing. At best, this is wasteful. At worst, it is disrespectful of our efforts and a bad use of limited financial resources." A pattern of questioning the ethical commitments of a company can start from the cynicism bred from these well-intended false starts.

Knowing how to plan for and look at the behavior of employees, from the senior leader to the front line, takes a certain kind of skill that is very often missing in the quest for a new initiative, theme, or mission. Over and over again, new initiatives are tried, only to be discarded after intense effort by many people. These initiatives are then replaced by other, seemingly better or brighter ideas—while all the time, the solution to the underlying problems lies in the mundane and everyday prediction, detection, and control of what is best referred to as *performance variance.*

ADDRESSING HUMAN PERFORMANCE

The high rate of failure of initiatives in corporate America is not necessarily inherent in any particular initiative but usually occurs because managers lack knowledge and skills regarding human behavior that would allow them to attain desired results. People are the real drivers of business success—even process redesign involves the careful use and reinforcement of activities required to sustain a newly designed process. Knowing how to increase and sustain positive performance is the most essential management skill.

People behave (in the main) logically and predictably. When they behave in ways other than those we want, they are, usually, still behaving logically and predictably. Managers need to manage the conditions of the workplace that set up good occasions for work and the kinds of consequences that employees respond to, including consequences related to dealing with the managers themselves. In behavioral terms, these are the antecedent processes (elements such as directives, values and mission statements, training, and procedural guidelines that precede and prompt behavior) and consequence processes (reinforcement, punishment, or extinction that follow behavior) that operate in every workplace.

Antecedents precede behavior as a signal and consequences follow behavior. Behaviors change as the consequences for words and actions reinforce or punish responses. It is our observation that company leadership almost always focuses on antecedents to influence behavior. Effort is directed to setting up the rules, giving directions, making suggestions, and providing training to produce the desired behavior. All too rarely do company leaders focus on consequences, the heart of behavior change. More will be said about antecedent and consequence control in Chapter 15.

Even more rarely do company leaders understand where the source of real control lies in creating successful change: it lies in managing human performance variance. Instead they work to design-in success, to design-in error-free approaches to the workplace, to redesign and then redesign again. Change is a constant in the workplace. Remember that managing the variance in human behavior patterns is the stabilizer that prevents change from leading to chaos or inaction.

DESIGNING INITIATIVES TO ADDRESS ROOT CAUSES

Your company may be considering a new performance initiative. What are the performance problems to be addressed? Believe it or not, that question is sometimes not the first question asked at the beginning of a new initiative. Instead, companies look for solutions outside the company—in the press, in new books on business, or in the way the competition addresses an issue. They search for elegant, engaging solutions, and then they find a problem as regards a chosen solution. You may doubt that this strange approach to performance change occurs, but it happens frequently.

The increased frequency of proposed solutions such as high performance teams, SAP software solutions, new sales approaches, total quality management, Six Sigma, or Covey's Seven Habits—all have been suggested and implemented on occasion without clearly defining the reasons for implementing any of these programs. Such popular and worthy programs, after a period of great fanfare and often high levels of success, end up failing to address the root causes for which they were initiated.

Let's say that your company actually did begin with a well-researched issue and then began to look for solutions. Good! The next question, again before searching for solutions, is "Why do you have the problem?"

The answer to this question appears simple but again is often neglected. It is not explored to the degree that it must be in order to uncover engrained practices. If such practices are not uncovered and addressed, they will continue to exist long after the initiative is over and the company has returned to the status quo.

People in organizations have predictable patterns of action, what behavior analysts would call behavior at habit strength. These patterns must be addressed if any initiative undertaken by the corporate leadership is to direct new behavior to the point of habit strength. Changing performance at work is just as difficult as changing people's habits in any other domain of life. Real effort must be directed toward change at the single-performer level as well as in quick-fix initiatives introduced through slogans and training. Training is good but training alone will not change behavior.

Stating problems in such high-level ways as, "Our competitors have introduced immediate rebates for service quality mistakes and we need to do so as well," does not work. Another high-level statement might be, "Our sales force is being outsold by the Johnson Brothers Corporation, even though they are selling exactly the same products we are. We have looked our account executives over and they are just not real sellers. Let's find ourselves a real sales force and let our current sales staff go."

If you drill down in each instance, you may discover the fundamental root of almost every problem: people behave given the contingencies that surround them, and their behavior spells either success or failure for a company. To implement changes without addressing the consequence systems that sustain poor or less than adequate practices will only reduce the likelihood of real change and real solutions that last.

The answer may be that your company would have been the first to anticipate the market advantage of rebates if your company had encouraged more brainstorming. Maybe your company would have been ahead of the competition if employees had been recognized for innovative service delivery, allowed to respond more freely to resolving customer complaints, and, most importantly, reinforced for doing so. In reality, it may be that whenever people in your company suggest new methods, they are reminded of the organization's founder, Joe Schmidt. "If it was good enough for Joe, well, it's good enough for us today."

Company leadership may have been reinforced for years for following the old book rules, and those old ways will still be there even as you introduce rebates. Most probably, your competition, which apparently nurtures creativity, will come up with another innovation while you work to catch up. The answer to your problem is not, in this case, rebates, but rather, establishing conditions to encourage and reinforce those employees who demonstrate genuine customer awareness. If you simply design an initiative to copy the competition, you may never discover that the root cause of your problems is that your management systems punish people for suggesting novel ways of doing things. In the end, the real change needed is a different way of managing your human capital so that employee ideas can float easily and quickly to the top for action. This solution requires a system of management that does not punish the expression of ideas.

Firing the old sales staff and hiring a new sales staff can also mask core issues related to skills in sales management that will continue long after the fresh, eager, responsive sales personnel are brought on board. The question, why do we have a problem? can affect multiple levels and has multiple answers. As a company seriously examines why it has a problem, other problems are likely to surface, most of which have been there for a long, long time. If this question is explored in detail, then the outcomes you are seeking and how you attain them have a much better chance of success. Unfortunately, most leaders will tell you they already do this, when in reality they are only reacting to symptoms, not searching for the causes.

What do all of these observations about change have to do with a book on ethics? The lack of understanding about human behavior can cause, as we are seeing, many faulty decisions about who, what, and how—placing blame on people who, with the right management skills, could have succeeded. This failure to understand and manage performance can lead to firing, to reassignment of personnel, or to costly redesigns when a simple fix would do. None of these efforts to find more effective ways of doing things (as most initiatives are intended to do) are ethical flaws in their own right, but they can lead to a generalized sense of incompetence in both employees and management, and, if not addressed, to wrongful acts that harm people and the business.

Now, to return to the company that is initiating a new change. The need for change can almost always be traced to practices that have been deeply entrenched and are often unexamined. These practices usually reflect a deficit in the knowledge and skills needed to 1) see performance clearly, and 2) address the uncontrolled and undesired variance in human performance that causes most business problems.

Businesses try many initiatives to improve performance and employee relations but many of the initiatives fail. For example, one person has commented on teams and reorganizations as follows:

> We trained hard, but it seems that every time we were beginning to form into teams, we would be reorganized. I was to learn later in life that we tend to meet any situation by reorganizing, and a wonderful method it can be for creating the illusion of progress while producing confusion, inefficiency, and demoralization.

This modern-sounding quotation comes from Gaius Petronius, author and satirist, in AD 66!

Managing change well requires careful thought about the messages and expectations sent to employees and the performance follow-through required to be successful. There is another aspect to designing a workplace that promotes, by its very presence, successful ethical action by employees, particularly during times of change. It is a key element in any design where not only ethical behavior is to be encouraged, but also innovation and creativity. It is what distinguishes us most as humans: the use of words, and especially the open expression of ideas. We address this topic in the next chapter.

10

CHAPTER

Speaking Up: Defining Loyalty Anew

Every organization should tolerate rebels who tell the emperor he has no clothes.

—Colin Powell

THE OPEN EXPRESSION OF IDEAS IN THE WORKPLACE

American companies have frequently taken a shortsighted view of what it means for employees to be loyal to the company and they have, very often, focused their shortsightedness on the issue of speech. Both employees and managers are often unclear about what should be expressed by a loyal employee. Some managers and some employees may believe that a loyal employee will never publicly criticize the company on ethical, legal, or practical grounds. At the same time, these same individuals may not be skillful at inviting debate and discussion inside their companies.

The history of whistle-blowers tells us that such individuals almost always try to express their concerns first to people inside the company. Thus, if managers could be taught how to handle divergent viewpoints in a respectful manner, they could save themselves and their companies from much expense and embarrassment.

Very often employees who want to address problems or raise uncomfortable questions are loyal, and they want a chance to present to their leaders what they believe will be helpful information. By the actions of their managers, they may be convinced that they have no choice but to take their concerns to someone else who will listen.

Consider the following examples. Management that encouraged internal discussion, and had learned how to listen and act on such concerns could well have changed the course of events in two highly publicized disasters: the explosion of the space shuttle Challenger on the morning of January 28, 1986, and the release of deadly gas from a Union Carbide factory in Bhopal, India, on December 3, 1984. In both instances employees raised safety issues and were ignored by those in authority:

> Fatal flaws in management and authority structures, problems in the interactions between the scientifically minded engineers and political managerial systems, and lack of ethical consideration are at least partially to blame for both of these events [loss of the Challenger and the Bhopal accident] as well as others like them (O'Connor, 1987).

Without a formal process for attending to and evaluating concerns objectively, in either instance, the response may well have been something to the effect that the issues in question were not the concern of the employees who spoke up, and indeed many employees did speak up in a variety of ways in these examples. We think it is safe to say that it would have been at least somewhat more likely that someone who did step forward would have been heard had corporate policies strongly encouraged such behavior rather than actively discouraging it.

The sorts of corporate policies that we are talking about must go beyond the paper they are written on. They must contain clear examples provided by management—examples that demonstrate that speaking up is a valued and safe thing to do. Indeed, if employees had been told it was their responsibility to speak up as soon as they saw an actual or even potential problem, and that they would be listened to carefully, the underlying root causes for the disasters mentioned above might not have existed in the first place.

Employees who are told that they are free to bring any workplace concerns to management, and that they are free to speak out publicly if management does not address the issues, will probably not end up going public—not if management listens and responds, even if not exactly as the person might have hoped. It is certainly possible that some employees will go public anyway, despite enlightened management/employee interaction. In doing so, they may seriously harm the interests of the corporation, even if the corporate leadership has good intentions. This risk from having in place policies that encourage open expression is minimal, however, especially when weighed against the alternatives. In our opinion, taking such a risk is morally necessary in any case.

A thorough commitment to ethical conduct is essential for any corporation concerned about the effects of its actions, and employees must come to know just how serious that commitment is. Such a commitment requires that employees be included in appropriately structured systems for review of corporate policy and be given the right to speak about their concerns, doubts, wishes, and insights.

A distinction should be drawn between freedom of speech in one's personal life and freedom of speech in one's life as an employee. This distinction should be fully articulated by the company. As with free speech granted to American citizens, consequences need to be attached to slanderous statements. In addition, employees can be restricted from disclosing proprietary information, such as competitive strategies, plans for development of products and services, and personnel information.

Employee rights and responsibilities regarding speech can be written into company policy statements. Where such documents exist, the focus is usually on speech that is restricted, not on speech that is protected and encouraged. The latter is, in fact, the most important part of a company's freedom of speech statement. Of course, such a statement, or such a policy, by itself is not enough. In order for it to be genuinely beneficial to the company and its employees, managers must know how to encourage and reinforce the open exchange of ideas. Unhappily, skills in this area are severely underutilized in today's corporate world.

WHISTLE-BLOWING

In America, we tend to police ourselves well once we are aware of violations. As a society, once we become aware of our mistakes, we often openly and vigorously publicize them, and increase the pressure on those who do wrong to at least redeem themselves by acknowledging their errors, serving jail terms, or in some way repaying the community. Most Americans believe that catching the wrongdoer is a good thing, and if asked, will applaud those who stand up for ethical conduct at work. But do our actions match up with our professed beliefs? Let's look at the fate of a few brave people who are commonly referred to as "whistle-blowers."

> Jeffrey Wigand, a high-ranking executive and researcher in the tobacco industry revealed that the tobacco industry was deliberately hiding facts about the dangers of smoking. Wigand was eventually the admired subject of the movie *The Insider*, but not before he lost his career and marriage and received numerous death threats.
>
> Shelley Davis' revelations about wrongdoing by the Internal Revenue Service (IRS) inspired a congressional investigation. She did the right thing, but she lost her career of 16 years and her retirement.
>
> Karen Silkwood, subject of the movie *Silkwood*, died in a mysterious one-car accident after blowing the whistle on safety violations at the plutonium fuels production plant where she worked as a chemical technician; arguably, not enough was done to investigate her death.
>
> Randy Robarge, formerly a radiation protection supervisor, lost his job when he exposed procedural violations at Commonwealth Edison's Zion nuclear power plant.

In addition, hundreds of whistle-blowers merely disappear into obscurity, unrewarded except for the knowledge that they told the truth as they perceived it and possibly made a difference.

Many issues relate to whistle-blowing, including questions regarding truth and evidence, the confidential nature of much of what the whistle-blower does, questions about how whistle-blowers can validate themselves, and debate about the methods whistle-blowers use to bring problems to management's attention. Even the term *whistle-blower* raises the question of whether we are to perceive that the standing of the person who speaks up has been enhanced or diminished. It is probably fair to say that the general idea of speaking up directly about concerns is still perceived as dangerous by most employees, because the consequences for speaking up are so often personally disastrous.

Brian Martin (1998), a professor and writer in Australia, has studied hundreds of whistle-blower cases over the past twenty years. He writes: "Whistle-blowers typically are conscientious employees who believe in the system. That's why they speak out, after all: They expect the problem will be dealt with. Therefore, they are deeply shocked when the response of managers is to attack them rather than investigate their complaints" (p. 10).

The point is that when a person behaves ethically in whistle-blowing cases, positive consequences do not automatically follow—a dilemma for all of us when we are faced with difficult decisions. But doing the right thing does not have to bring negative repercussions.

Acting ethically has its own rewards regardless of what else may happen. Striving to be ethical can give us peace, even in the midst of terrible events in life. Behaving ethically frees us from regret and from that most severe type of pain—shame. After all, to be embarrassed when we fail to do the right thing is in itself a good thing. Being ashamed, embarrassed, provides a powerful source of self-knowledge about how bad it can feel to disappoint others when we fail to live up to our own standards of conduct. The existence of such feelings helps to corroborate that such standards actually exist; such a state of affairs is not only a good thing, but entirely necessary if we are to create a culture that strives to be ethical.

Indeed, we talk too little about shame. Some ethicists and psychologists argue that we need to elevate the role of shame as a guiding factor in our lives. *Webster's* dictionary equates shame with pity, disgrace, ignominy, attaint, and dishonor. For purposes of this book, a more relevant definition of *shame* is "to bring dishonor upon, with the consequence that a person will feel the tremendous burden of disgrace." In clinical psychology, this burden is often manifested as a withdrawal of social interaction—a kind of social hiding. In behavioral terms, shame can be explained as the sudden and severe removal of those things that matter, that are reinforcing and valued by the person—affection, recognition, and so on.

For many people, a personal sense of shame can occur through their associations with those who abuse and dishonor relationships for personal gain. Experiencing direct personal shame for our actions, and shame that comes from associating with those who do wrong acts often provides enough punishment to keep people from actively continuing to violate generally accepted codes of decency and respect. Certainly, a dose of shame might have helped the Enron executives, who, after ruining the lives of thousands of innocents by acting unethically, requested (shamelessly) that the courts still grant Enron's year-end executive bonuses.

MIXED MESSAGES

Some companies deliberately suppress the speech of those who report wrongdoings, as with the whistle-blowing examples cited above. There are also companies that unintentionally suppress speech. One well-known company wanted to achieve the goal of *increasing personal accountability in the workforce* in part by espousing a set of values describing what the company's employees should do to be good corporate citizens. As part of that initiative, they used many easy-to-learn slogans such as, "Don't be a Victim: Bring Solutions, not Problems." In some instances, however, these few words worked to produce the opposite consequence of that intended.

On one high-performance team, for instance, an individual's request to discuss a problem was rejected because she did not bring a solution to the problem she had pointed out. Almost immediately, in an attempt to help her develop a greater level of personal ownership, the team labeled her a *victim* for her lack of accountability. She quickly fell silent and plunged into a deep well of anger. What if her problem had contained ethical overtones? The immediate impact of this particular set of slogans, at least on this individual, was to suppress verbal risk taking.

Corporations sometimes use such slogans or rules of conduct as ways to bind people together as they kick off new initiatives. Slogans provide a shorthand method for prompting action. The slogans used in the above example were acceptable on the surface and inspiring as well, but they had bad effects because of the destructive ways they were implemented by some managers. Probably not everyone in the corporation suffered because of these slogans, but clearly for several managers, assumptions about how to create high-and-steady rates of positive accountability were misguided. Leaders did no prior analysis of how such slogans might impact performance. No alternative slogans or, better yet, realistic ways to increase positive and accountable behaviors were taught to managers who were, in many cases, unskilled at managing others.

Doubtless, no one had thought about how the slogans might encourage team members to label one another in unhelpful ways. Some managers produced a hyper-vigilant atmosphere by praising employees who identified those who did not act as they should according to the slogans. Few thought about the possibility of creating such an atmosphere, which did a lot of damage in the name of increasing accountability. No one understood the high degree of negative reinforcement that their system created. (In Chapter 15, the impact of negative reinforcement on employee behavior is more fully described.) In this case, because management did not understand the real impact that their program had on behavior, the desired behaviors in some instances were pushed aside and replaced by minimal compliance.

Certainly, the corporate decision makers who wanted to increase accountability wanted to encourage their employees. They did not mean to create even a minimally coercive workplace. Still, behavior is lawful and predictable based on the consequences in place for doing one thing rather than another. It is naïve to use slogans or other kinds of rules if you do not carefully examine what those slogans or rules produce, as well as suppress. Especially, you do not want problem-oriented speech to go underground. All companies most urgently need open communications if they are to address ethical concerns effectively.

Unnecessary rules about personal conduct can create very inhibited workplaces. With many more companies at the present time attempting to emphasize ethics, the danger exists that management will simply produce more rules designed to get employees to do or say the right thing. A code of conduct, if not carefully considered, may mean that doing something other than that stated specifically in the rules is, by default, understood to be unethical. A code of conduct as a signal for what is wanted in professional conduct is a very good thing. Improving management skills in applying such codes to shape more effective performance is an even better thing.

SHARING INFORMATION

For the open expression of ideas to be most effective, managers must inform their employees of the company's goals, of precisely what the specific corporate intent is so that they, the employees, can address real issues, and not speculate about what may be happening. Product design, systems for delivering services, and performance expectations, make up one part of corporate direction. Another is the broad corporate philosophy, the company's strategic goals and its value system. If employees are kept in the dark about significant company policies and viewed simply as cogs on the company wheel, they will not be able to contribute as bona fide team members.

Managers of American companies have frequently worried that an open information dissemination policy would let company "secrets" leak to competitors. Certainly that danger exists. However, reasonable inclusion of employees as regards the company's direction and concerns is valuable, and more can often be shared than might seem appropriate on first examination. Performance accelerates as individuals are encouraged and recognized for their contributions. The satisfaction of workers is directly tied to how much they feel their performance (words and deeds) makes a difference that matters in how work is done.

SPEAKING UP: LOYALTY THAT SHOULD BE REWARDED

Rewarding employees for supreme loyalty to the company is a frequent but dangerous practice. All too often *loyalty* is perceived as the unstated but clearly understood code word for a person whose chief talent lies in saying yes to the boss.

There are dedicated employees who are both highly productive and loyal in the sense of having a positive attitude and a willingness to provide extra effort when it is needed. This is the kind of loyalty that should be rewarded. Complete, blind loyalty has no place in management philosophy. Rewarding the blind loyalty of an employee while ignoring other aspects of performance can violate that person's autonomy and produce resentment in others. It is but another form of coercion.

The important question is not how loyal (in the first sense) an employee is, but rather, in what ways do an employee's actions further the objectives of the company? All too often, managers encounter poorly performing individuals who are loyal beyond measure. Companies that do not want to be challenged often reward these people by keeping quiet about less than desirable performance. To management's way of thinking, such an approach reduces dissension. However, in reality this approach illustrates the fact that until loyalty is specified in behavioral terms and is measured by its positive effects, it has little contributory value to the company.

All too often, employees are afraid that they will be perceived as disloyal. Management must examine closely how the corporate culture is structured. Are employees allowed to speak out in defense of unpopular positions? Are they encouraged to take risks and bring to the attention of other employees, and also supervisors, decisions on the part of management that are not good for the company? Management must reward this type of assertiveness because it benefits the company.

What else should management consider if it wants to encourage the highest degree of ethical behavior in its workplace even if it has designed a safe, secure, pleasant environment, encouraged the open expression of ideas in both policy and practice, and modeled such behavior itself? We will close this chapter by discussing two of the answers to this question.

LESSENING INTERNAL COMPETITION

Actual head-to-head competition within an organization can be quite destructive. Management can overcome negative internal competition by adopting policies that assign more value to individuals themselves—well before they have succeeded in producing a new product design, a new sales plan, or a new investment strategy. For example, rather than have management tell three people to each produce a complete sales plan from which the best will be chosen while the other two will be discarded, a better strategy in most situations is to tell one of the three to produce a draft plan. All the people involved then conduct a brainstorming session to determine how to improve the initial plan.

This method gives a strong vote of confidence to the one person who is asked to write the draft, while other interested parties are not denied their chance to address the issue, and can be given credit for all their help toward producing the final plan. In certain kinds of tasks where individual creativity can go off in quite different and disparate directions (such as in developing a new design theme for a line of products) competition among individuals or teams may be the best way to uncover and assess a range of new possibilities.

Excessive internal competition hinders team efforts. Walls are built between units of a company that could do a better job if they shared their knowledge. Short-term competition, such as contests between teams, can be enjoyable if the contest has a set duration and the reward is not of such high value that dissension, sabotage, and resentment occur. Generally, it is better to reduce competition among employees within departments and divisions and to focus the competitive spirit on the organization's external competition in the marketplace.

INNOVATION AND JOB SECURITY

No one in the workforce wants to suggest a labor-saving innovation for the company if the labor saved means the elimination of that person's job. Employees are inclined to contribute more when they feel secure in a company because of its employment history and clear policies. They believe themselves genuinely to be part of a team effort. They are likely to enjoy solving work problems and are more likely to welcome increased automation and innovation.

Every company should work carefully to ensure, if possible, that no one in the organization will lose a place in the company simply as a result of suggesting a more efficient way to get a job done. If the suggestion eliminates the job of the person who made the suggestion, then management should find a new place for that person if at all possible.

Security is one of the most important values in life, directly tied to happiness for most people. One requirement for job security is to know the skills and behaviors that are required for success in the job. Furthermore, a secure employee expects fair treatment, that credit will be given for effort made, and that the company will honor all of its commitments. Secure employees also view candor about the direction and stability of the company as signs of a secure relationship. Such security increases the likelihood that employees will invest in their companies, giving their best advice and guidance, and approaching the workplace with energy.

Employees know the conditions for business success and that their jobs can be eliminated even when they are acting in ways that increase efficient and effective outcomes. Honest and direct discussion, searches for alternative solutions, and candor when decisions are made are fundamental when a company invites its employees to help shape its destiny. No promises need be made about security in an absolute sense, but employees do value being secure in terms of inclusion and information.

In all of this, human behavior and its prediction and control are critical to business success. Companies must arrange conditions to help employees speak out clearly about what they are experiencing and share their ideas for change if they are to 1) optimize performance, 2) celebrate steps taken to reach goals, and 3) relish the open exchange of ideas, improvements, and finding of errors.

Replicating good practices across a wide range of conditions within the workplace and its external environment tests the commitment that corporations have to an ethical framework. Some of the greatest challenges occur when the conditions are international in scope—which is the topic to which we turn in the next chapter.

11
CHAPTER

Workplace Ethics in a World Setting

For what shall it profit a man, if he shall gain the whole world, and lose his own soul?

—The New Testament,
King James Bible,
Mark 8:36

Moral dilemmas faced by businesses at home are faced on a different scale by businesses that span the globe. This is especially true when cultural and economic differences between countries are great. A wide variety of customs and cultures exist throughout the world. Abroad, America is seen as both a friend and an enemy, often within the same country.

America, in its foreign policy, has tended to use words that convey a broad moral perspective when engaged in international dealings. We have taken on, some would say, the mission of bringing our way of life to other countries less fortunate than we are. That can be a very big burden indeed when working to both respect and convert people to our values system. Sometimes that line gets murky when a business is our only representative, and when that business acts counter to the values we state as a nation, undermining both message and method. How American business shows up in the world is a critical topic as regards ethics at work.

Many of the issues are complex and governed by international and national law. We have prohibitions against bribery and involvement in the political life of foreign governments. Other matters require that American business keep a keen eye on the law. Some areas are vague and invite interpretation. Some areas are open and allow multinational businesses to determine their own approach to ethical issues, sometimes deciding strongly in favor of self-interest. Since we, the authors, are not experts on international regulations and standards, this chapter focuses on pointing out some of the dilemmas that the global economy raises for American businesses abroad. Many of the ethical approaches that can be done at home to ensure understanding of both intentions and effects of actions should be considered in international relations as well. These ethical plans should be developed and designed with the guidance of those who are alert to the law and to the moral issues raised for Americans involved in providing or producing goods and services in another land or with foreign workers.

BRIBERY AND GIFT GIVING

A company that does not respect the people in its host country will probably not be welcome there for long. Worker morale, the cooperation of local governments, local people's enthusiasm for buying a company's products—all are jeopardized when the company's representatives do not respect the host country. Respect requires sensitivity to a country's customs and culture, and an ethical philosophy that guides the international goals of the company operating in that country. Respect can be undermined by a number of different business practices that occur all too frequently. Among the worst of them is offering bribes to government officials.

In 1996, the International Chamber of Commerce (ICC) adopted The Rules of Conduct to Combat Extortion and Bribery to help businesses everywhere develop a clear standard that prohibits bribery and brings sanctions against companies that participate in such practices. Paying bribes is illegal under the Foreign Corrupt Practices Act of 1977, updated most recently in 2002. The practice of bribery is morally wrong. Americans must show a willingness to accept some unfamiliar practices but not the practice of bribery. Business forfeits fundamental and irretrievable integrity when, to gain access to favors, it conducts its affairs according to someone else's unacceptable definition of right and wrong.

If bribery is wrong, then what about practices that may resemble bribery, such as the custom of giving and accepting gifts when engaging in business transactions? Such gift giving is common in many foreign countries and some of these gifts may be quite expensive. In some cases, gift giving is a part of normal business expenses or business etiquette. In some cultures, an individual's dignity or standing may be recognized via gift giving.

The Japanese custom of exchanging gifts is widely practiced. Often, a number of different individuals expect to receive gifts in the course of a single business transaction. In some countries the custom of gift giving can be compared to the American custom of thanking vendors with gifts at the holidays or thanking a host with a small gift. Americans working abroad need to thoroughly understand the habits and customs of business in the country they are visiting, and from that understanding determine where they stand. Giving a gift openly and as part of a custom is not an act that will necessarily lead to favoritism, and not giving a gift may violate customs of courtesy and respect.

Understanding the role of gift giving in various cultures helps to open doors and ensures that our biases about gift giving as bribery are put away when we are in a culture where the practice is not about buying a relationship but demonstrating respect. In contrast to gift giving (in the most usual situations anyway), the point of giving a bribe is to ensure that you get the permit or contract while someone else who did not offer a bribe or as large a bribe will not get the permit or contract.

The Foreign Corrupt Practices Act (FCPA) recognizes a distinction between relatively large payments to higher-ups in government for the presumed purpose of influencing their decisions, and smaller payments to lesser officials who do not have the same decision-making powers. Only the former payments are illegal under the Act. Payments of the second sort may be treated generally in the same way as the custom of gift giving in various countries. Obviously, business must keep up with the changing terms of the FCPA and gain a fully researched understanding of international practices.

POLITICAL INVOLVEMENT IN FOREIGN COUNTRIES

Should a multinational corporation attempt to sway the outcome of elections in a host country? Some writers on ethics say flatly that a hands-off policy ought to be followed, because corporations have a vested interest in the results. The mere existence of potential conflicts of interests does not justify a hands-off policy, however. The interests of a foreign corporation may well be at odds with the interests of the host country, and those same foreign business people may be tempted at election time to finance their favored candidates on this basis. Such efforts, which are a form of bribery, will almost surely backfire. It is true that some companies may well back the right candidates from the perspective of the good of the country, not a corrupt perspective. Nevertheless, the principle of non-interference by such business entities must still hold since it is very difficult to determine how the future will turn out, regardless of who is elected.

At best, political involvement in a host country by foreign businesses is risky. It is done all the time, however, and the argument for doing it, a pragmatic one, is that by strengthening economic security through jobs and opportunity, US businesses are providing a countermeasure against corrupt regimes. Other forums for getting one's voice heard are available, and these other means are far better than direct interference in the politics of the host country through bribery or other tactics that do not hold up in the light of day. These issues are not small ones and they have the potential to turn nations against the United States for decades into the future—as well as advance causes that the business entity may know will damage future opportunities to work in those countries. Here the notion of self-interest and common good become easily confused and are sometimes expressed with patriotic fervor.

LAW VERSUS MORALITY

It is not enough for corporate managers—at home or abroad—to say in defense of their policies that they have adhered to the letter of the law. Laws and regulations alone are inadequate in many cases. As emphasized throughout this book, the pursuit of profit within the law must be tempered by other values. This is all the more true when corporations conduct business in countries whose laws are less strict regarding pollution, unsafe work conditions, and products that pose health risks. Do American companies have a moral obligation to adhere to American legal standards when doing business in foreign countries?

The general answer to this question is no. American laws and regulations are not in themselves moral rules. Morality sometimes means going beyond laws. Substituting American laws for those in another country will not automatically produce morality; that would be both too easy and too difficult. It would be too easy because it would relieve American corporations of the need to wrestle with the moral dilemmas themselves. They could say, "We have followed all of the legal standards that apply in America, so we must be doing the right thing." In reality, in some instances they ought to be doing more than the American legal standards require.

At the same time, it would be too difficult. American standards may be impossible to implement in foreign countries because of the extent to which certain resources are available in those countries, and the extent to which industrialization has progressed. Consider, for example, American Food and Drug Administration (FDA) regulations. FDA regulations may be difficult to implement in a developing nation for a number of reasons:

1. Developing or poorer countries may not be able to afford what, in some instances, we can describe as the "Cadillac standards" mandated in the United States.
2. Like all regulatory policies, FDA regulations are established in response to a variety of different pressures, some of them essentially political. Hence, the regulations are compromises and not always best even for Americans.
3. Beyond economic and political differences, many important differences exist between the United States and other countries. For example, the prevalence of a particular disease in a poorer country could affect the urgency and priority for approving and marketing a new drug.

Multinational pharmaceutical companies have a difficult task in their efforts to distinguish between ethical and unethical business practices. They have a greater temptation to cut corners in their business dealings in foreign countries than in America—a temptation heightened by the fact that consumers in developing countries may be less sophisticated than consumers at home. Some foreign consumers are not even able to read or understand the instructions on pharmaceutical packaging. This contributed to scandals in the 1970s involving foreign sales of infant formula; babies got sick and many died because illiterate mothers could not follow the directions for mixing the formula.

Many examples show that the ease of distribution has lead to some products being released in other countries before they are approved in the United States, and before an adequate assessment of adverse side effects has been made. However, the argument can be made that where great urgency exists for finding new treatments—as in the case of escalating HIV infection rates in countries where current cutting-edge treatments are too expensive—US rules are too restrictive and too many people die waiting for further trials on medications and treatments.

Consumers in developing countries are usually not able to carry out comparison shopping to the same degree as is possible in the United States. Multinational corporations thus have all the more responsibility to implement a positive vision of their corporate mission that embraces the best interests of customers, suppliers, workers, and the host country over the longer term.

The moral injunction "Do what is best for all concerned" is not going to be particularly helpful in a multinational corporation whose governance is split among executives, boards of directors, and investors. Every multinational is faced with competition from around the world. Many multinationals are owned by Americans as well as other investors, with differing sensitivities on various issues.

What steps should be taken to make it clear that multinational corporations, such as pharmaceutical companies, must conduct themselves in an ethical manner in whatever country they find themselves? One answer lies in the continued creation and implementation of international industry-wide standards.

INDUSTRY-WIDE STANDARDS

Two kinds of such standards are available, both of them necessary to support ethical decision making both at home and abroad.

First, moral standards should be included in industry-wide codes of conduct that are developed for all companies that sell similar products or services. When designed and accepted by all the companies that normally compete against each other in a segment of the market, the standards are more likely to be embraced. One reason for industry-wide participation is that no company alone will necessarily have to bear disproportional expenses if, at time of audit, they are operating according to accepted practices. A second reason is that individual companies that adopt such policies earn a certain measure of protection in times of dispute or litigation. Managers can say, "We did adhere to ethical standards recognized by the entire industry. We were doing our best at the time, acting in good faith."

Acting in good faith is strengthened if each company evaluates its own standards against those that apply industry-wide. If the industry-wide code is incomplete or vague, then the company's own code can make up for these deficiencies.

The second kind of standard is for the performance of products. Such standards range from standardization of thread types and sizes for screws and bolts to target figures for miles per gallon in cars, quality standards for materials, underwriting requirements, accounting practices, safety standards for operating machines, and so on. Again, companies are given a measure of protection when disputes arise, but more importantly, customers are likely to receive better products and services at lower prices. Standardization can increase efficiency, effectiveness, and safety. It may increase costs initially, but industry standardization over time should reduce labor, materials, and replacement costs.

The key ingredients for setting standards of both types are goodwill toward employees, suppliers, customers, and competitors, both at home and abroad, and the attitudes and negotiating skills that cooperation requires. Industry-wide standards provide essential benchmarks. The more that industry-wide and worldwide standards are taken seriously, the more that competing companies must join the same camp regarding product safety and performance, working conditions, and responsible use of resources. Adoption and oversight implementation of such standards will diminish opportunities for individual companies to exploit people in developing countries. Also, when standards transcend the policies of a single company, those who follow the standards are less likely to receive criticism from other sources.

American businesses cannot force global acceptance of standards adopted initially for local or regional application. They can, however, set an ethical precedent by not circumventing American law and/or taking advantage of more lenient laws in other lands that compromise product quality and safety, the environment, or human rights, even if doing so would bring economic benefit to the organization. At the present time, many US companies are taking the high road, losing a bit of profit but gaining much both in international and national reputation. However, there are some problematic examples, such as in the field of agriculture.

At the present time, many developing countries are banding together to take an assertive stand of their own, saying that select policies toward agriculture inside richer countries can doom poorer or underdeveloped countries to poverty and economic woes of all kinds. As the world moves to embrace a sense of interlocking global economic destiny, US policies and protectionism for our own people will receive stricter evaluation, and we can expect that negative reactions to our protectionist policies will become stronger. As economically depressed countries band together, we must redefine our worldwide economic policies. While many US corporations are taking on additional responsibilities and meeting higher standards than required in numerous countries, many are not.

Sooner or later, as economic sophistication grows worldwide, the welcome given to Americans will increasingly be determined by our commitment to ethical actions. At no time has it been more important for Americans to examine current policies for what the future implications of those policies may be. At no time has a public commitment to buttressing economic policy with underlying moral values been more crucial.

Of course, even when industry-wide standards have been established, businesses must seek to understand the cultures within which they operate and the people with whom they do business.

PUTTING YOURSELF IN THE SHOES OF ANOTHER

In seeking an understanding of other cultures as preparation for answering moral questions, a good place to begin is with application of the Reversibility of Roles test, the basic idea for which goes back many centuries in the history of moral philosophy. The requirement is to put yourself in the shoes of all interested parties prior to making any moral decision. Critics have asked, "Is it possible to reverse roles in this way? Can I genuinely place myself in the cultural and ideological shoes of all other interested parties?"

To reverse roles with employees, customers, and suppliers in foreign countries, managers of multinational corporations can begin by asking themselves pertinent questions. Although many questions can and should be asked, the following are illustrative examples.

1. If I lived in a country without a democratic government, would I want the existing government to be kept in power by foreign corporations that bribe public officials?
2. Would I want a multinational corporation to operate in my country with its only concern to make as much money as quickly as possible, regardless of the harm to local communities in terms of pollution or other resource drains?
3. If I lived in a country with an unstable government, would I want a foreign corporation, acting in its own interest, to undermine efforts toward political reform?
4. How would I feel if a foreign corporation purchased extensive agricultural holdings to raise crops for export, with the result that malnutrition in the host country increased because the remaining agricultural land was inadequate for raising sufficient crops for the local market?

The very existence of multinational corporations dramatically teaches the moral requirement for everyone to walk a mile in the other person's shoes. This lesson from the world scene applies also to operations at home.

CHEAP LABOR AND THE AMERICAN WORKER

When should our boundaries be permeable and when should they be restrictive? The question of hiring Americans first or redirecting business to places outside the United States is at the heart of much of the debate America now faces and will continue to face as a participant in the global marketplace.

Replacing American workers with foreign workers, even on their own soil, has raised many questions. Concern grows in many quarters that corporations have made the decision once again to place profits over people. Is the drive toward cheap labor at all costs one of those things that it is naïve to attempt to control? Are we doing an injustice to free enterprise when we attempt to establish a moral sensitivity to such a business practice?

The economic realities of an emerging global economy require that numerous American businesses hire foreign workers (both those who live in foreign countries and those who come from foreign countries to work in the United States) in order to be competitive. Sometimes as well, social and political pressures can motivate American corporations to not use offshore labor at a time when our own workers are without work—in other words, to not necessarily follow the least costly option. Moreover, competitive advantage can sometimes exist in opposition to issues of American workers' security.

The question of allowing foreign workers to come to America is further complicated by questions that pertain more generally to US immigration policies. The debate is most vocal by those who want to ensure, first, that Americans have the work they need to sustain themselves and their families before wages go to foreign workers.

Numerous US businesses are currently replacing American workers with foreign workers at a time when skilled workers are struggling to find employment. Regardless of the profit advantage, some would say that doing this is immoral since it appears designed to line the pockets of executives and stockholders with excessive profit at the American workers' expense. Such a judgment is not necessarily correct. Many businesses indicate that such practice allows them to stay competitive and healthy, returning through taxes and corporate sustainability, a benefit to the larger US economy.

There are those who argue that the numbers of jobs lost to both foreign shores and foreign workers in the United States is small and that in a fee-enterprise and global economy, adjustments must be made about where the workers reside. Foreign companies (Bayer, Roche, BMW, and many others) are, after all, offering employment to our citizens by establishing plants and distribution in the United States. The future state of the world economy is just too intertwined to assume that national borders define who should work for whom. From self-interest and decency, some would argue, US businesses must ensure that they are working as much as possible to give anyone who wants to work the opportunity to work right here in the USA.

The challenges of this new century in regard to a worldwide marketplace create new and troubling moral issues for all of us. American businesses are challenged to find the appropriate balance among competing values. American executives must consider that hiring foreign workers with special US work visas when our country's workers are idle undermines American workers' confidence in American business and robs eager workers of employment. There is, however, no assurance that the leaders of business will act as we might want them to act—certainly there is no guarantee that compassion alone for the American worker will limit their activities. Sometimes the faces of greed and poor judgment are all too evident.

A recent news report, for example, highlighted one company that made hundreds of its employees (prior to being laid off) train their own replacements (Indian nationals with special US work visas), as a condition for receiving severance packages. There are many problems with this action, and it is highly questionable on moral grounds.

There is another moral dimension that cannot be ignored. American policies protect some of our workers in unique ways. The Group of 21, an evolving political movement, is composed of developing countries that have banded together to protest certain global economic policies. They contend that countries (like America) with policies that protect their own farmers with subsidies, or that in other ways reduce the competitive edge of the marketplace, make it impossible for developing countries to ever break out of their impoverished state.

> The $300 billion in subsidies paid every year to the world's wealthiest farmers undermined the livelihoods of millions of poor farmers around the world. ... [the Group of 21] said the proposals made by the United States and Europe to redress what the developing nations regard as a major injustice fell far short of their expectations (*New York Times*, 15 September, 2003).

In fact, such policies doom some peoples to a life of abject poverty. A consideration of the common good beyond our immediate shores means that we must be concerned about the well-being of people in developing countries for our own sake as well as theirs. The World Trade Organization talks for 2003 were disrupted by a failure to reach agreement on the very issues of agriculture and other trade restrictions and subsidies that put such underdeveloped countries in jeopardy.

INTERNATIONAL GENDER ISSUES

Gender-related moral questions arise frequently when American companies do business in countries where women are treated very differently than they are treated in the United States. It is important to note, as an example, that in many Muslim countries, women do hold executive positions and even run governments. Some of our perceptions about the role of women in other countries are cloaked in our own biases. Yet, it is unquestionably true that women are treated differently than men in much of the Arab world and forbidden from doing many of the things (such as driving cars in countries like Saudi Arabia) that women in the United States do as free and equal citizens. These differences appear to many Americans as not simply differences in religion nor necessarily dictated by religious doctrine, but cultural and moral differences that affect the rights of women as human beings.

Should Americans in Saudi Arabia, for example, adhere to Saudi attitudes toward women? The answer to this question is both yes and no. Our reason for hesitation—for not flatly opposing sexist practices wherever they occur—is not that we believe in the cultural relativity of women's rights, any more than we believe in the cultural relativity of bribery. Nevertheless, bribery and gender discrimination need to be treated in somewhat different ways.

One important difference has to do with how the two practices are perceived by people in the foreign countries where Americans do business. In those cultures that do not recognize the equality of men and women, there is likely to be a widespread, culture-based belief regarding the proper role of women. This belief will be shared by a much larger segment of the population than is the acceptance of bribery. In Saudi Arabia, for example, gender discrimination pervades virtually all aspects of life, but bribery is not official policy. Even in cultures where bribery is widely practiced, people do not judge it to be morally correct in the way that gender discrimination is judged to be morally correct.

Why is this so? Presumably, the reason is that bribery is not consistent with standards for honesty and truth telling that lie at so deep a level that virtually every culture accepts them. Regrettably, a belief in the absolute and total equality of men and women does not lie at so deep a level. Often, in other cultures the roles of men and women follow the prescriptions of particular religions, and are held to be as sacred as is the American belief in equality of opportunity. (Even in America, some religious and social groups view women as being different in terms of fundamental rights and opportunities.)

Gender equality is fundamental to our value system. However, another value exists that competes with female equality—namely, respect for human beings in all their cultural diversity, regardless of whether or not they share the values that we hold dear. Therefore, Americans living or doing business abroad must both hold fast to their beliefs regarding the rights of women, and respect people who belong to other cultures. One way to do both of these things is to engage in progressive compromise.

Progressive compromise calls for an American company in Saudi Arabia to show respect while keeping some visible or tangible focus on its commitment to gender equality in a way that does not mask or deny faith in that concept. For example, a company could assign women executives or office workers to its Saudi branch, but not place them in front of Saudi executives and officials if that is considered a bad practice based on the religious and cultural norms of that country. We do not want to be ugly Americans, insisting on doing things completely according to our system of belief while in another country. We have little tolerance for companies that come to America and behave in ways that violate our sensitivities or cultural beliefs.

A company should make the presence of women workers known if the women desire that, and if their culture will not punish such women later. At the same time US companies must use discretion both for the sake of the women and in recognition of the religious or social customs of the country. When it comes to hiring local people, the company should attempt to strike a balance between the standards of the host country and the company's own standards.

The approach advocated here is an example of the same moral nudging urged upon salespeople in Chapter 5. The basic moral requirement is for taking action that will improve the situation in an area of business that traditionally has fallen short of strict adherence to the highest moral norms—to become better, not perfect, but always striving toward perfection. Consistent incremental change is often the only legitimate requirement in this delicate area of ethical decision making. Demanding either perfection or no change at all will, in almost all cases, lead to no action at all.

That said, change in gender attitudes and relationships is coming to all of the world's countries; we urge American corporations to play their part in determining the direction for change.

RAW MATERIALS

Some have argued that it is morally wrong for multinational corporations to set up operations in developing nations for the sole purpose of exporting raw materials from those countries. Such a practice amounts to exploitation, critics say, because each country has a right to the development of its own materials, for its own people. Otherwise, the host country becomes simply a supply depot for richer countries: its oil, gas, timber, minerals, and other natural resources support the living standards of people in richer countries while people in developing countries are left with next to nothing because rock-bottom prices are paid for these valuable resources.

In response, we observe, first, that different countries have different economic strengths and weaknesses. Some can do better selling finished products, while others are more effective when they focus on, for example, mining or the timber industry, neither of which are inherently exploitative. However, both the mining industry and the timber industry can easily become exploitative. When resources are taken from a developing country, the questions to answer first are these:

1. Who possesses title to those resources and/or are those resources in control of inhumane leaderships?
2. Are the people who have titles to land and resources the ones who really own them?
3. Who receives the money paid for resources by multinational corporations?
4. What policies exist for the replacement of resources when this is possible, as in the timber industry?

In the worst cases, multinationals are guilty of receiving stolen property, because the politicians who sell the resources have no right to them whatsoever. Even if these politicians do have a legal right to the resources, the fact that a business transaction involves no bribes or coercion is no guarantee that it is moral. Land and resources can be controlled by corrupt governments or by individuals who have acquired the land or resources through the actions of a corrupt government or through their own wrongful actions. Some countries exclude certain classes of people from ownership of resources, keeping these people forever in the debt of a landed class or other privileged group.

Here as elsewhere, an acceptable moral test is whether or not individuals or corporations have, in their business transactions, taken into account the best interests of all the people in the country involved. Achieving morality in managing natural resources is perhaps more difficult than in any other area of business. Expanding regulations and international law are providing clearer guidance in such practices; however, many decisions are still left in the hands of individual business leaders.

On the positive side, when resources are sold on the world market, a developing country will receive currency that every developing nation badly needs. Many American corporations work to ensure that profit will return to these countries in ways that are of some benefit. On the negative side, because the economy of the exporting country is by definition (as a developing nation) in its early stages, the market price of the resources will almost surely not reflect the value that these resources will acquire once the economy of the nation has developed further. Eventually the country may be able to develop its own resources, but by that time it may be too late as regards to nonrenewable resources. The resources may be depleted or wiped out and the opportunity for the people of the country to become players in international competition may be lost or significantly diminished, especially if the profits from sales of the resources have fallen into the hands of corrupt government officials.

What can be done to help safeguard developing countries? Leaving aside the few instances where philanthropy may play a significant role, the best safeguard may be a genuinely competitive worldwide market in which resources are protected from both corrupt governments and the individuals and corporations allied to those governments. At the same time, undergirding such a genuinely competitive market with a code of ethical conduct based on moral pluralism is vital. Rights, justice, the common good, and self-interest must all be taken into account. Justice, especially, in the sense of addressing the interests of those most in need, is problematic when we consider our own country first—as we have in the past and will in the future.

We are not yet a world without borders, and we are very much dependent on our commercial enterprises to support and sustain the life we have. We can, however, look at these issues with greater creativity and sensitivity than we have in the past. Market forces that are not grounded in values-based principles will operate in exactly the opposite way of moral pluralism, especially if a corrupt government controls the resources or if the political situation is so unstable that no long-term investments are secure. Both of these circumstances lead to an attitude of take the money and run, which is disastrous for the people left behind.

What can a multinational do here in the interest of morality? It can refuse to deal with corrupt governments, whether by buying resources from them or by paying them bribes. It can support political reform toward more democratic governments, as we mentioned earlier, and it can support governmental policies that strengthen market conditions. It can refuse to take advantage of special treatment that it would not receive in a genuinely open market. It can seek out the best people in a host country with whom to have business dealings. It can support land reform. It can work toward extending industry-wide codes of conduct to include strict guidelines for the acquisition and development of natural resources.

HEALTH AND SAFETY

Industry-wide codes can be especially effective for improving workplace conditions, as for example in foreign mines. In past years, some multinationals have been guilty of gross moral violations in the treatment of foreign miners; some companies and their countries are still reaping the consequences of ill will generated decades ago. As we have stated before, financial success in any area of business can be achieved at too great a cost. Nowhere perhaps is this more true than in the cases of employees at the bottom of the employment ladder working in hazardous jobs in countries where far too little is done to protect them.

American Occupational Safety and Health Administration (OSHA) standards or their equivalents cannot be applied automatically in foreign countries. However, a company that knowingly supports health-endangering practices is acting unethically. A continuing moral commitment is required by all multinational corporations to treat employees at home and abroad with respect. Hopefully, this practice will continue to evolve internationally, and American business can be at the forefront as it has in many instances, implementing high-quality safety protections and environmental safeguards.

LIVING UP TO OUR WORDS

Other countries expect us to demonstrate ethical business practices—in part because we have tied a message of morality to much of what we do. Trust is a fragile thing and is built in part on consistency—matching what we say with what we do. When trust is lost, America, its citizens, and its businesses have a much more difficult time achieving international business goals. Unquestionably, we depend on the goodwill of other nations. To be successful in commerce, to achieve lasting world peace, to optimize global health and safety, we must recognize that we are linked to everyone on the planet. Our founding principles and our consistent efforts to meet those principles in action can help us succeed in our relationships with others, especially as we work to ensure that our workplaces provide dignity, respect, and some degree of economic freedom. Historically, America has a mixed moral record in what it has done internationally, both in business and in covert activities designed to support certain political agendas. We need to remove our myopic lenses and put on lenses that allow us to see the value in other countries, their people, and their resources, and treat them not simply as we would want to be treated, but as they would want to be treated. George Bernard Shaw, playwright, once said, "Be careful in applying the Golden Rule, treating others as you would treat yourself. Some people's tastes are different than your own." We need to carefully consider these words when entering foreign lands.

The next generation must demonstrate a commitment to integrity as the guide to American dealings internationally while remembering that inconsistent messages and actions can impede or destroy a secure and peaceful future. It is a complex task to take the American way of business to other countries while minimizing or eliminating the possibility of doing harm at a cultural and individual level as well as at an economic level. In most ways, international trade has been good for us all, but the issues raised in this chapter are just some of many issues to be addressed in the ever-changing world economy. The next section deals with how to establish ethics as a habit, both at a personal level and in the practices of the workplace. The first step to achieving an ethical approach in business requires that employees—from senior leaders to those on the shop floor or front line—learn how to manage their own behavior.

3
PART

INCREASING ETHICAL BEHAVIOR

12

CHAPTER

THE POSSIBILITY OF ETHICAL CHANGE

We cannot become what we need to be by remaining what we are.

—Max Dupree, *Famous Quotes*

To change and to change for the better are two different things.

—German proverb

BEFORE PROCEEDING TO CONCRETE steps for achieving ethical change, it is important to consider, as a reader of this book, what biases you bring that may inhibit or distort how you perceive the idea that people can change. While change comes through practice, not by simply reading about how to change, it is important to be aware of how our assumptions about the possibility of change can color what we read as well as what we do.

BELIEFS THAT IMPEDE ETHICAL CHANGE

Changing behavior, whether one's own or that of someone else, is not easy. When the desired change is toward behavior that is more ethical, special problems arise. Indeed, so many impediments exist that some people believe that alteration of personal ethics is impossible or nearly impossible. At the same time, in contrast, numerous popular books and tapes attempt to convey the message that behavior of all kinds can be easily changed, including our ethical sensitivities and actions. Let's examine a few beliefs that may inhibit the process of ethical change.

1. The belief that merely understanding behavior is enough to change it.

Behavior change requires much more than knowing the behaviors that need to be changed. An understanding of the benefits that derive from changing either ourselves or others, though important, is not enough to bring about significant changes. If it were, the need for most of the popular self-help books would disappear! Nor is it enough to have good understanding, or insight, into the causes of our behavior. Knowing and doing are two different things.

An unrealistic outlook based on assuming we know how to change can keep us from doing the hard work necessary for actual ethical change to occur. This work includes designing or redesigning work settings, creating incentive systems, and modifying patterns of interaction.

2. The belief that ethical values cannot be changed.

This belief is the opposite of the one we just discussed. "You can't change character," people sometimes say. They assume that change in ethical behavior is impossible to any significant degree. They believe that once set, personality and the values reflected in it cannot change. On the contrary, character can be understood in terms of personality traits, and personality traits can be changed by changing a sufficient number of the behaviors that constitute a particular trait. A personality trait is a group of individual behaviors to which we attach meaning by a label that describes standard ways in which an individual usually behaves across conditions or settings. A *personality trait* is not an individual behavior but a name for a cluster of behaviors which have something in common. For example, being shy can be described in terms of specific acts of the individual—the extent of eye contact, posture, and frequency of conversation. Similarly, we can understand what a person labeled as *honest* does in terms of the frequency of certain behaviors such as making and keeping promises, telling the truth, and paying debts punctually.

To change a personality trait is to change a significant number of the individual behaviors that define it. When personality traits are thought to be more complex than the composite of clearly identifiable individual behaviors, we may feel helpless to do anything about them. Such helplessness is an impediment to success in changing ethical behavior. Individual behaviors, our own and those of others, can be changed. Still, there is no getting around the fact that personality traits are difficult to change for one reason: because a large number of individual behaviors define any one personality trait. Moreover, these behaviors occur across virtually all settings: at home, at work, in public places, in private circumstances, and so on. When we correctly label a person as having integrity or honesty, we do so expecting the person to exhibit predictably honest and principled actions in many different settings.

Is it possible to change a large number of interrelated individual behaviors? Most of us believe that it is when we think in terms of concrete, limited examples, as for example in the case of a typist overcoming errors. Likewise, a generally passive person can learn to say no assertively. A new manager can learn to run a good meeting. In each of these cases, change involves many discrete individual actions. Accordingly, this is the model that we employ regarding ethical change: Consider character and the values that reflect it as summary statements for a large number of small individual behaviors. Day in and day out, these behaviors are preserved to a significant degree by the consequences of our acts. Change strategies, therefore, must focus on the consequences of individual actions across settings. If we give sufficient support for the small changes a person makes, over time these small changes tend to redefine who the person is. In turn, the person's values will change in support of the new collection of actions that demonstrate his or her character: honesty, integrity, and respect for others.

3. A belief that we should not force our values on others. As a society, we have an ambivalent attitude toward ethical behavior, especially in the world of business. We do believe in ethics and we admire those who practice it. But we also are as likely to believe that advocating ethical behavior or ethical improvement makes us appear judgmental, uncompromising, or unrealistic.

Part of the problem has to do with the belief that business is, and ought to be, amoral. In reality, as discussed in Chapter 2, business is subject to the same moral rules as other spheres of life. Another part of the problem lies in the belief that ethical decision making leaves no room for compromise or the possibility of disagreement among informed and sensitive individuals. On the contrary, the essence of ethical decision making is finding a balance among conflicting values with room for compromise and rational disagreement. Moral pluralism, discussed in Chapter 6, is a model for ethical decision making that emphasizes the need to balance conflicting values.

An additional part of the problem lies in a faulty assessment of the extent to which advocating ethical change in the workplace addresses matters that are personal in nature. No one wants to invade privacy. Hence, management tends to review only the technical skills of the individual. It is important to realize that the overall manner, the style by which employees conduct themselves, can be reviewed by management as appropriately as tasks involved in the particular position.

We can be held to ethical standards in the workplace that are even higher than our usual standards. This is not an invasion of our privacy or of our right to be our own person. Once the individual enters the workplace, he or she makes a commitment to uphold the standards of the workplace. Both interpersonal and personal aspects of a person's workplace conduct, as well as technical skill, are part of the right and duty of managers to shape and direct.

4. The belief that advocating for ethical change involves large risks. Of course, change of any kind involves risk. In our opinion, supporting ethical change in the workplace actually involves fewer risks than a great many other types of change. Still, it is understandable that defending what is right may appear to jeopardize our jobs, our families, or our security.

In many situations, we overestimate risk because the behaviors we need to exhibit are novel and uncomfortable. There can be risk in ethical actions, but when we approach them sincerely and assume that the other person is just as ready to act with integrity as we are, we reduce the risks. When we stand up for what we believe, rarely will we have to pursue a course of action where the only choices are between extremes. Not every injustice in the workplace requires that we quit our jobs.

The model for ethical decision making described in Chapter 6 will help you approach troublesome situations in a way that poses relatively few risks. Look for evidence that those with whom you have disagreements or conflicts embrace at least some of the basic values of moral pluralism, which, as you may recall, involves finding a proper balance among rights, justice, the common good, and self-interest. Finding common ground when involved in conflict is critical to achieving better understanding and, more importantly, conflict resolution.

Keep in mind that two individuals both of whom are ethical can adopt the same basic values while assigning to them different degrees of importance in specific situations. Argue for your own position by saying, for example: "I'm glad that in this case we both believe in protecting rights and helping people in need. But let me suggest why I believe we need to do more for those in need than we are presently doing."

The processes of demonstrating ethical conduct and defending one's actions need not be threatening to others, or to one's self. There are many ways to create a more ethical environment. Flexibility, listening to what is presented, and inviting others to find challenging and effective new ways of approaching problems are all part of the opportunity.

We advise taking relatively small steps—addressing individual and/or organizational behaviors one by one. The potential impact one can have differs at the various levels of influence. The relative risks differ as well. For example, an office manager may encourage her employees to get involved in community service. A supervisor may invite his employees to participate in monthly planning meetings. At a regional sales meeting, a sales manager may speak out about the need to reassess incentive plans because they unfairly reward his unit without any recognition for the efforts of other departments. A senior level manager may tell her CEO that senior managers are mishandling the human side of a recent acquisition and have thereby failed to provide clear leadership.

In each example just described, the risks for confrontation and disfavor increase somewhat as the issues involve wider constituent groups. Nevertheless, the more responsibility assigned to an individual, the greater the need for actions or comments that have the potential to clarify and resolve ethical issues. In each instance, taking small steps increases the likelihood that further progress will follow. These examples are about the common good, fairness, honesty, and justice. They are not about achieving extraordinary levels of moral character. It is in ordinary activities that ethical action is most frequently required.

5. The belief that labels accurately describe individuals.

A fifth and significant impediment to ethical change has to do with the use of labels in describing or referring to people. If we attach certain labels, as when we describe someone as "shy" or "a bore," we will impede the process of change. However, if we attach other labels, such as being *bright or a team player,* we may enhance the process. The role of labels in ethical behavior change is complex; the main point to keep in mind is that customary ways that labels are used almost always hinder rather than help the process of change. In any case, labels color our view. When undertaking to manage people most effectively or to change ourselves or others, we are usually better off if we don't attach labels at all.

It is easy to attach labels that do not describe people accurately—with bad consequences to them, to us, and to the organizations of which we are a part. At the same time, in order to bring about ethical change most effectively, our goal is not simply to attach the most accurate labels. Labels of any kind can draw our attention away from the specific behaviors where change needs to occur. Yet, the use of positive labels, such as being a *leader,* for example, can help in positively changing a person's ethical behavior—as long as we are not taken in by our own labels. We must see others for what they are—that is, what they say and do across time and situations.

The use of labels of all kinds is widespread because attaching labels to people's actions is a handy and efficient method of grouping individual actions into an understandable whole. Labeling is inevitable. Others know us by what we say and what we do. Over time, our actions take on a certain predictability and offer a quick way for others to describe us—as "shy," "talkative," "earnest," "the life of the party," "aggressive," "a bore," "a leader," and so on. Once such labels are attached, others usually believe that they know how to interact meaningfully with us. In a sense, we have become our labels.

We all recognize the fact that it is often easier to begin interacting comfortably with people we have just met if we can first observe and then label their interactions with others. We attach meaning to a person's social behavior. Based on our past experiences with similar actions, we anticipate how a new person will act. In reality, the labels we attach to the new person describe only a small portion of the skills and actions that the person might demonstrate. The use of negative labels is especially problematic; we discuss them in the next section.

6. A belief that* negative *labels reflect who the person is.

Negative labels are often ascribed too quickly to others. For example, at work we might label a person as *lazy* because that person always arrives late to meetings and once there does not participate. Labels are summary statements intended to describe what is observed, as we said. However, they go beyond simple description when they summarize who the person is understood to be—in this case, lazy. In reality, whether our experience is quite limited as it usually is, or even quite extensive, we often do not know who the person is.

The disservice we have done is perhaps greater than we realize, because this inaccurate generalization is likely to follow a person everywhere. From the perspective of management, we have made change appear to be more difficult to achieve than it actually is. For example, it may well not be laziness at all that needs to be overcome, but merely a few specific behaviors that, if changed, would no longer generate the label of *lazy.* All too often, the use of a label such as *lazy* is based on a small sample of behaviors. Then, once the label is attached, different people will read into it different meanings depending upon their individual experiences in the past with lazy people. Thus the significance attached to the original specific behaviors—in the original example, lateness and a failure to participate—may end up being much weightier than it should be.

Obviously, it is more difficult to change laziness than merely to improve punctuality. Laziness is a trait of personality, after all. A manager or a peer may give up before getting started. This is one reason that inaccurate, negative labeling can be counterproductive. A second reason is that people too readily believe the labels that have been applied to them. If you call a tardy person "lazy" once too often, the person may fulfill your characterization. You have, in any case, reduced the person's potential.

Furthermore, we have injured ourselves by reducing our ability to see the real person. We stop responding to the person, and begin responding to the label no matter what the person does. He or she is judged to be lazy inside. If we do observe the person working hard, we may say, "Oh, that's not George. That's just a front. He's working hard to finish that report only because he knows we're watching." George has been hurt and we have been hurt. He must overcome a deficit that does not exist, or would not have existed. We must overcome our own misunderstanding as well. We have limited our view of George's potential, treating him quite differently than we would want ourselves to be treated. Perhaps most important, we must repair the injustice of what we have done to poor George.

We tend to act toward others in a manner that complies with our expectations. But if people have been assigned negative labels, we will ask less of them. We may deprive the workplace of potentially valuable contributions when we don't assign such people important projects. We may not even consider them when assigning new projects.

7. A belief that* positive *labels reflect who the person is.
Negative labels cause the most problems in limiting the approach to behavior change. But even ascribing positive general characteristics can be problematic. One reason is that doing so can lead us to expect from others more than they are able to achieve. We will have set them up to fail.

However, if we label someone as potentially better than he or she is, and we are realistic in our expectations, we are acting with sensitivity regarding change. One of the requirements for any process of change to occur is to set up expectations that elicit the change and reward small steps toward the goal. Ascribing realistic, positive attributions can help to begin that process. Seeing what people are capable of, rather than what they do not do, is a good characteristic of a strong coach.

Seeing the possibilities in others is essential for effective management, as long as we are not misled. The strongest base for building positive change occurs when we see who a person is by what the person actually does, not by what we wish he or she did. First, we must correctly observe others, and then support them in their efforts to surpass current performance.

8. A belief that who I say I am is as important as what I do.
As well as mislabeling others, people may label themselves inadvertently and inaccurately through the language they use. We have all encountered the grouch, someone who constantly complains about others, yet demonstrates by his actions that he in fact cares for others. The words he speaks tell one story, his actions tell quite another. He uses grouchy language and takes pride in calling himself a grouch. But if the word *grouchy* is replaced with *caring,* we may well be closer to describing who he is and the effect he has on others. Most of us learn from others what to call ourselves. Children learn to call themselves bullies, babies, shy, or awkward.

As adults we sometimes preempt the ability of others to attach a negative label by giving them one to use when thinking about us. When the label we offer becomes effective, determining how others respond to us, we sometimes then, illogically, are doubly assured that we can be nothing else. Conversely, if we have tried to avert criticism by labeling ourselves with positive words that we do not believe, we may then judge others unfairly as fools or liars when they adopt our words to describe us. Over time and circumstance, however, it is in what we say and do that our real selves emerge. Labels become less relevant when we consider that they simply reflect what we have learned to say and do. We can change those things and, in the main, we can change the associated labels as well.

Let's turn now to what the self-change literature can tell us about behaving ethically. We will then look at how to make such behavior a habit, gaining skill that leads to fluency in application across diverse settings and situations. From a behavioral analytic perspective, most people can change in very significant ways. To do so in a sustained manner, however, often requires an interaction between the environment and the individual. As you will see in the next two chapters, individuals can practice certain skills until they become habits, but the workplace may also need to be changed so that those settings are actively directed to bring out the best, not the worst, in everyone, from the top leadership to the entry-level employee.

13

CHAPTER

BEHAVING ETHICALLY

God knows. I'm not the thing I should be. Nor am I even the thing I could be.

—Robert Burns

There is very little difference between one man and another; but what difference there is, is very important.

—William James

PERSONAL CHANGE

The first step in establishing personal change around any set of behaviors is to have in place a method for pinpointing precisely what it is you wish to change. Let's say that you are a manager of a sales and service unit. You want to increase the number of times you discuss the ethical implications of how your people approach current customers and the marketplace, and you want to modify any behaviors that do not meet your unit's ethical standards. Your goal is to have at least three ethical concerns or issues raised and addressed each month and to ensure as well that everyone on your team makes at least one comment on one of the issues at each monthly meeting. To do this you may well have to look first at your own behavior.

Do you ask questions of an ethical nature? Do you remind people of what your goal is for the team? Do you examine new service and product-design plans against a standard that evaluates any potential conflicts? For example, do you inform customers that a new machine may fail to interface with the current equipment without a costly upgrade? Do you ask a salesperson if he has ever turned down an order, and then seeing that he did it for the right reasons, do you praise that action? Do you find yourself talking to your team about how you might make your own commitment to ethical conduct more visible? Do you celebrate yourself and others when the right course of action has been chosen even though it is costly (at least in the short run)?

Begin by pinpointing what the team and you want as an ethical outcome in your operation. (It could be increased customer awareness of product changes and their implications for current product operations prior to purchase of new units.) Pinpoint two to three behaviors that you may need to change or eliminate altogether—behaviors that may inhibit others from alerting the customer to any potential product problems. Next, look at each person on your team and examine the approach taken to customers and meeting the quotas you have set. Look as well at how members of your team talk about the limits as well as the benefits of new products, and make sure they are skilled and fluent in both types of speeches. Reinforce everyone for any noted changes they make to increase their ethical behavior; reinforce them for the words and actions you can see and hear. Track the impact of this discussion on sales, both from the perspective of a subjective assessment and in terms of your record of actual sales.

SELF-MANAGEMENT

You may have problems pinpointing the things you need to do differently. Begin with a private and yet quite effective process of self-assessment. The sort of exercise that we have in mind is *Stop, Start, and Continue.* It is something that you can do privately or involving others who can help you evaluate the accuracy of your self-assessment.

Take a sheet of paper; draw three columns, and in the first column, write down the things you want to *stop doing*. If you are already doing something that you believe interferes with your goals, then in all likelihood you have been, and perhaps still are, receiving reinforcement for that action. You may not be able to see or touch the reinforcement. It could be a part of your history—perhaps a rule you learned early in life, such as the comfort that comes from avoiding mentioning problems: Don't tell someone they are deviating from the plan. It is rude to deliver such messages, even though it is clear that their deviation deliberately sidetracks the team.

You want to stop reinforcing such action by your silence, and start telling the person that she is sidetracking the team. You must stop yourself from condoning the messages you want to stop. Have a colleague observe and tell you to stop when you inadvertently reinforce the wrong behaviors.

Next, write down those things you want to *start doing*. It is always difficult to get new behavior going. No matter how successful you believe yourself to be, you must have support to get new behavior going. It takes prompts, direction, and persistence, and often, prior success at engaging in new behavior. You need to arrange the conditions for your success. For example, prior to a meeting, you might publish an agenda that includes a discussion on ethical issues. Once the team has seen the agenda, it will be more difficult for you to avoid the whole thing without a very good excuse for doing so. Please set up this *start doing* process in such a manner that others will encourage and reinforce your efforts to establish new behavior. The new behavior might be something like talking about the ethical situations you have experienced and wish you had handled differently, or publicly praising good work in others.

Finally, fill in the column for those things you want to *continue doing* in regard to your role in creating an ethical environment in your unit of responsibility. You might engage others in the definition of how they will support you for the actions you believe are critical to continue. In each of these areas a coach or a candid and good friend can be a big help.

Once you have completed your own *Stop, Start, and Continue* list, you will need to share this list with a trusted friend who can help you identify when you are engaged in the relevant behaviors. It also helps to share such a list with your team if you are a manager. They will tell you if you have it right, as well as alert you to other behavior that you may wish to add. After a period of time, you might cascade this down to the next level and have them do the same thing. A little self-assessment, calibrated by the team, is a useful and humbling experience in relation to establishing the conditions for ethical success.

ESTABLISHING BEHAVIOR CHANGE

You will want to measure your targets for change, examine data on how well you are doing (review the count for the number of times you reviewed an ethical issue, and how members of your team contributed to the discussion), and reinforce and evaluate the pinpoints you establish both for yourself and for others. As you progress in this manner, you will want to revamp your self-management program based on what you have learned. To learn more about how to do this successfully in your workplace, we suggest you read *Bringing out the Best in People,* perhaps the best introduction to achieving managerial change in the workplace (Daniels, 1998); as well as the seventh edition of *Self-Directed Behavior: Self-Modification for Personal Adjustment* by David L. Watson and Roland G. Tharp (1997). While neither of these books addresses in detail the issue of ethical practice, they do address creating and sustaining behavior change.

All of Daniels' books include pragmatic ways to create a culture that can sustain the changes you are seeking. Watson and Tharp make the following important point in *Self-Directed Behavior:*

> You can change the way you relate to your environment. You can learn to change it more effectively. You can assist

> that learning by the use of contingent rewards as you go along. In the long run, success in changing [yourself] will depend on your setting up a new, improved reciprocal relationship with the world and the people around you (p. 222).

If you are a leader in your organization, you will want to ensure that your people practice ethical behaviors until these behaviors become habits. For this to occur, you must ensure that practices are reviewed, products are examined, and consequences are applied through systems of reward and recognition. You must absolutely ensure that you build in a process for ethical behaviors that you reinforce generously, and you must create the consequences that say these are valuable behaviors. Your company must train your managers and supervisors in the principles of human learning and ensure that they understand how to shape and guide ethical development, and then you must apply all of this to everyone.

Once you understand what is involved in shaping performance, you can begin to use certain tools to increase the likelihood of creating lifelong habits in yourself and others.

Nuts and Bolts: Steps Needed to Produce Real Change

The steps outlined in this section apply equally to organizations and individuals. Most people can begin the process of change by following the steps outlined below. However, there are no instant remedies. Maintaining ethical change requires persistent and behaviorally sophisticated efforts across the organization.

1. Identify the ethical change required.

Before we can bring about change, we must first identify what needs to be changed. As we said in Chapter 12, when identifying the targets for change, we must focus on specific behaviors that are problematic, not general labels. "We must get Sam to be more reliable" does not describe the behavior we want. Instead, we should say, "We must get Sam to turn in sales reports on the day they are due." The statement "Mary is disrespectful" is not pinpointed. Instead, the statement should be "Mary frequently interrupts others in a loud voice." Saying "Ed is not committed to the good of the group" is not specific enough. Say "Ed needs to state his opinions during planning sessions."

Before you can embark on producing behavior changes, you will have to ask clarifying questions about which precise behaviors you want, especially when a desirable ethical outcome is the aim. Look to current actions and their consequences. Ask yourself what, for example, maintains the current behavior you do not want or reduces the behavior that you do want.

2. Outline the specific steps required to achieve the targeted outcome.

Describe where you want to go (the destination or outcome to be achieved) and outline how you want to get there (the steps to be taken). Use a process similar to goal-setting where objectives, steps to achieve results, by whom and when, and methods of evaluation are identified. This component of personal or organizational change is sometimes fuzzy, often left to our good intentions, rather than described in observable and measurable terms.

It is often helpful to first analyze the conditions for change in general terms, and then progress to examining specific issues. For instance, one person contributes to a meeting by offering opinions and speaking eloquently. Another person may talk just as eloquently to a colleague off the record while exiting the conference room; he has the general skills but does not apply them in the setting required. It is not an ethical shortcoming when one does not speak in a team meeting. However, it takes on ethical significance when one who has something to say keeps quiet during discussions that have moral consequences regarding rights, justice, the common good, or self-interest; that can become a problem for you, as well as diminish the effectiveness of the group. In the specific instance of teams, we each rely on one another to point us in the right direction and support us. Learning how to communicate clearly, as a matter of course, with good humor and sincerity, involves skills that require a hospitable environment and successive support for steps in the right direction.

Once such observational information has been collected, you will have a good indication of which behaviors need to be increased.

These should be broken down into specific steps, as concretely as possible. It is not possible, in most situations, to identify every aspect of the needed changes, nor is it usually necessary.

3. Use every avenue available to establish conditions to promote ethical change.

If you are a manager, you have a number of different options available to reach your objectives: building group understanding through team meetings; examining company policies and procedures that support the actions you want; conducting regular performance appraisal sessions to allow both you and others a way to evaluate change.

If your goal is ethical behavior change for yourself as an employee, you often have to rely more on yourself to make such changes. Still, others can help, including your manager. Tell your manager what you want to do. It may be that you want to demonstrate more respect for others by improving your listening and communication skills. Your manager can help you introduce effective strategies into daily practice and can help in the evaluation of change. Also, fellow employees can be asked to support your efforts.

In addition, there may be company policies or procedures that provide an orderly way to bring to the attention of senior management recommended changes that could improve the ethical atmosphere of the company.

Depending on your position in the organization and the resources available to you, you might do the following: Characterize the nature of the ethical issues, the areas you interact with directly, and how you might structure your plan of action to address meaningful aspects within your areas of influence.

Inform others of your goals. Ask for their advice about both your and the organization's actions and how most constructively to increase overall sensitivity to the ethical implications of actions.

Hold meetings in which case studies or other methods are used to increase for yourself and all employees, ethical sensitivity to issues. Use the comments to evaluate the level of awareness and to refine current steps and better define needed next steps.

Build into the performance review system an assessment of the ethical conduct of employees in achieving objectives. Make sure, if you are a manager, that your manager holds you accountable in the same manner.

Require an ethical analysis in any planning documents at the unit, department, office, or company level and establish clear review dates and procedures.

Be clear about the details required to move you further toward your goal. Examine barriers that get in the way, such as empty excuses—"I have other responsibilities"; "I am too busy"; "I must look after new customers."

4. Practice the new behaviors.

After you have pinpointed the target for change, identified what was maintaining or keeping the needed actions from occurring, outlined the steps needed to remove barriers and reinforce new performance, you must then set up conditions that produce the newly defined, desired behaviors.

The example above about speaking out in meetings on ethical issues provides a useful framework for establishing the organizational conditions to evoke the new behaviors. Learning to talk about important matters, especially in a group setting, can be difficult.

First, announce your goal. If you are doing this as part of a system-wide change strategy, then the commitment to open discussion must be publicly stated to all employees, comments must be sought, and when small increases in the occurrence of such comments are made by people who generally may not make such statements, the manager must actively encourage (and hopefully reinforce) them. At the organizational level, the incentives for producing and increasing the desired behaviors rest, not with the individual, but with the conditions of the workplace.

The manager must understand that he is evaluated on how well he increases employees' positive, constructive talk about significant business issues of an ethical nature. The manager's approach to such issues is perceived often as the voice of the company, the norm.

If you are making such changes by yourself, set up the conditions by first telling trusted others what you want to do and how you want them to respond to you. Small steps can be practiced first; for example, before speaking up wholly on your own, you could speak in support of a statement made by another member of the discussion group, or reword the statement to be sure it is understood. This practice will help prepare you to confront and expound upon controversial issues in various settings.

You may need to actually go into the conference room alone and practice speaking out loud, to increase your level of comfort in that setting, which may remind you of, or actually be a setting where you have been inhibited about expressing yourself in the past. Previous experience can be recalled all too easily when walking into the environments where such actions occurred, and cause unanticipated emotional responses that interfere with the goal.

A suggestion: Take a trusted friend into the aversive setting. Have that friend listen to you in that setting. Sometimes, the new association—being with someone you like in an unpleasant setting—can help in reducing aversion.

5. Invite feedback and instruction.

When we undertake change, it is important that we have someone to oversee the new actions closely and provide feedback and analysis for the developing changes. This person can make positive comments and, when necessary, tactfully suggest a mid-course correction.

A company that really wants to improve its ethical sensitivities needs to expect that such change is difficult to implement, particularly if managers have become accustomed to other strategies that up to this point have always worked. Organizations need to avoid having the blind leading the blind. Sometimes it is worthwhile to have an outside observer provide comment. Sometimes peer managers or someone from a different area of the operation may recognize what is needed and be good at defining its presence or absence in others. These are the people who may make the best coaches. Remember, changes in style are unlikely unless the contingencies applied actively reinforce the right actions.

Managers can, as well, seek the evaluative critique of their employees. They can ask directly for comments about what they need to do to promote a more open environment. They can also make meetings open to evaluation. At the end of a representative meeting, a survey of two or three questions can be distributed, asking the group to describe what worked and what did not. Such a system does not require that everyone in the meeting get their way, nor does allowing employees to evaluate the boss undermine the boss's effectiveness. In fact, if correctly designed, this system can provide appropriate feedback to the manager and demonstrate the reciprocal nature of the company's genuine commitment.

You might want to select a colleague who will support your efforts during the meeting and help you assess your actions afterward. These steps may seem unnecessary, but there is no better way to change expectations and promote behavior change than to actively involve others in the plan. Such public commitment puts in motion another contingency that helps most of us persist—the contingency of other people's expectations. Positive feedback and constructive criticism that offer alternatives can reinforce our ability to change actions or attitudes of ourselves and others.

Placing the evaluation of our effectiveness in the hands of others is threatening. Commitment to treating managers and employees with respect and assuming they are trying to do the right thing is important to such a process. Both giving and getting feedback in such a system must be designed to be constructive and focused on solutions.

6. Reward yourself.

Tell others when changes occur. If a department or an office or an individual helps you achieve a change that you have been working toward, thank them. Positive feedback is a two-way street. Others are more likely to consistently treat you as a person who has truly changed when you tell them about your success and your determination to continue to behave differently. They are more likely to make positive comments without prompting. They become part of the natural consequences that help you maintain change.

When you are in the role of providing support for other people's change, be generous, genuine, and specific in your praise and/or criticism. Evaluate what you say according to what actually happens. This point cannot be emphasized enough. It is not in what we want to have happen, but rather in what does happen that we best define the kinds of actions we take in supporting change.

In whatever aspect of the change process you find yourself, never assume that there are rules about how you are to act. You must observe, intervene or not intervene, and observe once again. Do whatever it takes to help your colleague(s) reach the goal; that includes praising or constructively criticizing their effort and providing clear direction as needed. It also may include supporting the change through your own actions—such as by speaking in support of someone who has just spoken at a meeting.

What we tell ourselves privately can either reinforce and strengthen, or punish and decrease significant actions. For targeted behaviors, we must chart our own progress and reward ourselves through an internal system of private assessment—what we tell ourselves through our thoughts—or through the use of notes or actual graphs to record improvement. We must be fair and honest with ourselves, without being overly negative, when assessing our own actions. An example would be to say, "I really tried and I was able to tell the boss that I supported Joe's argument during the meeting. Next time I'll do better and make an independent comment."

7. Evaluate the effects of ethical change.

If you achieve the outcome you want, consider your plan for change a success, at least in the short run. If your plan does not work, then identify the point at which it failed. Begin working again from that point.

Regardless, over the longer term if the change is to be sustained, it must become part of how you respond in given situations, of how people see you, and part of what is supported in the environment. It must become a habit.

14

CHAPTER

Making Ethics a Habit

How use doth breed a habit in a man!

– Shakespeare, *The Two Gentlemen of Verona*

Watch your thoughts; they become words. Watch your words; they become actions. Watch your actions; they become habits. Watch your habits; they become character. Watch your character; it becomes your destiny.

– Frank Outlaw, *Quote Me on It*

THE WAYS IN WHICH WE approach ethical issues at work are, to a large extent, shaped by the experiences we have had long before we entered the workplace. Throughout our lives, people will attribute to us aspects of character, good and bad, that we may neither understand nor deserve. In the lives of virtually everyone there are numerous examples of both good and bad decisions.

In research on moral development, children are often observed to say the right things about ethical decisions, while their actual behaviors have to do more with the effects they experience than with the words they use. These findings do not change significantly as people age. Early training is important, but what happens in terms of the consequences of our actions is central to maintaining an ethical perspective throughout life.

Based on what is known about choice in regard to ethical decisions, it is critical that company leadership build in safeguards and practices that increase the likelihood of doing the right thing in spite of the temptations for doing the wrong thing—such as providing positive recognition when someone makes an ethical sale, giving a needed bonus to an employee who takes on someone else's work, sanctioning a service representative who brings a customer's issue to quick resolution without addressing the root and soon-to-reoccur cause of the problem, or sanctioning a sales engineer who changes a balance sheet in order to meet the demand for profit.

Rules demonstrate little direct effect on actual behavior if appropriate consequences have not followed the learning of rules. Commitment to ethical choices over other choices has a great deal to do with what happened to a person over and above the person's knowledge of the rules or what the person may say about the rules. How consistently did a person's parents give praise or show displeasure regarding childhood acts that can be called ethical? How much support, if any, did a person receive from parents, school, peers, and others in society whose behavior was modeled? Were early years full of reward and recognition for deceit, for doing something "this time only," for shortcuts, and similar patterns? If so, these patterns could well become self-reinforcing, and eventually could far outweigh any other consequences for the person's action that might be applied within the workplace.

By contrast, children who are trained and recognized early for trying to act ethically will continue to act ethically as adults for long periods without receiving any visible recognition. For such individuals, particular events at work or elsewhere will not likely reduce such patterns of striving to do the right thing. The important point to keep in mind here is that ethical patterns are learned, in large part, from the history of reinforcement that an individual has received from significant events and people. It has much less to do with how a person expresses belief in rules of conduct.

Accordingly, we are faced with important questions: Can workplaces be designed to bring out the best in those who have strong histories of reinforcement for doing what is morally correct, as well as in those whose histories of reinforcement have been much less exemplary? Is it a hopeless cause to introduce the idea that ethical behavior can be taught by the time a person enters the workplace?

The answer is that the conditions of the workplace can help to shape and increase the ethical sensitivities each person exhibits, regardless of the past. But it does matter how a person demonstrates ethical sensitivity across a lifetime.

It is simply easier, less labor intensive, to select employees who have had a good introduction to ethical behavior and have consistently experienced the consequences of such behavior. Employers must be careful in their selection of new employees, paying special attention to how a prospective employee has actually behaved, and determining whether there is evidence that he or she has a history of reinforcement that includes doing things that may benefit the company financially but rob it of its ethical framework. We advise you, in your hiring activities, to work on the questions you ask and the references you seek.

This chapter briefly reviews what is known from the psychological research about developing morality in children as the foundation for how such experiences do and do not control the actions of adults. We examine some of the systems, processes, and structures that support or impede the path to personal and corporate excellence.

REDUCING THE PRESSURES OF THE MOMENT

If company leaders understand what is known about conditions that support or impede ethical decisions, they are better able to set up an ongoing *cultural inoculation program* to ensure that no one assumes that unethical acts simply will not happen at their place of work. Virtually everyone is to some degree vulnerable to the pressures of the moment. Leaders must not reject the possibility of their own vulnerability to commit unethical acts just because they have behaved ethically up to the present time. Virtually no one is outside the range of the seductive Siren songs that were described in Chapter 1. Faced with temptation, not everyone will do the wrong thing, but virtually everyone is vulnerable and needs to recognize that this is so.

So, how do we create ethical habits in ourselves? What happens when we are young? Much of the research on early childhood learning indicates that children learn to discriminate between what is right and wrong from an early age and can, depending on the modeling around them, provide rather complex answers to questions of right and wrong at various ages across childhood. There are age-specific discriminations pertaining to given types of moral decision. The earlier that children learn how to move from the rule to the generalized principle, the better their discriminations will be in later life.

EARLY LEARNING

Behaving in a manner that others judge to be ethical requires that individuals consider the needs of others and themselves. But first they must differentiate between themselves and others. Ethical behavior demonstrates awareness and concern for others. Piaget's research looked closely at how children begin to differentiate themselves from others, and other developmental psychologists have pursued such research as well. Children say distinct things at certain stages to describe themselves. When we are very young, our first method of identifying our "self" is to talk about what is me and what is not me (Alcock, Carment, & Sadava, 1998) and to define self by what I do—for example, a favorite activity (Keller, Ford & Meacham, 1978). A very young child might say, by way of identifying himself, that he plays ball or runs fast or kisses mommy or puts on his blue shoes.

As children age, they begin to identify unique facts about themselves. They are able to describe themselves in terms not only of what, but how much or how well they do things, adding judgment to description (Peevers & Secord, 1973). Finally, in late childhood, relationships with others become important, qualities of personality and stable traits can be defined, and children can differentiate such things as who they consider and also value themselves to be. In adolescence, the full aspect of the self begins to take shape, and children can describe in principled and abstract terms the unique qualities of who they are as individuals and their impact for good on their immediate family, friends, and community, as well as answer questions about their value to the larger world. The evolution of self is important but is not a sufficient condition to create people who are ethical.

MORAL CODES AND MORAL ACTIONS: SAY/DO CORRELATIONS

How does the moral person emerge? What is it that we as parents or as individuals can do to increase the likelihood that our children's actions will be judged to be moral? What about ourselves? Many of us believe that if we teach a particular moral rule, consistently and without fail, we will develop moral children.

As Hartshorne and May (1929) reported in *Studies in the Nature of Character,* there are inconsistencies between the moral beliefs of children and their actual behavior. The situations in which children found themselves, not what they stated as their values, determined who yielded to various experimental temptations. Knowing what was right and wrong expressed in words was found to be significantly unrelated to what the children actually did. Other researchers have found the same thing—a weak link at best between moral thought and moral action, not only among children but among adults (Forsyth, 1980).

Donelson Forsyth has been engaged for several decades in research on moral codes of conduct and the relationship between what one says one believes and what one does. Currently a professor at Virginia Commonwealth University, Forsyth has written about two broad categories by which to classify adults in terms of judgment and behavior: relativism and idealism. Idealism entails a belief in universal truths, while relativism entails the belief that so-called absolutes must be assessed according to the context or the situation. Forsyth went on to subdivide people into four further refined categories regarding personal moral beliefs, examining how idealism and relativism impact predictions about actual conduct based on someone's personal moral philosophy. His work, among that of others, helps us define the shades of grey in how individuals actually demonstrate the link between what they say they value and what they actually do.

Many research projects explore different ways to characterize one's moral beliefs and the relative likelihood of moral actions. Many different categories have been used to label people who express different beliefs regarding ethics. We believe that Forsyth's four-dimensional coding system in which an individual is categorized in terms of a personal moral philosophy is useful particularly in helping us gain an understanding of the relationship between what people *say* and what they actually *do.* The words people use are related fairly consistently to what people do, but only in the most unexpected ways. What people say they will do in certain situations rarely reflects what they actually do. In his writings, Forsyth offers a test that helps determine where you stand in terms of your personal moral philosophy, and what guidance that might give you in learning about yourself.

Following is a broad interpretation of Forsyth's work. The labels that he attaches to each of the personal moral philosophies tell us almost nothing about what people do in a given situation but rather, they tell us what people report about what they will do in relation to ethical events.

PERSONAL MORAL PHILOSOPHIES

The label *absolutist* in Forsyth's system characterizes people who are, first, idealists, and who, second, hold to the hope of achieving good ends and positive consequences for moral acts. Such people believe there is an absolute right or wrong response to questions of an ethical nature. Context or situational variables are not relevant. The ascribed-to moral rule plays the dominant role in determining what an absolutist says that people must do, and the rule is used in judging the goodness or correctness of others' actions.

Absolutists are hard judges of other's actions, tending to see unacceptable actions as evidence of character flaws. They state that there are only right and wrong ways to act. Actions are either moral or immoral, with no shades of grey. As adults, absolutists tend to be more conservative about lifestyle and contemporary moral issues involving the toleration of people whose behavior they believe to be wrong. Absolutists' actions are described as being moral when they produce positive results by conforming to moral rules (Forsyth, 1980). Jean Valjean's protagonist, Javert, could be considered an absolutist. Javert, a policeman, made it his life's work to capture Valjean, an escaped prisoner convicted to hard labor for stealing a loaf of bread (Hugo, 1862).

Situationalists are both idealistic and relativistic. They believe that, while people should try very hard to determine the overarching right thing to do, there are no hard-and-fast moral rules; rather, the unique aspects of situations should be considered. Decisions as to correct actions are determined relative to promoting the best outcome in a given situation. Situationalists seek contextually true moral actions and do not ascribe to absolute truths. In general, situationalists are more liberal about matters that are often called *life-style choices* or involve a personal decision as they see it, such as taking one's own life when seriously ill.

The third group is comprised of *subjectivists.* Like situationalists, these individuals do not attribute their conduct or that of others to rules; but unlike situationalists, they assess the rightness or wrongness of an event based on their feelings of the moment as to what will do the most good or least harm at that time. They believe that individuals must make the best judgments they can at any given moment based on personal history rather than relying on a code of conduct. Needless to say, such individuals do not believe in moral absolutes.

Finally, there are *exceptionists.* Exceptionists are not relativists or idealists. They believe that moral rules should guide our behavior almost always, but sometimes negative actions should not be condemned. These individuals make exceptions (when needed) to their moral code according to the details of the events in which immoral actions occur, according to their ascribed rules. Killing in a just war is one example. Stealing medicine to help a sick friend who has no money might not, in their worldview, be condemned.

ASSESSING MORALITY IN PATTERNS OF BEHAVIOR

In assessing individual moral actions, the field of psychology must grapple with many variables, not the least of which is how people who do certain acts interpret those acts. For example, sometimes people who state that we should help one another above all else, may do something that is not right according to the common code of right and wrong (such as cheat), but their action is intended to help others. They then justify their behavior as moral, even though their actions, by all external criteria, are wrong. However, in a group setting, having just one person model inappropriate, wrong actions (such as cheating on a test) will increase by large numbers the people who cheat on the test. The reason why the person performed the inappropriate action will in all likelihood not be perceived by the others in the group. But without the personal example of cheating, the opportunity alone to cheat will prompt some, but fewer, people to cheat (Forsyth, D. & Berger, R. 1982).

One condition that most people understand as a good principle to live by is telling the truth. In a series of experiments, individuals were assessed according to where they stood on a moral rating scale. They were then asked to engage in lying during an experimental condition (Forsyth & Nye, 1990). Situationalists and absolutists usually lied no matter what the consequence, if asked to lie by the person in authority. Exceptionists were less likely to lie if the reason they were given for lying was that they would be given money if they lied. Subjectivists were even less likely to lie if they stood to gain from the lie and their act was labeled *lying.* Why is it that we can be so sure of how we will behave in ethically demanding situations, even state our convictions firmly, but then do the very things that fly in the face of what we report to cherish about our own code of conduct—such as not lie? We will return to this question later in this chapter.

TRAIT VERSUS CONSEQUENCE HISTORY

It is important that readers understand the issue of trait theory. The work described above supports, to some extent, the persistence of general and predictable ways that people respond to the issues that they face. Importing of this kind of psychological work is very popular in company culture, often showing up in testing employees to see who they are—in terms of those rather stable traits of personality that show up in such tests as the Myers-Briggs. If you have had a classification assigned to you that is based on the use of the Myers-Briggs, especially a classification that you find personally true as you see yourself, you may be tempted to ascribe to the notion that people are their traits, just as you are. Unfortunately, this process works in reverse as well. People who feel constrained by the label given to them, who disagree with it at some fundamental level, may find that others use the label to define them. All too often the label becomes the person, at least in that setting, and there may seem to be no way out. These individuals will not be eager to accept the notion that people are their traits. The idea behind the use of personality traits is to accept the trait as true, to respect the person, and thus to work with the person as is. While the intention behind this use may be the desire to seek out and promote a diverse and rich cultural setting where people can be who they are, in all too many cases such an approach will forever limit a person's potential—even when the label is quite positive.

The Myers-Briggs test is one of the better tests out there in terms of its sample and design. However, in the September 20, 2004, *New Yorker Magazine,* Malcolm Gladwell wrote broadly, in an article entitled "Personality Plus" about the notion of assessment center approaches and specifically about the Myers-Briggs. Here is what he had to say about the stability of the results in regard to the Myers-Briggs:

> The Myers-Briggs has a large problem with consistency: According to some studies, more than half of those who take the Myers-Briggs a second time end up with

> a different score than when they took it the first time. Since personality is continuous, not dichotomous, clearly some people who are borderline Introverts or Feelers one week slide over to Extroversion or Thinking the next week. And since personality is contingent, not stable, how we answer is affected by which circumstances are foremost in our minds when we take the test.

Another troubling aspect of trait theory is the more dangerous use of invention by people who believe that if the Myers-Briggs works, then a much more simplified test of traits should work as well. At one company, for example, individuals at a meeting were asked to place themselves on one of four squares that best described each person's overall characteristics.

Once everyone had done that, the members of the team then moved each person in one direction or another until the person was in the square seen as most appropriate. Once that humiliation was over, the team leader then described the positive and negative attributes of the particular square the person was standing on. Everyone had the opportunity to offer advice about how best to support the personality now standing on an isolated square. Feeling the pain of discovery about the impact of one's behavior on the crowd, the humiliation of not getting one's own personality right in the first place by having to be moved, and then discovering that the right square, the really highly desirable personality square was not the square one had been placed upon—well, the reader can easily see that great harm can come from the application of naïve notions about human capabilities.

Many of you may have experienced such events and looking back, said such things as, "Well, there was some truth to that" or "I loved it—they really got me right." It is good to know how we come across to people when the characterization seems to come out right. That part of the lessons learned is rewarding. However, as was discussed in Chapter 8, the misuse of psychological testing is a very distressing trend in terms of the earnestness with which the results are often applied. Most disturbing is the mistaken notion, often conveyed, that no matter what you do, you will always be the personality on the square. You might work to break out but you will always be the label. If you should try to be like the upper right-hand square, less analytic and more intuitive, well, perhaps you have a problem with self-esteem, but bully for you for trying, and so on. What makes the situation even worse is that these barely understood tools are applied by people who invent labels and have no real competence in such testing. Corporate America seems to contain a great many folks who love to do this kind of thing.

In the next chapter, personality and traits are discussed further. We recommend that you not use trait descriptions of those you work with to define who they are, what jobs they get, and how best to arrange the workplace. Instead, adhere to a more functional view of human potential. It is unavoidable that, in some fashion, we will generalize about individuals in the workplace, based on certain traits that appear across conditions. Care must be taken, however, not to limit what a person might yet do based on what a person has been doing.

It is true that personality is broadly consistent across a variety of situations. It is true that we have patterns of behavior that show up in ways that lead others to think of us in certain ways. It is also true that new patterns of behaviors can replace those perceptions and can even change the label that is applied to us. Overall, we may still be the person we seem most generally to be, but the label has done nothing except impede the optimal progress that we could be making.

Of course, it is a good thing that human beings are generally predictable, or else the workplace would be a chaotic place, with people constantly presenting themselves differently from what was expected. Problems arise when it is believed that traits are what and who an individual is because then, in all likelihood, when a person is undergoing positive change there will be no recognition that this is occurring. Instead, we will say, "Oh, well. He had an unusual day. He really isn't that outgoing, you know." Then, on the next day, as if by magic, he is not that outgoing and we will conclude that we were right all along.

If you are a manager who wants to bring about change in others, or if you wish to change your own ethical behavior, then you must believe that there is the possibility of real change, occurring through the consequences that can shape and build new patterns of behavior. The change may be subtle in some cases, but without the underlying assumption of the possibility of change in who the person is, each person's potential is defined by a prior history of success or failure in identifying and living an ethical life. Therefore, it is important that trait theory be applied very carefully. Traits give us valuable clues about how to respond and how to guide others, but they are very limiting if we assume they mean that change is not really possible. In most workplace situations there is the possibility of making small changes every day—changes that lead to a new definition of our ethical sensitivities—and perhaps even a new definition of our personalities.

People are not their labels. They are complex human beings who generally behave consistently, but not always. The variance in behavior may be very small indeed, and then we are especially prone to tell ourselves that the larger trait is the person. So we say that Mary is selfish and Joe is a deal maker; it is part of their character (traits). We are not being fair to Mary or to Joe, and this is especially true when Mary and Joe behave in ways that are slightly different from what we had expected, but we brush this aside in applying our labels to them. We must remember that while people are generally consistent in their actions, individual behaviors are always changing, being shaped by the opportunity and general conditions of the moment.

THE ROLE OF CONSCIENCE

Finally, what about conscience? In raising children, parents try to help them understand that there are consequences when they do wrong, and these consequences can generate bad feelings. These bad feelings, along with good feelings produced when children do what is right, are then translated into a conscience that is expected to guide children and help them sort right from wrong. And it is true that individuals who say that they adhere to very high moral standards (who are absolutists, for example), but who do not live up to their own moral standards, will express greater self-loathing and disappointment when they fail (pangs of conscience), even when they are working to benefit others, than will other individuals who ascribe to less demanding moral standards. Thus, it can be said that what each of us calls our *conscience* may either possess no shades of grey or be multicolored; in either case, a person will say, "I am following my conscience" when making ethical decisions, and that guide, alone, may not be enough.

In each of the four broad categories discussed in an earlier section, experimental conditions have been arranged to find out who is most likely do the right thing based on what they say about the rules of conduct. When people talk about conscience they may say such things as, "My conscience won't allow me to do the wrong thing" or "My conscience tells me this is right." Nevertheless, when specific actions are looked at, those who say, "I never tell a lie; my conscience won't let me," do, in fact, sometimes lie. For example, when asked to lie for the sake of a greater good, the absolutists were much more likely to lie than were the exceptionists who evaluated the circumstances, not the rule, in determining their answers. This research tells us that even those individuals who are most certain about what the rules are, and usually reference a higher order guide (namely, conscience) may not do the right thing at the right time in the right way as judged by external criteria. We can count on them, however, to follow the relevant moral rule.

Thus, because telling people to follow their conscience can lead to many very different outcomes, relying on the control of conscience is inadequate unless we know what the people we are dealing with will do in given situations. Children need to have a strong sense of right and wrong, and the same is true for adults. Nevertheless, in general, conscience is too personal and too private for appeals to conscience to function effectively as the tool for shaping the behavior of employees.

ENSURING ETHICAL ACTIONS: MOVING BEYOND MORAL RULES

If a general conclusion can be drawn from the research discussed in this chapter, it is that the usual method of teaching ethics, which is to teach moral rules, does not ensure ethical performance in particular circumstances. On the contrary, if you want to ensure that I do the right thing consistently, you must ensure that I experience positive consequences for doing the right thing, and those consequences should begin as early as possible in my life. It is so important that children receive praise and cheer from Mom or Dad or sister or brother when they do the right thing. We must not make the teaching of ethics an event that occurs only when the child fails to do what we consider the right thing. When parents only react to failure, children often learn to lie to escape negative events and to attempt to receive their parent's favor. We should celebrate any act of sharing, even if it is accidental, or celebrate when a child expresses empathy by comforting another child who is crying. We should not just reinforce the stating of the rule—which is a large part of why some people find it hard to do the right thing. When children learn to merely state or follow the rules about how they should behave—politely, listening to authority, and so on—without understanding or even believing in the validity of the rules, then as adults they are more likely to cheat or do something wrong as long as they think they won't be caught.

Of course, as part of my moral development, I must also experience consequences for actions that are not right. These consequences must be firm and clear and punishing enough to redirect my behavior, for example, making comments such as, "No, that hurt Sam" or "Do not take Bobby's toy away from him. It belongs to him," or "I am sad that you pushed Mary off the swing without waiting for your turn." In each such instance, if I love my mother who is saying these things to me and I care about her affection, the words "no," "I am sad," and other such expressions of feeling and the impact of my behavior on her and on other people begins to open my eyes to the impact I have when I do the wrong thing. Such instruction needs to be paired with steps taken by my parents or others that direct me back toward the right actions.

Children must learn to feel embarrassed and ashamed when they commit selfish or mean acts. We should not protect our children from coming in contact with how their behavior affects others, particularly when they disappoint or harm others. Children must understand why parents or teachers or neighbors believe what they did was wrong, not simply that their behavior was wrong because they were caught and punished for it. Efforts to teach children about the reasons for actions should begin just as soon as children begin to understand the language required for the lessons to be taught. As early as possible, children need to know that what they say and do can either help or hinder others. Sharing a toy is an act of generosity and a focus on another's well-being. In words that the child can understand, she needs this larger lesson.

It is not enough simply to teach children to share. They must know why it is good to share, and that adults in their lives are disappointed when they do not share. Such lessons must be done in a manner and to a degree that is appropriate for the age and experience of the child. Without experiencing those sad feelings that come from disappointing people who matter to them—their parents or teachers, for example—the motivation for young children to change behavior in a positive direction will probably not exist. Learning early in life such lessons as feeling embarrassed by the ways our parents and others respond when we disappoint them enables us to practice behaviors that help us later avoid the awful depths of despair that we experienced as children.

Having said all of this, it is very important to emphasize that as a young child and in our adult life as well, we should be made to experience consequences that are tied to the idea that we can do things better, that there is complete faith in our ability to do things right next time. We can all hope for parents and supervisors who believe that, with practice, we will improve and our capability to improve is not in question. Our work with young children should take a developmental, shaping approach, helping children toward the right responses—as opposed to being focused on teaching children a lesson through punishment for failing. If we don't help our children as well as ourselves generalize from one condition to another, we will have real difficulty using broad-based rules to help us make ethical decisions. In other words, ethical behavior will not become a habit.

Taking back the candy bar I took from Smith's store and apologizing is important. Being complimented by someone I care about for sharing a favorite toy with another child is important. Requiring that I complete a promise (such as visiting a friend on a certain day) is important, even if another offer comes along that I would rather accept. Moral character is built upon small everyday actions. Moreover, what is done, not what is said, is the best predictor of whether future actions will look like current actions. This very same point applies within the setting of the workplace. In fact, many workplaces offer developmental coaching for adults that is very similar to the type of ethics training required with children. Many times that developmental focus will consist of what can be called a *shaping process,* the goal of which is to help the performer move incrementally toward better ways of doing things the next time.

It is also very clear that sometimes we are managed so tightly that the workplace rule is all that is really reinforced, not the actions we take to implement the rule. We are not taught why we are following a particular rule, and indeed we may learn that the good action does consist simply in following the rules, because that is what a good person does. The classic example illustrating how deficient this approach can be is the infamous good soldier who does what is asked by people in authority, even when this means committing atrocities. As we said earlier in Chapter 3, rule following is not necessarily representative of a consistent code of conduct that will operate across all relevant situations. In the next chapter, we have more to say about consequences and how they operate.

USING PUNISHMENT TO ENSURE THE RIGHT ACTIONS

It would be humorous, if it were not so debilitating, to think that many people believe that punishment teaches positive lessons about living. In reality, punishment mainly teaches what not to do in the presence of those who punish. It teaches how to hide, deceive, and protect oneself. It does stop certain behaviors. If severe enough, it can stop all kinds of associated behaviors, including the targeted behavior, from reoccurring even for many years to come. The lesson that is taught, however, is not a lesson in living life well, but in suppressing action. Punishment, which we discuss further in Chapter 15, will likely stop anything that is judged to be wrong in the presence of the punisher, but punishment alone will not build new behavior, behavior that is on the right track. Punishing others is reinforcing to those who punish insofar as it stops what is not wanted. For parents, it often seems a quick and effective fix.

Since the use of punishment can easily escalate (much research exists regarding how using punishment affects the person who is doing the punishing) and since using punishment often seems to be the easiest path, it is indeed a dangerous and lazy way to direct children, to teach them to do the right thing. This same lesson applies to the workplace as well. To maintain good behavior, that behavior must consistently be reinforced and praised, ideally from the very beginning—small steps shaped along the way. Then once such behavior occurs on a routine basis, the behavior pattern itself becomes reinforcing and builds new behavior from its own reinforcing properties.

Parents need to understand and use well the power of positive reinforcement to build strong patterns of behavior without fear. By contrast, the damage in using punishment to raise our children is enormous. We as a society do not pay enough attention to the negative impact on the behavior of children who are constantly threatened with the possibility of punishment. We need to better understand both punishment and the freedom and responsibility that are more readily taught through strategies of reinforcement and shaping toward success. The same general point applies as much within the context of the workplace as within the context of child rearing.

Ethical actions will occur only insofar as there is freedom to act. Because it stops freedom of action, punishment alone (without positive reinforcement for other behavior) makes it unlikely that strong moral codes will develop. This is true in regard to child rearing, and it is true also in regard to a sound managerial philosophy in the world of business. Following rules, judging others harshly, and beating in "goodness" leads to rigid rule-following and behavior driven by the desire to escape punishment. This kind of behavior pattern rarely enables a person to act ethically when acting unethically means the possibility of immediate personal gain.

It is interesting to note that some of the people who are most strongly supportive of punishing children corporally are also, often, absolutists in their moral views. "Spare the rod, spoil the child" they say. But this is mythology. Sadly, ill-equipped parents pass down mythology to more ill-equipped future parents who do not know how to look at and learn from the information available about raising well-adjusted and happy children. Similarly, ill-equipped managers pass on their bad practices to the next generation of managers. Both the parents and the managers are locked into their own bad habits and faulty assumptions.

PERSISTENCE

If we are to teach our children to sustain good habits such as honesty, we must understand that persistent and positive recognition of the desired behaviors such as telling the truth is crucial. Eisenberger has written extensively about learned industriousness and its importance in creating adults who are reliable, persistent, and creative. Several extracts from his important paper, "Industriousness: How Can It Be Learned?" are reproduced with permission here.

> The Romantic tradition in Western civilization, as reflected in the writings of humanistic psychologists, values the gentle nurture of unique talent as a means to individual success. This romantic view gives insufficient recognition to the difficult work needed to become proficient in a field of endeavor (Eisenberger & Cameron, 1996).
>
> Some individuals work harder than others who have equivalent ability and motivation. One student consistently

> studies more for various courses than another student with similar life goals. A teacher carefully prepares lessons whereas a colleague relies on old, incomplete notes. A factory employee completes tasks rapidly and efficiently whereas another dawdles. Learning may contribute importantly to such individual differences in industriousness.
>
> Almost seven decades ago, J. B. Watson (1930) argued that "the formation of early work habits in youth, of working longer hours than others, of practicing more intensively than others, is probably the most reasonable explanation we have today not only for success in any line, but even for genius" (p. 212). If Watson exaggerated for emphasis, individual differences of industriousness do have an important influence on achievement.
>
> Recent research has shed light on mechanisms that contribute to the learning of industriousness. When a difficult task is followed by reward, the effort would become less aversive; increasing the amount of effort the individual subsequently chooses to spend performing this and other difficult tasks. If the experience of effort is similar across different tasks, then learning to tolerate high effort in one task may increase toleration of high effort in subsequent tasks. Reward of high effort could help sustain a person's subsequent performance in difficult tasks when the opportunity arises to achieve the desired result by dishonest behavior. By concentrating on working for a desired goal, rather than dwelling on the goal itself, a person would be less inclined to resort to dishonest shortcuts (Eisenberger, 1999, p. 24).

There is a good reason to challenge our children to focus on the process of working hard, of doing the right thing even if we cannot get to the end goal soon, and of making achievement a worthy and recognized event by celebrating the small steps along the way. Over time, Eisenberger's research implies, the ultimate achievement of a goal may be less important to sustained performance than the reward and recognition for the effort to get there. We recognize this with sports. However, we do not always recognize the role that hard work can play in creating honest self-evaluation. Some people still do not understand why taking shortcuts and misrepresenting facts takes the fun out of achieving a goal for those who have learned to value the effort as much as the outcome.

Eisenberger states that sustained effort, learned industriousness, with intermittent recognition of effort, has much to do with helping our most celebrated scientists and creative innovators work through long, painful years, even when not producing visibly tangible results related to the target goal. The same applies to the factory worker who stays at work longer whenever she thinks it is necessary to solve a problem, or the employee who quietly takes on extra duties to learn a task more efficiently and thus provide better quality work, and so on.

The most intriguing aspect of Eisenberger's work for the purposes of this book is in regard to improvements seen in reports of honesty by those who work hard for a desired goal.

> An experiment with college students tested whether rewarded high performance would increase the subsequent resistance to cheating on a different task (Eisenberger & Masterson, 1983). One group of students was required to solve difficult mathematics problems and perceptual identifications. A second group received easier versions of these problems, and a third group was given no training at all. Next, the students were asked to work on a series of anagrams that were almost impossible to solve in the short time allotted for each word. The students were told that speaking aloud interfered with the anagram task and that they should try to solve the anagrams without speaking. When the time was up for figuring out an anagram, they would be shown the correct answer. They were simply to place a plus on the answer sheet if they had figured out the answer they were shown, and to put a zero if they had not achieved the solution.

> Cheating seemed simple to the students because they never had to supply an answer, simply to claim the solution after it was shown to them.
>
> Most of the students did cheat. However, the students who had previously been required to solve difficult anagrams cheated less than the others. Rewarded high performance on preliminary tasks reduced the number of anagrams that students falsely claimed to solve. These results suggest that an individual's honesty is influenced by the generalized effects of rewarded high effort (Eisenberger, 1999, p. 25).

There is something meaningful here about persisting at work, receiving reinforcement along the way, and staying true to the ultimate objective of building real character. If self-persistence is one clear quality that this society needs more of, that quality can be reinforced by alert managers, parents, and teachers. They should reward persistence and effort at least as much as they reinforce the end goal of solving problems correctly. Ironically, if we recognize the ethical effort/pursuit of the end goal, then achieving the end goal by ethical means becomes more possible and probable. The act of trying to "be better than we are" can be as or more reinforcing as actually claiming to be better. It is not what we say in this regard, it is what we do.

We need to shape one another to see that the real diamond in the "character pool" is not the person who simply says "I never lie," but the person, who, even in the most difficult of circumstances, does not lie. The ethical person is the person who refuses to lie even when no one around that person would know they were lying—and even when the social contract says "Do lie, just this once. You make me happy when you lie, and you are thus doing the (socially) right thing." We need to help people learn that the socially expected rule that one should always do what one's boss says to do should not be followed in ethically questionable situations. Reaching this goal can be a great challenge, especially for anyone who relies on their employment for financial survival.

15

CHAPTER

HARNESSING THE POWER OF POSITIVE REINFORCEMENT

Expedients are for the hour, but principles are for the ages. Just because the rains descend and the winds blow, we cannot afford to build on shifting sands.

—Reverend Henry Ward Beecher

WE ENVISION A WORKPLACE where no one punishes, threatens, or cajoles anyone else. In such a workplace, managers do not manage—at least not in the usual sense. They do not worry about performance on a day-to-day basis because the atmosphere of work itself promotes the kinds of performance needed to create the best products and services. In such a workplace, managers and employees support one another in a positive and non-coercive environment to achieve the best for all, including the customer. Respect for the intrinsic worth and autonomy of everyone is clear.

Such a workplace is achievable. Nothing less is acceptable on ethical grounds. Nothing less is acceptable as sound business strategy.

We are describing a culture and a philosophy of action within the workplace where every individual, as part of the workplace, has the right to expect to be valued "as a rational creature, seeking reinforcement" (Garret, 1987, p. 327). In such an environment, the corporate commitment is to find ways to reward people so as to maximize individual and group potential. Understood most broadly, it is a commitment to the existence of a moral society.

SETTING THE CONDITIONS FOR EVERYONE TO DO THEIR BEST

In the sort of workplace we are describing, rewards for positive actions are part of the usual and customary way that business is done. Each person examines the consequences of what he or she does and how those actions support colleagues as they strive to do their best. In such a setting, both managers and employees are evaluated according to their effectiveness in achieving this goal. The overall goal is to bring out the best in everyone in reaching business goals—to encourage a reciprocal view of our relationships to one another. Policies, procedures, goal statements, planning documents, and daily practice—all are colored by this cooperative effort.

Unfortunately, few work settings are designed with this kind of human engineering in mind.

It is time for managers to learn the necessary skills to manage people and themselves successfully and in as non-coercive a manner as possible. Managers must become proficient in the application of the most up-to-date knowledge about behavior management and change—just as they are now required to become proficient in technical knowledge, customer service, annual operational planning, and expense control. It is time for managers to recognize that a major and crucial part of their role is to ensure their employees' success.

A good place to begin is by examining differences between what managers say and what managers do in the workplace. For example, a manager says that high quality services and products are paramount; yet high production is demanded and no inspection for errors is made. At other times, service promises are made to obtain sales, but there is no review of customer satisfaction. These observable actions send a strong signal to employees about what really counts. Likewise, for companies to say that they value teamwork while paying bonuses only to those who close the final deals and without regard for the sweat equity of others on the team, sends entirely the same signal. When employees are rewarded only for their own deal making, it is unreasonable to expect them to put aside the prospect of personal reward for the greater good of the team. If they are self-serving, it is because they are merely responding logically to the contingencies of the workplace.

If the relationship between an action and its consequences is changed, then we can expect behavior change. Thus, if a manager wants team behavior, the manager must determine how the individual can be rewarded for individual actions, and how the group at the same time can be rewarded for team productivity. Both the individual and the group must be allotted some share of the incentive, and the shares need not be equal. Under the right system, individuals and groups seek to promote the best performance from everyone, both internally and in relation to customers. Such a system must be especially sensitive to the design of the spoken and unspoken incentives, maintaining a consistency between what is said and what is done, so that the commitment to external as well as internal customers drives appropriate behavior. Having such a focus is part of the ideal work world we envision.

How do managers go about learning what they need to know about behavior? The general answer is that they must be exposed to some of the key findings from the science of applied behavior analysis. The science of applied behavior analysis deals with human learning and how to arrange the best conditions for personal and group success. It is not based on hopes but rather on proven research about how to increase, maintain, or decrease behavior patterns—those we want and those we don't want.

Applied behavior analysis is based on data regarding observable events that can be recorded, graphed, and displayed. It is based on the reinforcement that is available for all actions—both those you want to keep and those you don't want to keep—and it requires an objective and persistent view of how to generate the best in people. Following is a description of the main ways in which behavior increases, stays the same, or decreases, depending upon relevant circumstances. An understanding of these ways, along with an understanding of some additional key behavioral strategies, is essential if one is to dramatically change performance. These strategies are particularly important to managers if they are to become good at what their primary job should be—but rarely is—to produce discretionary effort from each of their employees. Discretionary effort can be described as consisting of "want to" patterns of behavior, as opposed to "have to" patterns of behavior.

FOUR METHODS FOR CHANGING BEHAVIOR PATTERNS

The following paragraphs describe methods by which behavior change occurs. The four methods of change are *positive reinforcement, negative reinforcement, punishment,* and *extinction.* Both positive reinforcement and negative reinforcement increase the probability of a behavior occurring. Punishment is a process for eliminating the occurrence of a behavior. Extinction is another way to eliminate behavior by no longer providing the reinforcement that previously sustained the behavior, or failing to provide the reinforcement the performer seeks to sustain the behavior. Extinction is often used unintentionally—by failing to notice effort, for example. When used deliberately, extinction is difficult to maintain for as long as is often required since it is the act of doing nothing at all in response to annoying, disturbing, unwanted, or unnecessary patterns of behavior. As with punishment, extinction is measured as effective or ineffective in terms of whether or not the targeted behavior stops.

By contrast, positive reinforcement is not coercive, and is the only one of the behavior-change methods that uses recognition and reward to change behavior. Positive reinforcement increases the occurrence of behavior and makes it more likely that the person whose behavior is reinforced or recognized will continue to demonstrate actions that lead to such reinforcers in the future. With positive reinforcement, not only will the desired behavior increase, but associated positive actions will increase as well.

Notice that all of these methods are defined in terms of their effect on behavior, not in terms of the intention of those who apply them. This is an important point! Even when we intend to positively reinforce, if the behavior we want does not increase, we have not rewarded it; positive reinforcement has not occurred. Similarly, if the behavior continues, we have not punished or extinguished it. Saying that rewards or punishers do not work tells us more about our skills (or lack thereof) in applying techniques of behavior change than it does about these techniques themselves. If we do not increase (or stop) the behavior we want, it is not the rewards or punishers that fail. Instead, we have failed to correctly identify the relationship between a person's behavior and the consequences that we provide.

COERCIVE BEHAVIOR-CHANGE TECHNIQUES

Negative reinforcement and punishment, two of the ways in which behavior can be changed, are coercive. They get results through the threat of, or the actual delivery of, punishment. Extinction can be an effective method of behavior change, but when applied correctly, it is only effective for stopping behavior, and, while not openly negative, it can be perceived by the person who is "on extinction" as coercive or shameful. Let us look at each consequence system in more detail.

Extinction

Extinction reduces and ultimately stops behavior. Extinction is a less direct and less immediate method of eliminating behavior. It is the elimination or reduction of the occurrence of a particular behavior or group of behaviors attained through the absence of attention or reaction to that behavior. Extinction is a technique that managers often use in the workplace when unwanted behavior occurs. An example is ignoring someone who drones on and on during meetings, and not calling on that person to speak in future meetings. Over time, if the manager continues to ignore the behavior, it is likely that the person will probably not only stop trying to talk incessantly, but will stop trying to contribute at all.

Now, the person's long-winded habit is extinguished but so is his desire to contribute or even attend meetings. His enthusiasm for work in other areas may also diminish. Emotional reactivity, a predictable event that is formally called the *extinction burst,* is a strong side effect of having one's previously reinforced behavior ignored. People will increase their talking or do other things to see what it is that is no longer working. They report the embarrassment of being ignored. The manager might say that she is not ignoring the person but simply the behavior of talking in meetings. Unfortunately, unskilled managers often do not see how extinction is perceived by the individual on the receiving end; these managers do not see how they have cut the person off from other kinds of reinforcement, such as a manager's and the team's attention, the pleasure of being listened to at least in that environment, and so on. All of these negative side effects result from the single act of ignoring a person in meetings when a simple directive from the manager to the individual is much fairer. The manager can speak privately and directly to the person with an explanation of the problem, such as the following:

> I am going to ask you to monitor your talking during meetings. Often you interrupt others, talking for as much as two minutes at a time on points you think are important, even though people look away or frown or in other ways indicate they are not listening. You do not check for understanding and your behavior appears rude in that it takes time away from others to respond or continue in our meeting. Please observe yourself and see if you can find a quicker and more succinct method of contributing. I will help you as I see you doing this, and I'll let you know when I see improvements.

Now these words may seem rather awkward to say, but in almost all instances of difficult performance, a direct approach is required. Even if you then intend to ignore the troubling behavior, you have given the person a forewarning and conveyed trust that they can handle their own behavior. You have made clear that what you do is not a generalized response to their personality but to the specific behaviors under question. People need to know if something they are doing is not working, and how they can or should improve.

Because extinction is so readily available and sometimes unintentional, managers may use this technique without understanding the powerful effect they are having on behaviors they want to jump-start, increase, or simply maintain. For example, managers may fail to acknowledge new ideas or suggestions from an employee. If attention from the manager is important to the individual, its absence will eliminate idea-generation over time.

Extinction is often viewed as a benign process of withholding feedback to eliminate troublesome behavior. Extinction can, however, also eliminate behaviors of value to management. While it is an easy method to use—if the manager can handle the process of ignoring a wildly waving hand in a meeting, for example—extinction is often slower than the direct punishment or negative reinforcement strategies discussed below. Extinction can, as with other coercive strategies, have side effects. One of these may be a negative response directed at the person using the technique. For example, because being ignored may be embarrassing and unpleasant, an individual who feels that someone has extinguished his or her behavior is less likely to seek out that person for any reason. The negative feelings may remain and result in unwanted aftereffects.

Punishment

Punishment occurs when the immediate and direct use of words or actions stops a specific behavior or pattern of behavior from reoccurring. Docking a person's pay can be punishing; so can firing someone. Saying no to a request or removing privileges, such as a company car, can be punishing. Whether or not any of these actually constitute punishment depends on the reaction of the individual for whom punishment is intended. Punishment, as we said, is defined as occurring only if the specific behavior in question stops as a consequence of the action.

With punishment, incidental behavior can be as greatly or even more affected than the targeted behavior. For example, if the boss tells an employee that she is stupid, the effect may not be a decrease in her stupid behavior, but only in the frequency of her approaching the boss.

In addition to the danger just alluded to, employees resent managers who rely often on the use of punishment. Furthermore, punishment strategies demonstrate a lack of respect for autonomy. Unnecessary control over individual action is usually born out of a failure to understand how to increase independence. Punished individuals are generally more passive and take fewer risks. Punishment suppresses both the targeted behavior and other, similar behaviors. Punishment becomes associated with the individual who uses it.

To be most effective, punishment must be immediate. For such immediacy to occur, the individual in question must be under the close scrutiny of someone else. This means that risk taking and new ways of acting are discouraged in a system that relies on punitive control. Such control often requires the application of an excessive number of rules, constant intervention, and micro-management of individuals. All of these together will impede, if not defeat, the benefits that come with increased skill and autonomy.

Negative Reinforcement

The third coercive method of controlling behavior is negative reinforcement. In contrast to punishment and extinction, negative reinforcement increases behavior, but it does so in an aversive fashion. Managers use this method with ease. "Do it or else" is the single most common strategy for change used by managers. However, the experience of being threatened reduces the frequency of contact with the individual who uses threats. The manager's intended goal is to increase certain types of behavior through negative reinforcement; but the conduct that also increases is that of avoiding interaction with the manager. The employee desires to escape or avoid the potential punishment. The use of fear as a management strategy may produce results, but the effects are uncertain and the cost is high. Also, under negative reinforcement conditions, performers will do only as much as is necessary to avoid the potential punishment. Negative reinforcement strategies never inspire discretionary effort and require almost constant vigilance on the part of the manager.

THE OVERALL EFFECTS OF COERCION ON BEHAVIOR

Coercive methods to achieve change instill aversion and avoidance. Generally, such methods take away from the dignity of others. They are often disrespectful. They diminish possible return on investment. In environments where coercion is used, it is unlikely that individuals will speak out about new ideas, cost-saving ventures, innovative applications, or—even more damaging and demoralizing—problems that exist.

At times, the behavior of a person in the workplace is so self-destructive or destructive to others that coercive methods should be applied. This is rarely the case. Only after the exploration of other options should the use of punishment at work be considered, and even then should be approached with much care. However, if an individual is threatening to others, commits an illegal act, lies about a contract or other company commitment, or does other outrageous and dangerous things, that individual needs to be told immediately to stop, and in some instances to be immediately dismissed.

A BETTER WAY

The point we wish to make is that in the vast majority of cases in which aversive control techniques are used either deliberately or unintentionally to obtain good performance at work (or anywhere); there is a better and more ethical way. If this better way is applied across the work setting, then punishment, extinction, and negative reinforcement as *a management strategy of control* are almost never needed. Individuals will still experience the normal daily effects of consequences as they learn new skills, practice old ones, or engage in behavior that requires change, but that kind of consequence management is built into the fabric of "doing" and is very different than a strategy of management that relies on fear and threat. The better way to manage others is to become skillful in the effective use of positive reinforcement to shape and sustain desired performance.

Positive Reinforcement

Positive reinforcement, like negative reinforcement, increases the occurrence of behavior, but it does so in a non-coercive way. When positively reinforced, people seek out the conditions that reward them. Examples of potential rewards include bonuses, kind words, time off, greater freedom, or better schedules. Just as with things we assume to be punishers, these intended rewards may or may not actually be rewarding, depending upon whether they change the behavior in question. Kind words, for example, may not positively impact the future behavior of a given individual, but may be rewarding to another person, who will increase future actions in order to obtain more kind words. Management strategies that focus on examining and rewarding behavior require an active process of observation and intervention to shape the desired responses; such a systematic process leads to mastery of skills and effective performance.

BECOMING SKILLED IN THE USE OF POSITIVE REINFORCEMENT

Knowing whether or not we are rewarding behavior requires perseverance, particularly when we are trying to develop new skills. It requires willingness on the part of managers to change. Managers must be willing to change their supervisory style by taking cues for adjusting their responses according to the actions produced in others—their colleagues and even their bosses. This commitment to using information about the effects of one's actions in producing the desired response places the primary responsibility for change squarely on management's shoulders. Managers are, after all, largely responsible for the conditions, particularly the systems of consequence management, that exist in the workplace.

Becoming skilled in the use of positive reinforcement requires consistent effort to build the skills of both observation and application. As indicated above, if, in using positive reinforcement, we do not get behavior that is closer to what we want, it is incorrect to say that recognition or positive consequences don't work. Actually, it means we have failed to correctly identify the contingent relationship between behavior and what we are doing to change it. For example, a manager thanks an employee for making the extra effort to complete a job, but the employee does not find comments from that particular manager rewarding. The result may then be the opposite of what the manager wants. The employee may discontinue making the extra effort in order to avoid receiving praise from that particular manager. The behavior, extra effort in this case, has in effect been inadvertently punished by the actions of the manager.

MANAGEMENT SKILLS

Most managers have their jobs because they possess technical skills, not because they are skilled in the use of behavior-change strategies. Many managers do not know how to change behavior by specifying and recognizing new, desirable ways of acting; instead they use coercive techniques that limit desirable behavior or eliminate undesirable behavior. Managers should be catching people doing the right thing (or approximations to the right thing) and rewarding them. Managers who are truly skilled at managing behavior replace punishment, negative reinforcement, and extinction with positive reinforcement whenever possible. They become skilled shapers (or coaches) of other people's success.

Managers may feel inclined to ask, "Why not leave it up to individual employees to figure out how to bring about needed changes? After all, haven't we hired them because they know how to do what we want them to do? If things are not going as well as they should, why can't the employees figure out how to improve the situation? Otherwise, why pay them a salary in the first place?"

Notice that when managers say such things they are placing responsibility for change completely on the shoulders of the employee who is doing the wrong thing in the first place and who moreover has no power in the organization to change what management is doing wrong. In either case, such managers are not accepting any responsibility.

If managers fail to produce desirable change in others through the management strategies they presently employ, they should try using other strategies. The definition of desirable change is a tricky one. It is about producing "want to" patterns of behavior from employees rather than "have to" patterns of behavior. It is not just about managers getting the quick fix they need at the moment. Managers should find methods that will clearly express the unfavorable consequences of unwanted behavior and hold responsible those explicitly accountable for needed change; but especially, managers should measure and reward the progress of positive change as their primary method of problem solving. When necessary, managers must change themselves. To be effective in changing the behavior of others, they must observe not only others' actions but also their own.

OBJECTIVITY

As a manager, becoming objective, not taking personally the responses one receives, is an important part of learning. If managers are to look at behavior to determine whether they have set up the right conditions for success, then interpreting behavior with words like "willful," "disrespectful," or "unappreciative" only gets in the way of good observation and change. Still, substituting language that is more neutral about why a person is doing a particular act that you do not want them to do—by saying something like "That non-specific and confusing method of describing his work is still occurring at a high rate in the presence of Joe and Bill, but changes dramatically to a much clearer report when Sam is present"—may sound less satisfying and not as substantial as "willful," "disrespectful," or "pain in the rear end." While difficult to accomplish, the more objective that managers can be about the effects of consequences on behavior, and the less interpretive, the better these managers will become at changing the targeted behavior. Objectivity is one of those core skills that a manager needs to learn. It will allow the manager to address many things in a much more productive way, including actions that have ethical or unethical consequences.

DATA-BASED ANALYSIS

The use of positive reinforcement requires steady commitment to change and a reliance on data-based observation to determine what must be done next. The process is difficult at first. For example, from the perspective of a busy manager, it may appear far more cost-effective to deal with mistakes when they happen by using punishment rather than waiting to catch someone doing the right thing. After all, punishment can be swiftly carried out, and determining when and how to use it is relatively easy in comparison to applying positive reinforcement. Determining the how, what, when, and where of giving rewards is a more complex matter. (The issue of timing is beyond the scope of this book, but more information can be found in the psychological literature on learning under the category of *schedules of reinforcement.*)

Delivering punishment in the workplace seems simpler, because the effects on those punished and on their actions are clearly and immediately visible. Managers all too frequently rely on coercive techniques to get what they want, doing things such as chewing people out when they make errors, writing them up when they miss a production quota, or publicly reprimanding them for stammering during a customer presentation. These techniques may have validity on the surface, because they appear to make the manager's job easier, but is making the manager's job easier at the expense of another person's dignity an ethical choice? Do such strategies actually change the behavior of the learner, the employee? Behavior may stop but more successful behavior is not necessarily mastered.

PATIENCE, PERSEVERANCE, AND THEN HIGH-AND-STEADY RESULTS TO BUILD ON

We confess that positive reinforcement does, on the surface, appear to be a less efficient behavior-change strategy. It takes time to determine whether we are effectively using it, and we have to continually monitor the situation and adjust our responses to what occurs after we do what we believe will reinforce future action.

In addition, the reinforcing event must closely follow the action it intends to reward. If you jump ahead and reward actions before they occur, you may be rewarding many things other than the behavior you are attempting to target.

However, once a manager breaks the code to the effective use of positive reinforcement, the entire work setting takes on reinforcing properties, and the rate and acceleration of positive behaviors, including shifts across a range of behaviors that are aligned, takes off. Positive reinforcement's effect is well worth the effort that such a strategy requires.

NATURAL CONSEQUENCES

Effective management means creating systems that shape behavior unobtrusively and maintain it over time. The systems themselves do the talking, as it were, while the workaday exchanges between managers and subordinates focus on tasks and ideas concerning design, production, marketing, efficiency, safety, and other aspects of work life.

Well-designed workplaces are arranged to lead naturally to desired behaviors. Positive change is built into the fabric of the operation. Employees themselves become instruments of positive change. The energy of everyone, including managers, is redirected from concentrating on problem performance to focusing on goal attainment and product/service enhancement.

An effective management system can be so rewarding that there is no need for the threat of negative action for non-compliance. Such a system sets up an environment from which positive reinforcement flows, whether or not a specific individual is present to praise or recognize performance. This type of work setting includes the pleasure of cooperative teams, the freedom to generate and express ideas, the certainty that management actions and requests will be reasonable, and the responsibility to set one's own pace to effectively achieve specific goals.

Constructive policies and procedures that are part of the furniture are less intrusive while being more effective than rules that draw attention to themselves. The former types are much less of a threat to autonomy; indeed they need not be a threat at all. As an analogy, the fact that a person will get wet in the rain without an umbrella is part of the furniture of living that plays a strong role in shaping people's behavior; yet no one feels threatened. Imagine how different it would be if prior to every storm a voice in the clouds said, "Get out your umbrellas now; we will punish those who do not do so by drenching them."

THE ELIMINATION OF NEGATIVE CONTROL

Whenever human beings have a choice, they seek environments that are rewarding and avoid those that are coercive. Allowing aversive control to dominate American management strategies is one way that we, as a society, are failing to harness the potential of the workplace. Too few work settings are designed to eliminate coercion. Company handbooks spell out policies and procedures that are typically reactive or defensive in nature. Policies for time off, sick leave, hiring, firing, salary administration, promotion, dress codes, attendance, promptness, neatness, cooperation, educational leave—all of these are too frequently spelled out against a background of coercion.

Environments that rely too much on punishment and negative reinforcement suffer from the fallout that results from such negative control. Frequently under negative circumstances individuals do a poor job but continue to work at the tasks at hand. Then the person stops working altogether after being told his work is no good. The unacceptable performance has been punished, but have any positive changes in attitude or performance been achieved? Withholding comments can have the same effect. The absence of comment may seem to others to be less harmful than telling someone their work is no good. In fact, both of these procedures are harmful. Both responses establish bad rapport between employee and supervisor. Both can lead to the likelihood that employees will view the person delivering the threat or the punishment as an aversive, punishing person. Avoidance and escape on the part of employees will likely follow. Managers sometimes believe incorrectly that to praise or to recognize good performance is to belittle achievement. "I hired them to do the job and, damn it, they better do the best job they can if they expect to be here next year. I don't give them M&Ms for just doing their jobs. And I do get results. You can't argue with results."

To that we say, nonsense! There are better ways to achieve results—better both ethically and as sound management strategy. Any senior executive who knows about the aversive styles of his or her managers and does nothing to change those actions fails to fully instill the values of an ethical workplace. Worse yet, as these kinds of consequence systems play out, they encourage the very behavior we see all too often—intimidation, silence, finger-pointing, hiding. If we are to curb the extraordinary excesses of unethical deeds in our corporate operations, then nothing is more urgent than for leaders to learn about human behavior.

16

CHAPTER

Accountability and Responsibility for Ensuring Individual Success

The measure of a leader is in the actions of the followers.

—Aubrey C. Daniels and James E. Daniels, *Measure of a Leader*

THE MANAGER'S JOB IS TO HELP an individual reach his or her fullest potential. In turn, we must measure a supervisor's effectiveness by the effectiveness of his or her employees.

Even with all of the current books and seminars on management techniques, American business managers generally are not truly held accountable for their management of individual and group success. Instead, the measurement of a manager's effectiveness is attainment of goals—above all, profitability. Many bullying, threatening, unpleasant, and arrogant individuals are judged to be successful as managers because they satisfy predetermined goals for profits.

We say that if a manager achieves results using primarily aversive control techniques, that manager is cheating the company, missing limitless opportunities, and behaving unethically or at least amorally.

The chief responsibility a company has is to enable its employees to be successful in an ethical fashion. If poor management strategies are accepted (as they all too often are) because profit is obtained, the company has failed to understand the consequences of such negative-control strategies. It has failed to identify the potential gain that can occur through positive management techniques. It has cheated itself and its people.

The following statements are all too frequently made by leaders in praise of results achieved:

1. "He puts the numbers on the board."
2. "She gets the job done."
3. "You can't argue with success."

Not only do these statements reflect the view that business is amoral, without regard for how results are achieved, they also reflect unsound business strategies. A great tragedy occurs when the price for success need not have been paid in the first place. If we as managers tell a subordinate "I don't care how you do it—just get it done" we are treating business as amoral, and in the process we are short-changing our companies, our subordinates, and ourselves. Aversive control can produce desired performance, but it leads to fear-based productivity, avoidance, and refusal to take risks. It does not promote innovation but it does promote deception. Aversive control implies that punishment is in store for non-compliance. The person using the strategy becomes aversive; people avoid him or her. Only the rarest of individuals will confront such a manager. Seldom is such a threatening environment necessary, however. Such an environment rarely allows individuals to achieve their greatest potential, even if it does force people to attain immediate goals.

Many managers achieve goals via the use of designs that cause the employee to view goal attainment as equivalent to the avoidance of failure. "Unless this goal is achieved, I will fail, be blamed, and possibly lose my job." Managers rarely consider not only what needs to happen to satisfy profitability demands but to address what is necessary to satisfy, or reward, the worker once the goal is achieved.

In settings where managers use coercion to achieve results, the only positive outcome of an employee's sustained good performance will likely be that the threat to him or her is removed for a period of time. Under such aversive management, employees are often not able to specify how their managers rate them, even when those employees are high achievers. They do not really know what their manager appreciates about their performance. They are always slightly on edge, never knowing when the next threat or belittling statement might occur.

What is the alternative? First, look for the causes of change. For example, look to see if the slow person has increased his or her rate of work output, and then determine whether that increased performance is linked to positive strategies such as your kind words. Is it linked instead to negative responses such as avoidance of your displeasure? Second, find activities that reward the behavior you want. The likelihood is that the person making the change will then begin to reward himself or herself for making the change. People around the individual will do the same. Positive actions tend to build upon themselves.

When employees fail to do their jobs, in almost every case more of the responsibility for the failure belongs to management than to the individual employee. Why? The manager and the environment for which the manager is at least partly responsible have not provided the necessary feedback and positive reinforcement to get the employee to perform adequately. We must look at the situation somewhat differently when mistakes are made in hiring, and when it may not be possible to teach the individual the necessary skills at a reasonable cost. Even here, management bears some responsibility for the employee.

When a mistake has been made in hiring, management should tell the employee candidly what the problems are and, if possible, help the employee find a more suitable job if there is no resolution without great cost of time or money to the employer and the employee. Sometimes some problems are just too large to fix.

We advocate a management philosophy that says to employees: regardless of what happens, we, the company, bear responsibility to provide instruction and feedback to you, the employee, to observe your performance as carefully as we can, and then respond in ways that are most helpful to you and the company.

INDIVIDUAL ACCOUNTABILITY

Individual employees are accountable for their own performance, their own success, and for taking needed actions to make improvement. While managers affect performance very directly, there is no way that individuals can be removed from observing and making changes for and by themselves when needed. They may need to arrange special conditions to ensure they stop bad habits or build new skills. They may need to ask for feedback from a trusted source. Every employee has a responsibility to understand and work on the impact of his or her performance on others. Every company has the responsibility to teach employees how to manage personal change effectively. Hire employees who already have this ability if you can, but coach them in this ability when it is needed.

The setting, how an individual is managed and the effects of consequences, can and do impede success for many. However, no matter how much a particular management strategy or particular culture can impact performance, the organization and the individual must understand that the ultimate responsibility when difficulties arise rests with the performer—to take action, to ask for help and to do what is requested or required. In some extreme instances, it is incumbent on the individual, if the fit is wrong, to resign without causing undue problems for the organization. That is a hard and very rare act indeed. It flies in the face of self-interest and so could not be expected to occur very often, but it may be the best alternative some individuals can give to their companies.

Given the responsibility for personal accountability by each person in a company, managers are still accountable for developing employees and thereby setting them up for success. Daniels and Daniels (2005) in their new book, *The Measure of a Leader,* define a leader through the behavior of the follower. If you think about that, then the sense of mutual accountability becomes clear. Employees who succeed and follow the path of an ethical leader, and who exhibit the right behavior in the right way along that path, define effective leaders. The measures identified in the book embody the concept of reciprocal accountability that exists in any system of leaders and followers. Leaders cannot be defined as successful outside the actions of those who follow them, namely *their employees.* A leader may be identified at any level and in almost any role by this test. Managers are often excellent leaders, but one doesn't have to be in a management position to be a good leader.

THE ROLE OF COACH

Is it fair to ask managers to be so concerned with all of the details of changing behavior? Absolutely! Managers now waste inordinate amounts of time, energy, and resources on ill-conceived and rarely evaluated change processes that ultimately fail.

Most managers believe that individual achievement occurs pretty much independently of everything else that happens. Even if managers are aware that contingent relationships exist among individuals that allow one person to make a sale, establish a legal title, or develop a blueprint, they do little or nothing to shape those relationships in the best way. Managers continue to think essentially in terms of individual goal attainment. Changing this mindset is perhaps the biggest challenge facing American management today.

THE MORAL PERSPECTIVE

When we look at the issues under discussion here from the perspective of morality, we face two challenges. The first challenge for those responsible for behavior change is to understand that the goal is increased freedom as demonstrated in a range of positive responses, a wider repertoire for "getting it right" in the workplace, not a restriction of behavioral choices. In this sense we are not talking about compliance or a task-specific action, but rather the ability to do the job right and skillfully at high-and-steady rates and with behavior that says they are enjoying the work—approaching the work setting eagerly, volunteering improvements, and so on. When management uses punishment, they only decrease the occurrence of the behavior; but do nothing to build new options. When negative strategies such as threats are used to produce behavior, there may well be an increase in desired behavior; however, the behavior occurs under duress and can have negative emotional by-products. Those by-products include reduced enjoyment, lowered long-term loyalty, harsh and angry feelings expressed to friends and family about work, and work habits that are inferior in unobservable ways. Such outcomes are not necessary.

The second moral challenge is that of finding ways to reward ethical behavior. Positive change toward more ethical actions must become part of the fabric, part of how work is done—an ongoing process, not one requiring continuous and immediate management.

Increasing the likelihood of ethical behavior at work must be managed through establishing clear consequences and by making ethical actions more likely to occur regardless of the immediacy of reward. Longer-term and more complex systems of recognition and support are required.

DESIGNING CHANGE INTO THE FABRIC OF THE WORKPLACE

Without question, numerous barriers stand in the way of business success. For example, frequently employees do not know why they ought to do a job, and much too often they do not know how to do the job most effectively. What should a manager do to improve the situation?

On the whole, the answer is to design workplaces to minimize or eliminate human error. But sometimes errors provide opportunities for instruction. So, when should a supervisor allow individuals discretion in reaching desired outcomes? If the boss's responsibility is to reduce errors or get to results more expediently, then it is important to provide direct instruction. If the goal is longer term and the manager wants to help the individual develop independent problem-solving skills, then allowing employees to reach a desirable outcome through error and corrective feedback may be advisable.

Desired Employee Outcomes and Performance Management Design

Some employees know how to do specific jobs, but do not know how those jobs mesh with work being done in other sections of their companies. They may not know exactly when to start or when to complete their own jobs relative to others. They may not know when they should suspend their assignments in favor of more pressing tasks, or how they should coordinate their tasks with those of others. The need for team meetings and discussions is important. Accordingly, managers should place a high level of focus on disseminating information. They should describe plans for the company's operations and how each employee's efforts fit in. They should invite debate, ask for suggestions for change, and implement such change where it is possible and practical.

Ironically, if an employee's behavior is tied to goals that are too narrow, such as focusing only on one specific component of a task, then rewarding the individual for task completion is counterproductive. The individual meets one or two specific task goals, but the entire task may not be completed satisfactorily. Suppose an employee doing repairs is rewarded primarily for fast work. This creates a strong incentive to play the numbers. The employee completes as many repair jobs as possible in a given period whether or not the repaired items stay fixed. Indeed, there may exist an incentive to do a sloppy job; when the thing breaks again the worker will already be familiar with it and will be able to repair it again in record time, thus adding another number to the daily tally. We may reward another employee for getting new customers, which provides an incentive for neglecting old ones. Or perhaps we only reward him for keeping previous customers; this may provide an incentive for not actively seeking new ones.

First, make task assignments more comprehensive, so that obvious one-sided incentives are eliminated:

- "Your job is to repair items in minimal time and do the work correctly; you are also to identify any flaws that might help us keep breakdowns from occurring in the future."
- "Keep old customers and pursue new ones at a pace that allows you to manage both groups successfully."
- "Work toward the success of your department and the company as a whole as well as your area of direct responsibility. We will set up times to observe and share learning with one another about how to improve overall."

Second, allow the employee opportunities to design, discuss, and implement goals that are within the scope of his/her skills and abilities. Research indicates that when individuals set their own goals, they frequently set higher goals for themselves, tougher than their manager might set. They will, in addition, aim at producing higher quality work if they are their own auditors. Provide the measurement tools and other evaluative data by which they can track their own actions and let them modify their own performance to do the best job. Reward them for showing initiative and also for achieving goals. Encourage employees to objectively examine their actions and evaluate their success in achieving quality.

THE CONTEXT OF CHANGE AT WORK

The rewards that a worker receives do not come entirely from management, nor do all of the punishers. Day in, day out, most workers are in contact with fellow employees, not managers. They are receiving feedback all the time from co-workers, and this feedback constitutes rewards and punishers. It is the manager's job to design an overall system that ensures sufficient encouragement and support for doing a good job.

When we think in terms of creating top-down strategies for change, the overall picture is even more complex than we have made it out to be. It is not simply the manager's job to design systems that ensure sufficient encouragement to do a good job, but rather, the company must consider its workplace a mutually reinforcing environment for all individuals who enter it, including senior executives, managers, and employees. The reciprocal nature of using positive reinforcement is fundamental to the company's capacity to rapidly increase the likelihood of positive and supportive actions. Every person in the organization should be able to say, "As I set up conditions for you to change, and you change, I then change. As we change, the company changes. As you are rewarded, I am rewarded. As we create positive outcomes, the customer benefits and the company is rewarded."

In such a setting, the manager's behavior is shaped by the positive responses of subordinates. To be accountable, the manager's performance must be measured by his or her ability to affect positive change as well as practice the strategies we have described in managing others. The positive effects of the managers' and the employees' interactions are reciprocal. Specific behavioral objectives should be built into each individual and group performance appraisal, as well as company-wide planning documents. Commitment must be visible to everyone.

In an earlier chapter we discussed the value of making the workplace as pleasant an environment as possible. If workers are treated with consideration, they will have all the more reason to want to be at work; they will enjoy their jobs more and be happier. Good feeling is contagious.

Even if the result is not necessarily increased productivity, having employees feel better at work is a positive end in itself. Treating workers with consideration is the right thing to do. If workers perceive that they will be treated well regardless of quarterly profits, this will probably lead workers to be more productive and to display greater team spirit. "Treated well" means to be treated with respect, not simply to be paid. Sometimes conditions do not allow the pay to be "good," but the relationship between manager and employees must always be good in that it is based on trust and respect.

As we said previously, the work setting—temperature of the workplace, lighting, noise levels, and the comfort of furnishings—plays a role in the workers' perceptions of whether or not management cares about them as human beings. Moreover, improvements in these matters belong to the structure of the system that we mentioned earlier in this chapter. A worker should not be told, "When you process ten more contracts per day, we will give you a more comfortable chair." Instead, the message should be, "We want your workday to be as productive and comfortable as possible, so if a new chair will help, we will get you one."

It may seem paradoxical, but allowing workers more independence can increase their team spirit. In general, a person who must follow a rigid, unpleasant schedule or procedure that offers no opportunity to make changes will not think about how she can do the extras that will help the organization. Instead, she will think about how to get through the day with as little pain as possible, or she may think about getting another job. By contrast, someone who experiences greater independence in decision making is likely to contribute to the team's effort and to make valuable suggestions for improving performance. Having a say in work procedures and increased responsibility for her daily work life contributes positively toward a more satisfied worker, a more productive worker.

However, it is not the case that everyone wants or is ready for independence. An essential part of respecting the individual is considering who requires greater guidance and who can operate independently. It is also not the case that everyone works best as part of a team.

Is the use of teams a better way to get work done than the use of individual efforts? In some cases, individual effort is required; at other times (depending on the tasks) a team is the best means to accomplish a goal. When to use teams and when not to do so is too complex a subject to treat adequately here. The important point is that a team, like an individual, can be motivated to do a superior job. The advantage of a properly utilized team is that there are greater opportunities for idea generation and problem solving. Teamwork is often desirable, but it is not necessarily always the better choice.

REMOVING BARRIERS

Divisions between units, unnecessary competition, unfair practices, and misunderstanding are some of the critical elements that may preclude optimal performance. If there are structural barriers that keep one unit from talking to another, or one individual from combining talents with another person, these barriers are serious impediments to excellence. Recognize and utilize teams and individuals; the employees need to know which combination is expected and why. To the degree possible, human performance should not be driven by a system of formal permissions but rather by incentives to get the job done in the best way possible.

If management wants to avoid undermining all of the employees' desires to do a good job, it cannot afford to treat employees badly, or unethically, even the one or two employees who may be very difficult to manage. Once an employee is treated badly and the word gets out, much more harm is done than the manager is likely to anticipate. It is difficult, and sometimes impossible, to rekindle trust in other employees when an individual is publicly fired and humiliated—especially if management seems to delight in the humiliation—even if the individual is widely known to have been an employee whose behavior was incompatible with the company's requirements. Such actions are corrosive.

Managers have been known to attempt to justify their actions in treating poor performers with a lack of dignity and respect as a way to show strong action, outrage, and a commitment to the employees who do not act in the same objectionable way. Such managers may well get immediate applause from those employees who have suffered because of the poorly performing employee. However, these same applauding employees will notice how that difficult employee is handled in terms of dignity and questions of privacy. A strong negative signal is sent to all employees. In a well-managed company, the exact opposite signal is sent—the message that in this company, even if an employee is terminated, he/she will be treated with respect. Holding to the higher standard does make a difference.

DEVELOPING THAT HIGHER CODE OF CONDUCT

In the next chapter, we summarize the steps discussed in this chapter and elsewhere in this book that have implications for how you develop your own code of conduct to put ethics to work in your company. We summarize the tools that will help you to identify the conditions that support either successful or unsuccessful actions in the workplace, and the conditions that support either ethical or unethical effects of actions in the workplace. We outline the steps to take to create environments that use positive and reciprocally beneficial management strategies to generate optimal and ethical performance from everyone.

17

CHAPTER

IMPLICATIONS FOR ACTION

I have faith that the time will eventually come when employees and employers, as well as all mankind, will realize that they serve themselves best when they serve others most.

—B.C. Forbes

FEW BOOKS CAN BE summarized easily. This book is perhaps more difficult to summarize than most because it combines insights from three quite different fields—moral philosophy, business management, and behavioral psychology. Yet, the interdisciplinary approach that we take is indispensable if the meaningful integration of business ethics and business success is to be achieved. We believe that nothing else is as important in the contemporary world of business.

The impetus for real change lies outside the pages of this book. It lies with all of the individuals who participate in the world of business. When a sufficient number of these individuals decide it is time to promote a cultural practice of ethical behavior in the workplace, the result will be a cascading effect of greater ethical sensitivity and greater trust among all those who invest in the business—customers, employees, stockholders, the community at large, and the wider world in which trade is conducted.

Each of you in the workplace will probably have a different starting point from which discussion and action must begin. You must determine the initial steps that apply to your own situation such as

1. the questions that should be asked;
2. advice that should be sought or given;
3. changes that are called for in office settings, assignments, or workplace expectations on a larger scale;
4. adjustments to your own expectations and behaviors;
5. skills that you may need to acquire.

In determining your kicking off point, look first at yourself as an individual and second at your position in the company that employs you. Everyone, regardless of job description, can make an important difference. However, senior leaders who read this book bear the largest responsibility since they control the antecedent and consequence conditions that most directly and immediately affect ethical decision making.

You have the power to arrange consequences to bring out ethical practices or to make them secondary to the way business is done. You have the power to either talk the walk or walk the talk—and in ethics you must do both—firmly and without equivocation. You must determine where an organizational response is needed in regard to structures, policies, and procedures; and you must ensure that your various management teams understand that you will, above all else, value ethical processes and outcomes.

The first four of the recommendations discussed below apply to everyone regardless of rank or tenure within a company. Any employee who enters a workplace must consider these steps seriously from his or her individual perspective. None of us is free from accountability to live a life that is ethical whether at work or elsewhere, even if no one holds us directly accountable.

The remaining six recommendations discussed below are directed to managers. If they want their workplaces to reflect a commitment to ethics, they are the only ones who can require the implementation of these recommendations, and they are the only ones who can ensure that there are real consequences in place for those who do follow the guidelines, celebrating ethical choices visibly and even, we dare hope, with real gusto.

Please remember, as we said early on, that ethics is too serious not to have fun with it. Make your workplace an ethical safe haven and see how much real delight you will generate, how such a perspective brings calm, security, and certainty to employees. Also, please reflect with satisfaction that long after employees retire they are likely to remember with fondness the company and the people who made it successful. Let us go about winning the Integrity Revolution through the actions of each of us, one person and then another, and then another. That is our collective best hope.

FOR INDIVIDUALS

1. Support the idea that ethical behavior is always possible in business.

Whenever you encounter someone whose words or deeds indicate that he or she believes that business activity is amoral, you should respond. Take a stand that is sensitive yet direct. Talk that perpetuates the view that business is amoral is cheap, easy, and frequently encountered.

People who are cynical believe themselves to be worldly wise, find it easy to repeat what others say, or are sincere and thoughtful but simply mistaken. Cynical people seem to find talking about the amorality of business as effortless as breathing. Like bad currency that drives out good, such talk sabotages efforts to present the other side. The primary point to get across is that the world of business is all of a piece with other aspects of life and therefore should not be conducted according to any special set of rules.

Honesty, kindness, concern for people in need, concern for society as a whole and for future generations, a healthy feeling of self-worth and respect for the rights of others—these values belong as much in the business world as elsewhere. The pursuit of profit in business is fine and necessary if tempered by these values.

2. Help people by being clear about what you value.

Your role in maintaining or changing other people's actions can be active or passive. If you choose to do nothing when you observe harmful words or actions, you are most probably weighing the safety of inaction against the varied costs of involvement. We want to encourage you to speak up, but from a perspective that endorses other people's ability to change and that lends support to the idea that increased skill in doing the right thing can be learned. For example, some people rarely if ever hear the words *ethical* or the phrase *a person of integrity* applied to them or to what they say or do. They may pride themselves on their tough, real-world posture. To catch such people doing something morally right for its own sake, or for the sake of someone else, and to point it out in appropriate terms may cause them to begin to see new possibilities. Remember the lessons about labels and how they can in fact change the possibilities about what we believe we can do.

While their new insight may not bring about a permanent change in behavior, helping them to achieve such a change even temporarily is nevertheless a kind and ethical act on your part. Endorsing the specific acts of a person does not mean endorsing the totality of a person's actions. Let a generous and forgiving spirit guide you in dealing with the selfish among us, while staying clear of involvements that use or abuse you or that increase an individual's success in behaving badly. We should all hope that in our moments of selfishness, someone else will help us become better than we are.

3. Follow the decision-making model of moral pluralism outlined in Chapter 6.

Whenever possible, seek a balance among the basic values of rights, justice, the common good, and self-interest in relation to individual autonomy and integrity. Practice thinking about these four pillars, as well as others of your own, and remember to balance as best you can your own self-interest across time and conditions. When you do need to protect yourself or do something that will clearly help you and not others, understand that you can do that and still be ethical.

Do not forget that in many cultures the welfare of the collective is more important than that of any one person; we can learn from these cultures, even though we will not want to adopt all of their attitudes in a wholesale fashion. Become better versed if needed in your knowledge about ethical decision making and its many shapes but establish your own standards measured by an overarching and relevant cultural standard such as the model in Chapter 6. Practice and discuss your efforts with colleagues and friends. Whatever your standard, make sure that you do consider in your decision-making process the needs of all against the needs of the few when making choices that may have different effects on various groups or individuals. Considering ethical implications can become second nature and can lead to actions that have a strong, positive impact on American business and your own immediate life.

4. Do not become discouraged if you appear to be the only employee who takes ethics seriously.

An important thought to keep in mind is this: the Integrity Revolution in the business world has only just begun, two decades at most having passed since its inception, and revolutions are rarely instantaneous.

The majority of senior business managers who are presently in positions of influence did not take a business ethics course in college and passed through their formative years at a time when prevailing attitudes were quite different from what they are now. So don't abandon the cause! In a few years, many others will catch up with you. A thoroughgoing commitment to ethics in business is the wave of the future.

FOR MANAGEMENT

1. Select and retain ethical employees.

Make sure that at the point of entry into the organization, your organization examines a person's ethical commitments, and as thoroughly as possible examines not only what they say they have done when faced with ethical dilemmas, but what they actually have done. Sometimes the reference source can validate character-commitment to ethical practice, personal values of rights, justice, and honor. The businessperson who is willing to cut ethical corners for the sake of profits may be tough and competent, but you should see to it that such a person faces great difficulty in being allowed to fit into the fabric of your workplace.

To avoid hiring the wrong people in the first place, evaluate how prospective employees define *treating others with respect* and *following through on commitments.* Make sure that such phrases, as well as others that demonstrate an awareness of one's ethical obligations, are contained in job specifications. The characteristics that we would like included in selection interviews and examinations are often handled as mere by-products, not the stuff of tough-minded interviews; but they should be viewed as necessary right along with the technical requirements for a job. If you want certain personal qualities in your employees, plan your interviews and ask questions along the appropriate lines. Remember though, that what we say we will do and what we actually do are often very different. Once a person is hired, use this knowledge to build into your early training lots of good examples of how your company demonstrates ethics. Make it the meat and potatoes of their early learning, along with technical skills and HR procedures.

2. Make ethical behavior part of performance review.

The majority of individuals in an organization are ethical. Most people desire to do the right thing and, day in and day out, they do the right thing. Some people act in ways that put short-term and selfish gain first. Some people are insensitive to the needs of others. As we have indicated, you cannot and you should not label them as unethical; but rather, you have an obligation to examine what you can do, at a reasonable cost to you and the organization, to change their behavior. You may have no choice but to remove such individuals, but that is rarely the case. As long as they remain working at their jobs, assign them performance goals that compete with their usual styles of behavior. For example, someone who does not demonstrate respect for others may learn to act differently by being placed in situations that require cooperation and trust, the give and take of working with others. Set up working conditions that require reliance on others to complete assignments.

Give employees a shot at modifying their behavior through well-designed processes of change that pinpoint the areas of development required. Measure them accordingly. Recognize and reward changes in ways that are meaningful to that individual.

Because the variance and subtlety of behavior along ethical lines can be difficult to manage, many managers do not tackle this area. But, just as with any behavior pattern in need of change, identifying where an individual needs help to increase ethical sensitivity is hard work. The more you pinpoint those actions that incorporate core values, and the more you work on identifying the times when you actually see other, competing behavior patterns, the easier it will be to help the person understand and change patterns that could, if unchecked, lead to unfortunate situations for the person and the company. Act quickly, point out the inconsistencies, and then adapt a shaping strategy to help the person make well-defined change.

3. Work on increasing moral sensitivity from as many different angles as possible.

Do not allow your work environment to be one that pushes the tough issues of business decisions under a mountain of numbers, technical demands, and marketplace surveys. Encourage people to look at the numbers in a budget reduction plan in terms of human costs. This will provide a solid guidepost against which individuals can measure the true costs of decisions, and it will help to ensure that decision makers are not removed (by walls, management hierarchies, or boardroom meetings) from the real repercussions of such decisions when measured in both business and human costs.

Bring ethics into your employees' workday by discussing the issues involved in the hardships of laid-off workers, disappointed customers, family members of employees transferred at short notice, mothers with young children who are not permitted flexible work hours, older employees who are still competent and capable of a full day's work if they are not rushed or intimidated, handicapped individuals whose contributions may be compromised by the difficulties inherent in areas of the work environments, and so on.

Allow and encourage others to take such concerns into account when weighing short-term, long-term, and human gains.

For example, George's increasing difficulty in hearing reduces his effectiveness in direct customer contact; but his hearing loss has no negative impact on his ability to do underwriting. Transferring him from one position to another allows him to continue working and to maintain effectiveness. True, his pace may be slower than that of other employees, but he makes up for it in his reliable work habits and thorough attention to the task at hand.

Evaluate the gain to the group at large in seeing that the company does care for its elderly employees and does find good ways to make them contributors. Such a gain may loom larger than the output count that goes to headquarters. It may turn out eventually that George will need to be replaced, but just as often such individuals can be supported with respect and dignity as they find their capacity to work diminished before their desire or need to work is completed.

Take on the structural and job performance issues faced by all companies that lead to good people doing the wrong thing, even if they consider what they are doing to be for a good reason. Consider how your company can require speed in reaching productivity targets without compromising safety, health, or legal issues. All too often, the people involved simply assume that such compromises happen only infrequently, and they simply assume that everyone already understands that management does not intend to have employees commit unethical acts in order to complete assignments. As a result, the very issues that most need to be discussed end up not even being raised.

Discuss these issues. Consider how compensation can drive behavior, just as productivity or quality targets can. Discuss the need for care in how goals are attained and invite people to raise ethical questions about time, quality, and efficiency versus the possible consequences that may come if one unit is slower than another unit, or if one division reports fewer closings or items sold or orders completed, and so on. Remember that the slippery slope can begin when individuals or teams set out to make the company, the unit, the team, as well as themselves successful, but their pursuit of success is not properly balanced in all of the ways that we have discussed. Remember that walking along that slope is among the most dangerous places for employees to be.

It is difficult to see the blind spots since most individuals in business start out working for success, not to create bad practices. So please, bring up the issues that we have raised in this book in your discussions. Put these issues on the table and keep them on the table. The natural extension of the ideas under discussion here is for companies to initiate ethics sensitivity workshops.

Depending on your role in the organization, it may be appropriate for you to conduct such workshops yourself after receiving training that would contribute to your own moral sensitivity and professional development. Or, you may want to consider bringing in professionals to do the job. A number of resources are listed at the back of this book. Also, if you type the words *ethics at work* into Google or other Internet search engines, you will receive over eight million responses within seconds. Many people are eager to help all of us. (We have recommended a few of them.)

4. Make ethics a fundamental part of workplace expectations.
If people in the workplace are rewarded for behaving more ethically, then they will behave more ethically—and their attitudes and beliefs will change as well. Moral leadership, the day-to-day pressures and influences of the workplace, examples set by managers and co-workers, statements of corporate values, vision statements, and the culture of a corporation—all can help make people more ethically alert.

5. Develop a public ethical code that promotes individual choice and responsibility as well as corporate requirements.
Business can become its own best policy setter, its own best overseer in ethical matters. Certain groups have begun in earnest to

carve out industry standards for ethical practices in their fields. Each business can do the same inside its own operation as well. Whenever possible, establish the expectation that individuals will evaluate and make decisions according to ethical standards. Most importantly, apply consequences for those who do and those who do not behave ethically. Make a person's ethical performance count!

6. Remember to use both social and tangible consequences that are visible to everyone. Reward effort to increase individual/team ethical sensitivity, and publicly celebrate those actions that have ethical implications.

A manager can take no more important action than to always be ready to reinforce and build on the positive actions of others. Make consequence management a part of the system, building formal and informal recognition systems for ethical actions. Take the time to learn how to do this well.

7. Use antecedents, those conditions and actions that precede behavior, to convey your constant commitment to workplace ethics.

Be clear from the start (in written materials and in other actions) that ethics count at your company. Share and publish your code of conduct and then talk pragmatically about how the company turns those words into actions. Invite people to assess you and to help you think through what you are planning or implementing as requested from your leadership. Let them know by their level of involvement that ethical concerns are part of that picture. Ask them what you can do to make the topic of ethics a driving force in the workplace.

Be open in your meetings—to dissent and other viewpoints—and invite, whenever possible, ideas to make the actions proposed or the strategies that are unfolding more effective. Be prepared to evaluate your actions and to reconsider them. Stay true to your course if you believe you are headed in the right direction, but then share with those who disagree with your decision why you are taking the actions required.

Remember, the investment of time involved in such discussions is relatively small compared to the cost to the company when employees who cannot challenge decisions and concerns go underground, or when performance compliance is minimal. Your role is to structure the work environment in such a way that you and your fellow employees can rest assured that you are each doing all you can to hold yourselves and the company accountable to the highest possible standards of integrity.

> *Judging by what I have learned about men and women, I am convinced that far more idealistic aspirations exist than is ever evident. Just as the rivers we see are much less numerous than the underground streams, so the idealism that is visible is minor compared to what men and women carry in their hearts, unreleased and scarcely released. Mankind is waiting and longing for those who can accomplish the task of untying what is knotted and bringing the underground waters to the surface.*
>
> —Albert Schweitzer

REFERENCES

Aguayo, R. (1990). Dr. Deming: *The American Who Taught the Japanese About Quality.* New York: Fireside.

Alcock, J., Carment, D., & Sadava, S. (1998). *A Textbook of Social Psychology.* (4th ed.). Scarborough ON: Prentice Hall Allyn and Bacon.

Allhoff, F. (2003). Business Bluffing Reconsidered. *Journal of Business Ethics,* 45, 283-89. Netherlands: Kluwer Academic Publishers. Also available online athttp://www.UCSB.edu.com.

Bavendam Research, Inc. (2000). Measuring Job Satisfaction. *Effective Management Through Measurement,* 6.

Beal, D. (2003, April 8). *Pioneer Press.* Also available online at *Pioneer Press and Wire services sources,* http://www.twincities.com.

Carr, A. (1968). Is Business Bluffing Ethical? *Harvard Business Review,* 46, 143-153.

Daniels, A. C. (1998). *Bringing Out the Best in People.* New York: McGraw-Hill.

Daniels, A. C. (2001). *Other People's Habits.* Atlanta: Performance Management Publications.

Daniels, A. C. & Daniels, J.E. (2004). *Performance Management: Changing Behavior That Drives Organizational Effectiveness.* (4th ed.). Atlanta: Performance Management Publications.

Daniels, A. C. & Daniels, J. E. (2005). *Measure of a Leader.* New York: McGraw-Hill.

Eisenberger, R. & Masterson, F. A. (1983). Required high effort increases subsequent persistence and reduces cheating. *Journal of Personality and Social Psychology,* 44, 593-599.

Eisenberger, R. & Cameron, J. (1996). Detrimental effects of reward: Reality or myth? *American Psychologist,* 51, 1153-1166.

Eisenberger, R. (1998, April 18). Psi Chi Distinguished Lecture. Combined meeting of the Rocky Mountain and Western Psychological Associations. Albuquerque, New Mexico.

Eisenberger, R. (1999). Industriousness: How Can It Be Learned? *Eye on Psi Chi,* 3 (3), 24-25. Also available online at http://www.psi.chi.org.

Forsyth, D. R. (1980). A taxonomy of ethical ideologies. *Journal of Personality and Social Psychology,* 39, 175-184.

Forsyth, D. R. & Berger, R. (1982). The effects of ethical ideology on moral behavior. *Journal of Social Psychology,* 117, 53-56.

Forsyth, D. R., & Nye, J. L. (1990). Personal moral philosophy and moral choice. *Journal of Research in Personality,* 24, 398-414.

Garret, R. (1987). "Practical Reason and a Science of Morals" in *B. F. Skinner: Consensus and Controversy.* Sohan Modgil and Celia Modgil (Eds.). New York: Falmer Press.

Gilbert, T. (1978). *Human Competence: Engineering Worthy Performance.* New York: McGraw-Hill.

Gladwell, M. (2004, September 20). "Personality Plus." *New Yorker Magazine.*

Hartshorne, H. & May, M. A. (1929). *Studies in the Nature of Character.* New York: The MacMillan Company.

Huffington, A. (2003). *Pigs at the Trough: How Corporate Greed and Political Corruption Are Undermining America.* New York: Crown Publishers.

Hugo, V. (1862) *Les Miserables.* Belgium: Lecroix and Verboeckhoven.

Keller, A., Ford, L. M., & Meacham, J. A. (1978). Dimensions of Self-Concept in Preschool Children. *Developmental Psychology, 14,* 483-489.

Kirp, D. & D. Rice (1991) as quoted by Joseph H. Boyett and Henry P. Conn in *Workplace 2000: The Revolution Reshaping American Business.* New York: Dutton.

Martin, B. (1998, July 22-28). Studying whistle-blowing. *Campus Review,* 8 (28), 10.

Miller, A. (1949) *Death of a Salesman. New York: Penguin Press.*

O'Connor, J. (1987). *The meaning of crisis: A theoretical introduction.* Oxford: Basil Blackwell.

Peevers, B.H. & Secord, P. F. (1973). Developmental changes in attribution of descriptive concepts to persons. *Journal of Personality and Social Psychology,* 27, 120-128.

Perone, M. (2003). Presidential Address. The International Association of Behavior Analysis.

Rachels, J. (1985). "Egoism and Moral Skepticism" in *Vice and Virtue in Everyday Life.* Christina Hoff Sommers (Ed.). New York: Harcourt Brace Jovanovich.

Rhoades, L., Eisenberger, R., & Armeli, S. (2001). Affective Commitment of the Organization: the Contribution of Perceived Organizational Support. *Journal of Applied Psychology, 86* (5), 825-36.

Royce, J. (1885). *The Religious Aspect of Philosophy.* Boston: Houghton Mifflin.

Shaw, G. B. (1903). "Maxims for Revolutionists." *Man and Superman.* Cambridge, Mass: The University Press.

Sidman, M. (1960). *Tactics of scientific research.* New York: Basic Books.

Sidman, M. (1989). *Coercion and Its Fallout.* Boston: Authors Cooperative.

Smith, A. (1776) *Wealth of Nations.* Edinburgh. Available online at http://www.adamsmith.org/smith/won-intro.htm.

Watson, D. & Tharp, R. G. (1997). *Self-Directed Behavior: Self-Modification for Personal Adjustment.* (7th ed.). Pacific Grove, CA: Brooks/Cole Publishing Company.

Watson, J. B. (1930). *Behaviorism.* NY: W.W. Norton & Company, Inc.

Wilde, O. (1890/1892). *The Picture of Dorian Gray.* Philadelphia: M. J. Ivers, James Sullivan Publishers. Also *Lady Windermere's Fan,* Act III.

INDEX

Many sources are available to help individuals and corporations design codes of conduct and set up consequence systems to increase the likelihood of ethical actions. We have included a few of the best in the References section. An interesting observation is that the growing focus on corporate ethics and ethical behavior in general is reflected by Internet content. Two years ago, a search for the word *ethics* yielded a little over 10 million references on the World Wide Web Google site. At the time of this book's publication, a Google.com search yielded more than 413 million references! We recommend the following helpful Internet sites:

www.josephsoninstitute.org
www.workingvalues.com
www.ethics.org

For an effective approach to behavior change, we also recommend that you read *Bringing Out the Best in People (1998); Other People's Habits (2001)* by Aubrey C. Daniels; and *Measure of a Leader (2005)* by Aubrey C. Daniels and James E. Daniels.

About the Authors

Alice Darnell Lattal, Ph.D., is President and CEO of Aubrey Daniels International (ADI), a management consulting firm that helps the world's leading businesses use the scientifically proven laws of human behavior to promote workplace practices vital to long-term success. ADI specializes in creating profitable habits from the executive room to the front line. Dr. Lattal is an adjunct professor of psychology at West Virginia University, a member of the Board of Directors of the Cambridge Center for Behavioral Studies, a member of the International Association of Behavior Analysis, and a member of the American Psychological Association. She is listed in *Who's Who of America* and *Who's Who of American Women*, and has served as president of her state psychological association. She has worked in a variety of consulting practices and also owned a company that specialized in the positive learning techniques of behavior analysis to increase literacy in children and adults. Dr. Lattal may be contacted at (678) 904-6140.

Ralph W. Clark, Ph.D., a professor of philosophy at West Virginia University, teaches courses in business ethics, current moral problems, and ethical theory. He has published in such journals as *Philosophy, The Monist,* the *Journal of Value Inquiry,* and *Philosophical Studies.* His other books include *Workplace Ethics: Winning the Integrity Revolution* (co-authored with Dr. Lattal), *Introduction to Moral Reasoning,* and *Introduction to Philosophical Thinking.*

Our ***Balance of Values Decision-Making Tool*** will help you sort out conflicting or supporting values involved in ethical decision making at work or in your personal life. It is a yardstick by which to measure and weigh ethical decisions, an external standard better than just listening to your own voice. To read more and use the tool, go to *www.aubreydaniels.com.*

ABOUT ADI

Aubrey Daniels International (ADI) helps the world's leading businesses use the scientifically proven laws of human behavior to promote workplace practices vital to long-term success. By developing strategies that reinforce critical work behaviors, ADI enables clients such as DaimlerChrysler Financial Services, Dollar General, and Blue Cross and Blue Shield achieve and sustain consistently high levels of performance, building **profitable *habits*™** within their organizations. ADI is led by Dr. Aubrey C. Daniels, the world's leading authority on behavioral science in the workplace and author of the bestselling management classic *Bringing Out the Best in People* (McGraw-Hill). Headquartered in Atlanta, the firm was founded in 1978.

OTHER TITLES BY AUBREY C. DANIELS

Measure of a Leader
Aubrey C. Daniels &
James E. Daniels

Bringing Out the Best in People
Aubrey C. Daniels

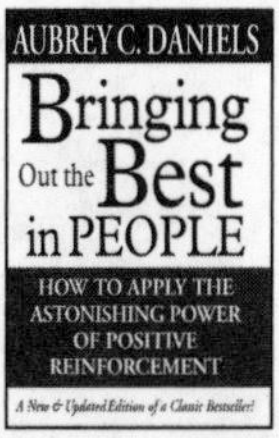

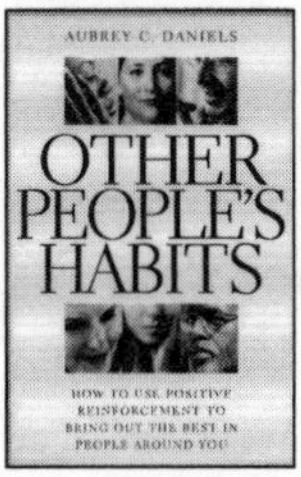

Other People's Habits
Aubrey C. Daniels

Performance Management: Changing Behavior That Drives Organizational Effectiveness (4th edition)
Aubrey C. Daniels &
James E. Daniels

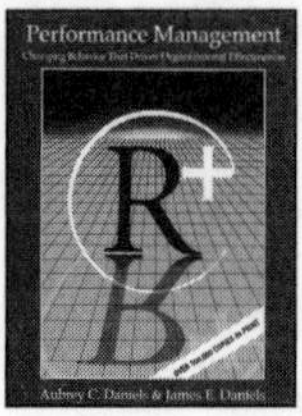

For more information, call 1 (800) 223-6191
or visit our Web site, www.aubreydaniels.com

REGISTER YOUR BOOK

Register your copy of *A Good Day's Work* and receive exclusive reader benefits. Visit the Web site below and click on the "register your book" link at the top of the page. Registration is free.

www.pmanagementpubs.com

A GOOD DAY'S WORK
INSTRUCTOR'S GUIDE

A complete Instructor's Guide for *A Good Day's Work* is available to instructors and professors in academic institutions.

For more information, call
(678) 904-6140, extension 131 or 113.